IN SEARCH OF

ADAM and EVE

A case for a theology of evolution

William G. Joseph

CreateSpace Publishing

cover graphics: NASA free library.

Background: Emission nebula NGC 6357 where the physical universe continues to evolve through star formation and heavy elements evolve through the death of stars.

Foreground: DNA molecule model, the key to the evolution of living organisms.

See http://apod.nasa.gov/apod/astropix.html

Table of Contents

In Search of Ourselves

Imagine being the first human being. Imagine it in great detail, not in general terms. You have two choices: you are an infant, the result of a messy birth and being raised by rather hairy parents or you are suddenly an adult, probably a surprised one. If you make the second choice, you are taking the more frequented path, the creationist option. Your challenge is to decide what life was like as a newly arrived adult human being in those initial days.

The biggest problem with this path is that you are governed by the biblical account of the first human being in chapters 2-3 of Genesis. Since you can name things, language already exists. You are the envy of all future generations since you have perfect control of your appetites. You will never get overweight or argue with your mate, that is, when you finally meet her. Best of all, your immune system is so finely tuned that you will never contract any disease or infection. Death is not possible and appetites and relationships are all in harmony. Your task becomes an exercise in accommodating an ancient metaphor rather than exercising your imagination about possibilities.

Because the details in the Genesis text are metaphors, we can take the snake and other elements with a grain of salt but those aspects about your physical situation must be real. The most important detail is the sin you and your helpmate commit. It has affected every human being since the act was done. While the first human is a creature made out of earth yet so unlike any biology we know of today, everything changes with one bad decision. We do wonder how much of all this that first couple understood as well as what kind of God would do this to his own creation.

If you take the first choice, the evolutionary one, there is fertile ground for imagination and not in the sense of creative science fiction but real, physical possibilities. Archaeologically, we know that you are in Africa. You grow in perception but your development seems much slower than the other siblings around you. You learn certain skills from parents but as you mature you find that you are more inventive than your parents and curious about a much wider world. The world is a challenge to understand and control where possible. Your primary interest, like that of every species around you, becomes survival.

You, however, are not easily satisfied. You are creative in your attempts at problem solving and tool making. You find a mate who responds to your presence, seems to share your approach to the world and the task of survival and the two of you develop a relationship and a language. You have offspring and in quiet moments you wonder why all this is so. For the next 150,000 years or so, those offspring increase in number and skills.[1] They migrate under the pressure of natural environmental forces and experience serious setbacks from natural disasters and the advance of ice over previously inhabitable regions.

With this evolutionary scenario, we will never know the exact details but we can certainly determine the constituent steps that must have been taken. Most of what we have been talking about can be explained by increased brain size in this infant. But we need also to face up to the difficult question of the presence of a spiritual dimension, an entity identifiable as the person, what we usually call the soul. Does it coexist with this enlarged brain? Is it part of the evolutionary continuum which resulted in a person? It does not advance understanding to create a scenario that eliminates the need for a soul, as some scientists are wont to do, or create a scenario that eliminates the need to ask the question as Genesis effectively does. We understand a question better by confronting it and dissecting it into all its parts. It does make it simpler if God created a fully mature adult with a soul but that does not seem the way God did everything else in nature. Either way, the first human person happened in a moment and everything needed—cranial capacity, organs, tissues, genes, etc.—is there in this human being so let your imagination run free.

Why should something that happened 150,000 years ago matter today? It matters because it is a question of who we are. It is how we explain ourselves and what we think we can expect from ourselves. It also strongly influences the decision of whether religion makes sense or not. In those places where religion has lost influence, what caused the lack of interest and the loss of credibility? In those places where religion is strongest, why is it so often characterized by a blind refusal to accept clear and obvious physical scientific evidence while tenaciously clinging to words penned in an age when there was no scientific understanding of our world.?

The thesis of this book is that science can help us dissect the question of our origin and nature and our understanding the human entity that is Homo sapiens, the creature that is vitalized by the soul. Science will not arrive at all the answers to all possible questions that can be asked about the physical world although it keeps on looking. Similarly, we should not expect theology to have all the answers concerning the soul and our relationship to God and our hope is that theologians keep on looking.

We do not hear anyone seriously talk about Adam and Eve today. We frequently hear churchmen remind us that we have a fallen nature but that statement does not explain much. In fact it seems to imply that this is a good as it is going to get because we are stuck in a flawed mechanism. Adam and Eve are more than a metaphor used in an ancient story to make a point about our importance and position in a created universe. They represent what we think about ourselves as persons living in social relationships within a divinely constituted environment. It is now time to reawaken interest in these two important characters. In fact we might well shout, will the real Adam and Eve please stand up!

Revelation

Religion turns to written revelation for the answers to these questions so we should start there. The first chapter of Genesis marks the beginning of what we call written revelation. This sacred texts comes from the *Torah/Old Testament* assembled during the two thousand years or so before the birth of Christ. The *Old Testament* and other biblical texts are regarded as sacred and containing the "word of God." At the fundamentalist extreme, the text is considered to be the literal dictation of God to his prophets and evangelists. Most non-fundamentalists believe the text contains what God wants us to understand about him and our relationship with him but is couched in human language which reflects the personality and culture of the human authors. In either case, the texts have the quality of God's wisdom and authority. Divine revelation, then, is the Creator giving humankind knowledge and direction; until that revelation was made, we might not know it with conviction or be able to arrive at it ourselves, at least not at the time it was written.

To start the chronology of humankind and revelation with Genesis is short-sighted. Written revelation has existed for a very short period of human existence. It is a little more than 2000 years during which revelation texts were being composed and another 2000 years until today during which time it has been studied as containing God's revelation. Let's put this into perspective. If we compare the total period of human existence to a 24 hour day, we can begin to see how short a time written revelation has been with us. If the first human person appeared on Earth at the beginning of our anthropological day, that is at zero seconds, then Genesis was composed at about 11:22 pm. Jesus Christ was born at 11:41 pm. If you are fifty years old, then you were born 29 seconds before the stroke of midnight, which is the time at which you are reading this text.

3

Did all the generations of humankind who lived their lives during the first twenty-three and a half hours of the anthropological day have no revelation? Were they just throw-away generations who simply lived in the dark? Any speculations we might make would be motivated by our discomfort at how this reflects on God. It is not sufficient to say that this is the way God did it and we must be satisfied with it. Are we certain that this is the way God did it? To have left humanity adrift for the vast majority of its history seems very much out of character for the Creator of all things who had a divine purpose in mind. Was there no revelation to guide primitive humanity?

From the moment a human being walked on Earth, there was a useful form of revelation which predates textual revelation and can be called natural revelation. This form of revelation has many new and important things to say to us today. What natural revelation said to primitive humankind was not a compendium of dogmas about the Creator. It was a collection of principles, attitudes and conclusions which helped satisfy the curiosity of the time and laid a foundation for future development of more profound understanding. Nature itself and not God pointed the way to these conclusions. This collection was derived from the process of encountering the physical world in daily life. Often the specific conclusion was faulty but it preserved an awareness of an idea central to reality and preserved it ready for the opportunity to improve on it.

This is a revelation that needs no prophets to articulate it or fixed text to explain it. In fact it was rarely if ever looked upon as a process of revelation but simply as a useful conclusion drawn from personal observation. After very many generations of humanity, some of those conclusions began to focus on a person causing the things which could not be otherwise explained and thus began our notion of a god.

In the thirteenth century, Thomas Aquinas used the philosophical concepts of Aristotle (384-322 BCE) to initiate a theological inquiry, motivated by faith, into God's existence. He was not offering proofs based on evidence from the natural world. He was demonstrating the connection between the theological conclusions and his experience of the natural world. If the physical universe had a creator, one would expect a connection. This reasoning underlines the reasonableness or fittingness of theological conclusions even though it does not prove them.

The term philosophy is the key here. As the scholastic philosophers who followed Aquinas defined it, philosophy is the science of all things, in their ultimate causes and reasons, derived using the light of natural reason. But reason cannot divorce itself completely from observation. Without it

4

there would be very little to think about. As a result, when Aquinas, in his first proof from motion, speaks about recognizing that whenever something moves, it had a mover, this is a physical observation. When he considers the necessity of a first mover, he is out of the realm of science and into the realm of philosophy. When he turns to divine revelation and introduces the words, "In the beginning God created..." he is in the realm of faith and theology, which is faith seeking understanding.

I include in natural revelation any support which the physical sciences give to philosophical considerations concerning the Creator. That support is the connection between nature and philosophy and without which these philosophical considerations could not proceed or correct themselves. Such corrections are often necessary. The Greek philosopher Plato reasoned that matter exists, but since nothing can come from nothing, matter is eternal. He could not admit the creation of matter. Of course at the time, there were thought to be only four elements in the universe: earth, fire, air and water. Scientific observations have corrected these errors.

Natural revelation shows us things like cause and effect, the stability of nature and the almost incomprehensible magnitude of our universe. From these ideas, our natural curiosity leads us to seek the first cause and the great designer. Natural revelation is all the implications we can derive from material facts and the philosophical or theological conclusions which they suggest. These conclusions are not just those concerning grand ideas about the Creator but can also contribute to our understanding of ourselves in relation to that creative God.

Early revelation

You and I may often quote biblical revelation but can we quote natural revelation? Conclusions derived from natural revelation by the generations of humanity which preceded the revealed texts can be clearly seen in the biblical text. The notion of the existence of a controlling being external to the universe was a longstanding assumption for hundreds of generations before the *Old Testament*. Pagan myths give testimony to this conclusion, albeit by way of sometimes petty and vindictive gods. We take these early conclusions for granted and never ask ourselves where they came from. Psalm 65 tells of a God, "who formed the mountains by your power, having armed yourself with strength, who stilled the roaring of the seas, the roaring of their waves, and the turmoil of the nations." These ideas come from the primitive recognition that everything we see has a cause. And because the natural forces are powerful, they must be controlled by a powerful being.

5

The most primitive cultures recognized the predictability and regularity of the objects in the heavens and the seasons. There were times, however, when the seasons were unkind and these had to be explained. Psalm 25 can say, "All the ways of the Lord are loving and faithful for those who keep the demands of his covenant." They assumed that when the seasons were not kind to them, it was punishment for disobeying the covenant. This notion was not unique to Israel. Pagans made human sacrifices to appease the gods just as Abraham was ready to sacrifice his son Isaac. This is simply a human reaction to a natural situation, to the evidence. If you cannot control something directly, the next option is to influence the one who has control.

These foundational concepts whose influence we can find in early religious faith were the result of natural revelation, the way things were perceived. They did not need to be the subject of direct divine revelation. Because primitive humanity's understanding of the natural world was so extremely limited many, indeed most, of their ideas about the natural world were in error.

Long before Genesis was written, the natural revelation was not how God made all things. That God did it was assumed. The important revelation tells us what God had in mind when he created these things. Since we can use many things to our benefit, it was concluded that the controller must have made them for that purpose. We see regularity in the motion of heavenly bodies so the controller must be trustworthy and faithful. We see beneficence in the ability of the land and weather to provide food so the controller must be beneficent and loving. God has our welfare in mind.

The basic tools used to deal with these questions were imagination and speculative logic expressed through the cultural assumptions of the day. Eventually, into this cultural environment came textual revelation. The human authors of the *Old Testament* were not describing specific events in exact detail. They were expressing their conviction that the Creator continued to have a hand in human history. They often made this point through the use of parables based on the memories and legends of past events. A local flood, for example, might be portrayed as covering the whole Earth. It was in fact the whole Earth for those people who experienced. It also makes for a better and more repeatable story that way. But the divine revelation contained in it remains the same whether it was universal or not. The conclusion to be drawn from the story of the flood was not that we should be impressed by such a great flood but rather by God's care for his chosen people through intervention in history for their benefit.

While the parables were primitive and imaginative, the conclusions derived from natural revelation remained constant assumptions. They were so seamlessly incorporated into textual revelation that they were considered a part of that divine revelation rather than natural revelation. This tendency to conflate natural revelation with divine revelation can distract us from what is being divinely revealed in the sacred text. An awareness of the influence of natural revelation can clear the air, especially in the book of Genesis where the text encounters the natural world.

Modern revelation

In the last 150 years science has made profound and fundamental discoveries about the physical universe. Relativity, quantum mechanics and the Big Bang can be described as revelations to the scientists. They can be revelations to the theologians as well. Since the Greeks and Persians used geometry to describe the motion of the celestial bodies, we have known that the constancy and regularity seen in their movement can be described with mathematical precision. But geometry could not tell us why. Isaac Newton's algebraic expression of the law of gravity told us why the geometry worked but did not tell us why there is such a thing as gravity which makes it work. His equations defined the physical world which impressed us with its stability and inevitability and seemed to admit of no exceptions. This gave mathematics an eternal quality not unlike the perceived stability and immutability of Christian truth.

But there is even more. Recent insights into the makeup of the physical universe can give us a new and more profound understanding of what was created. For example, in the Genesis account of the creation of humankind, we have been given stewardship of all creation. It is only in recent times that we have become aware of the full implications of this, how critically important stewardship is. This is true not only for our physical environment but social, economic and psychological environment as well.

As we read the Scriptures, we become aware of the evolutionary character of what it reveals. Some of the basic concepts found in the early books of the *Old Testament* are expanded in later books. The contemporaries of Genesis did not necessarily believe in only one God. They believed that by being faithful to their God, Yahweh, they need not worry about the other gods. In the early books of the *Old Testament* the idea of life after death was missing. The reward of a life faithful to God meant that you were rewarded in this life.

7

Today, in a sense, revelation has come full circle. It began with natural revelation, proceeded to textual revelation and we now have the opportunity to return to natural revelation for greater insights. Modern science has opened a window on our natural world. There is a whole new world of natural revelation to consider.

The Creator is being revealed through what was created just as artists reveal a bit of themselves in their collected works. The twentieth century philosopher and historian, Etienne Gelson, described science as thinking God's thoughts after him. We probe the mind of God by studying the physical things he brought into being.

Natural revelation can aid the process of understanding the sacred text as well as give us new insights into the nature of God. It can help us distinguish those things in Sacred Scripture which are the result of cultural influences on the human author from those things God intends all generations to understand and practice. It can also give us new insights into the character of the creative God as well as the potential and limits of the physical bodies we inhabit. It is like a forensic search for the fingerprints of the Creator.

All fields of human understanding have progressed more in the last four hundred years than during all previous human history. These include our understanding of the physical, social and emotional universe which resulted from that first creative act. Most of those advances have occurred in the last 150 years. A human being is understood through physical, biological, psychological and social laws of our human nature. It is true that most often this understanding has grown without any formal reference to the Creator. Yet any scientist who thinks that scientific conclusions have no impact on theology does not understand the nature of theology. Any theologian who thinks that recent advances in science have no capacity to impact their understanding of the creator God has neglected to keep in touch with what is happening in science. As science progresses and new discoveries are revealed, theology should feel obliged to make reformulated and deeper expressions of faith that incorporate these scientific insights. Physical science can be both a resource and a moderator for theology.

Our image of God

In the age of the *Old Testament*, humanity thought that God was awesome because he organized the chaotic world into what we see. You and I have seen the astronomical photos taken by the Hubble space telescope and satellite photographs of other planets in our solar system. We

8

are awed by the size, beauty and complexity of the universe in a way that the people of the *Old Testament* did not even have the vocabulary to discuss. Terms like quantum, black holes, gravity, light years, nebula, galaxies, supernova did not exist. This is the more accurate way to describe the world around us.

Today our scientific understanding of the natural world offers us a new level of natural revelation. It can help us improve our image of God. The first divine image which the *Old Testament* gives us is that of a Creator, or should we more accurately say craftsman on a colossal scale. There are two different creation stories in the first two chapters of Genesis. They are appropriate and effective for the primitive concept of the physical and life-filled world as observed and understood by the human population in the early Bronze Age. Theologians and natural philosophers for some 1500 years after the death of Christ shared that same view. It is obviously at odds with what physics teaches today. Furthermore, at the time Genesis was being written, there was no concept of a life after death. Should this matter?

When we consider the world from a scientific viewpoint, our image of God changes from an Old Testament craftsman putting order into a chaotic world to a creative mind so profound that it exceeds our greatest imaginings. The story of creation in six days is an imaginative one and speaks appropriately to the primitive experience. It made the listener feel comfortable in a world that can be extremely hostile. The Big Bang and other scientific understandings proposed by physicists today inspire awe and wonder and elevate the idea of Creator to a new level. We can benefit from both.

How we understand

For believers, formal texts such as the *Bible* hold a prime place as revelation but to limit revelation to these words limits some concepts to the culture and intellectual boundaries of the understandings at the time the texts were written. Textual revelation has benefited from advanced tools of study such as textual, form and historical criticism. In the same way, a more profound understanding of physics and the origin of the physical universe, what the creative act produced, are opening a new and more profound understanding of God as Creator. If theology wants to understand why God created, it will first need to understand the full extent and nature of what was created.

The *Bible* is not always easy to understand. If the sacred texts are the "word of God," we sometimes get the impression that God had some difficulty explaining thing and at times even changed his mind. This is obvious from the multiplicity of interpretations we find among those who consider these texts as a source of God's revelation. I once saw a cartoon of a young graduate devil ready to go out into the world to tempt the human population. He was standing before Satan who was pointing a finger at him and saying, "Now remember, quote a lot of Scripture!" To decide what these words are trying to tell us, we need to use every tool at our disposal, including our best knowledge of the physical world. This becomes especially true when we try to use the natural law as a model of the moral law. We must be very certain what that natural law is.

The need for a rational basis of our understanding of all revelation is urgent. On a very practical level, each advance in technology can bring with it a challenge to traditional Christian values. Accurate Scriptural interpretation, however, will never contradict accurate science. Science has the more rigorous method of proof yet little attention is given to the contribution science can make to our understanding of God. In part, this is because theology has preferred to consider God primarily as redeemer and not Creator. The focus has been primarily on personal salvation and less on creatively living our life for the benefit of all society. But it is the same God in both models.

When we want to learn about the physical universe, we don't turn to the *Bible*. God has given us the physical senses to be observers and the intellectual tools to discover and understand our observations. He gave us the ability to make inferences about what he is like based on what we observe around us. Why should God tell us things we can discover ourselves? Many of the things revealed to us both in nature and in the Scriptures are the things we cannot detect with our senses, things we cannot observe directly.

We are able to understand goodness by seeing things which are able to achieve their purpose. A person's actions are good if they contribute positively to the human community. We arrive at a concept of power and energy by experiencing things with power or energy. Perhaps the first lesson about the physical world every human being learns is the power behind the force of gravity even though it is the weakest of all physical forces. We learned it as a child the first time we fell down. While gravity was not defined until the seventeenth century, every human who existed before that definition knew about it and even used it to their advantage. Is it possible that our sense of immortality is also the realization of a reality we find difficult to explain? For us, revelation is in the conclusions we draw from the things we observe in nature or derive from the Scriptures.

How to proceed

We can see from history that whenever scientists and theologians attempted to understand physical nature, they often got it wrong: for example, how our universe began, the movement of the stars and planets or the arrival of living species. We will consider each of these three basic topics. They are the evolving record of our struggle with revelation, natural and Scriptural, and they document the dangers we can encounter in the process.

The main points to be developed in the following pages are these:

- With the maturing of experimental science, theology has much to gain by reassessing its past conclusions about the human person in light of current scientific findings.

- Taking the example of scientists, theologians need to learn how to deal with uncertainty rather than resort to authority and tradition. This is the only way to regain any credibility in the eyes of secular society and perhaps among church members as well.

- Abandoning the notion of original sin means replacing it with a renewed development of the revelation contained in the incarnation. This opens the possibility of rewarding advances to deeper understanding of traditional dogmas which have become static and mired in metaphors of the past.

- Finally, the concept of evolution applies not just to the biology of living organisms, humans included. It is also the method of choice used by the Creator for all that exists and is still driving changes in the realms of material substances, living organisms, social constructs, economics as well as religion's understanding of God and our relationship with that God.

In other words, religion is not simply a matter of God said it, I believe it and that ends it. Instead, it is the adventure of recognising the small revelations God offers us both through Scripture and nature and attempting to arrive at new insights about a God we know we can never fully understand.

We will start with the creation story in the first chapter of Genesis and look at the ways it has been interpreted. This defines for us the problem of the natural and divine realms and how they come together. We will continue by considering the contributions of Copernicus and then the long running saga between the Catholic Church and Galileo and their view of how the heavenly bodies move relative to the Earth.[2] We will consider what natural revelation has contributed to human understanding through

11

this controversy.

The works of Copernicus, Galileo and others marked the beginning of science as a true discipline. There followed a period in history called the Age of Enlightenment which forced Christians to rethink and clarify the way revealed texts are read. The methods which science established made possible the discoveries of modern science and thus new possibilities for natural revelation. For the first time in the history of humanity, we began to understand the reality of our physical universe. What we discovered contained as many mysteries as any theological investigation of the nature of God. It is helpful to trace the history of the development of physical science and the personalities involved. Only in this way can we begin to appreciate the enthusiasm of the scientist and the difficulty they can have with the closed and authoritarian system that is much of Christian theology.

The theory of evolution followed the Enlightenment and brings us back to the second creation story in Genesis 2-3. The problems generated by misguided religious fervor about what the Bible tells us of the origin of humanity were played out publicly in the court room during the famous Scopes monkey trials in 1925, in Dayton, Tennessee. Oddly enough the issue continues today in the creationist and Intelligent Design controversies waged predominately in the United States. We will also consider the work of a priest and noted palaeontologist, Teilhard de Chardin. Like Galileo, he was treated badly by the Church. What we will discover, however, is that the real issue in both cases was not revelation but authority.

Finally we will try to take the lessons learned from these examples and see how they can influence our response to modern natural revelation in the most practical terms. To this end, we will consider the twenty-first century implications in both morality and spirituality. That response must be supported by a theology which fully recognizes the implications of modern natural science, especially that resulting from evolution which drives all natural development.

Notes

1. Because we are not trying to develop an exact anthropology, throughout this book I will use this number as the time during which Homo sapiens has inhabited Earth.
2. I call it "long running" because, while Galileo died in 1642, the final verdict was not issued by the Catholic Church until 350 years later, in 1992.

2

In The Beginning - Genesis 1

If we could catch God in an informal setting and in a mood of reflection, how might he describe what he brought about in the act of creation? God might begin by telling us that he initiated an enduring and evolving physical reality we now call matter and endowed it with such energy, potency and quantity that for 13.7 billion Earth years it has spun, congealed, expanded and reacted to form a universe. Throughout that universe planets formed, spinning on their axis while in orbit around the warm glow of spherical nuclear reactors of overwhelming size which we call suns or stars.

On at least one of these planets, because of its fortuitous position and the potency of matter, there evolved living organisms. Their variety, stability and adaptability allowed them to flourish and evolve into forms more beautiful and intriguing than all the bodies spinning in the heavens. There then developed living beings with the imagination and curiosity to want to understand what has been happening.

This universe has suddenly changed from a clockwork model whose gears are the relentless laws governing its material reality to one that can choose, appreciate, empathize and plan. It is not just God standing at a distance watching with fascination this complex and ever changing universe. Now the model itself has begun to understand and appreciate itself. At this human level, it has become a universe in which each of these conscious organisms is an individual to be appreciated and valued in itself. They are persons not unlike God in that, as a person, they are able to to choose. Here may be the secret behind this development. God can watch this universe with greater interest and surprise. Its possibilities and creativity are limitless. You begin to suspect that God's purpose behind this was that he thought we would like it.

At this point God stops speaking. Clearly he could explain everything to us but that would deny us the joy and satisfaction of arriving at an understanding using our own intellectual ability and curiosity. It would also deny him the thrill of watching us do it. All persons are capable of being thrilled. Secondly, achieving understanding is a process, not an event. It requires accumulated experience to develop the necessary vocabulary and concepts. For this reason he patiently waited some 150,000 years for that experience to accumulate, a mere moment in his eyes. He then cleverly inspired a few individuals in the course of time to express in literary forms, using language understood in their society, subtle ideas to guide their conclusions and direct their thinking.

Some have thought that this inspiration was too subtle and resulted in an inability to see clearly his hand in the process of revelation. Others wanted more obvious involvement for the sake of a feeling of security about the revelations. Most of us see this light touch as a sign of respect for our individuality, creativity and free will. As a result, because of these textual revelations and what the physical universe indicates to us through natural revelation, we do have rich provisions with which to work out some of the meaning of it all.

The Genesis story

Textual revelation started out as oral tradition and became a collection of books which took some 2000 years to compose and collect and became known as the *Bible*. For our immediate purpose we will begin at the beginning with the creation story found in the first chapter of Genesis and try to read it as if we had never seen it before and knew nothing about where it came from or why anyone wrote it in the first place. We will pretend that someone handed us two pages of text containing some 770 words and suggested, "Read this." At this point, if you have not read chapter 1 of Genesis recently, you might want to do it again and then return here.

The story is about what God did when he "created" the heavens and the earth. I use quotations because at the time Genesis 1 was put into writing, the authors could not have understood our concept of the act of creating something, that is, making something out of nothing. In the story, even before God said, "Let there be light." there was "a wind sweeping over the waters." Darkness and chaos do not imply emptiness. The concept of "nothing" is difficult to deal with; it is not the same as "zero" or "nought".[1]

Our choice of translation becomes clearly wrong when we read on and discover that what God really does during the first six days is not make things out of nothing. Throughout the *Old Testament*, references to God creating really mean ordering. Isaiah uses the image of God as a potter molding clay but not creating it first (Is 29:16).

In the first three days God seized this "huge agglomeration of upset" and separated light from darkness, waters above (rain) from waters below (seas and rivers), and finally dry land from the waters below. In the next three days, he populated the dome holding back the waters above with

14

lights of the day and night. Then he populated the waters below with fish and the air under the dome with birds. Finally, he populated the dry land by forming from the earth – the potter again - animals and humanity, male and female.

When we read something we need to know what kind of writing it is. Is it history, a humorous story, newspaper report, poetry, a scientific paper? Clearly Genesis 1 is not a page from a science book. If by science we mean the study of material things, then this story simply tells us that there is stuff and it gets sorted out, organized. But how does one separate light from darkness? This is figurative speech. It is a result of the view of the world at the time.[2]

Our first question might be, where does this text come from? We would be told that it originated in the middle east some 4000 years ago. The best thinking says that it was probably handed down for centuries by word of mouth and underwent many modifications before it was committed to writing. It was influenced by the other myths of the time from Egypt and Mesopotamia. Those who finally put it into written form had the benefit of improvements made during many retellings.

To understand what was written we must try to put ourselves in the shoes of a person living at the time it was composed. They recognized that all these things actually happened in some way. They saw the world as the end result of some kind of activity. The evidence is everywhere so something had to bring it about; every effect must have a cause. Tents don't build themselves, animals must be led, wells must be dug and fires must be ignited. So how did all this organization come about? Obviously, someone did it. There was a plan.

Since to primitive people this cause seemed to act much like humans do, at times out of whim and at times, so it seemed, in response to prayers and sacrifices, this god must be a person very much like themselves. This gave them a person they might deal with and that gave them hope. Today, we may smile at the notion of a rain god or sun god, but given the original assumptions about causes and the severe limitations on observation, gods are the result of a reasonable chain of logic. People in that era did not need divine revelation to tell them that someone or something caused the order they saw around them. Humanity came to that conclusion long before Genesis was written.

It is little wonder then that in the Genesis story of creation in six days we find the God who fashions the world acting very much in a human way. He even needed a day to rest when it is completed. God's actions are so human that there is the implication that he worked with a committee of advisors. He says, "Let us make…" as he creates the first humans. All great endeavors in primitive society were conducted in this way. All the myths from ancient Near-East cultures presume this human-like agency as the cause of all things, even producing order from chaos.

To that primitive society which gave rise to Genesis 1, the satisfying, interesting and useful thing was not the science which it did or did not contain, nor the physical history of how it happened. Such speculations were of little interest in a nomadic society faced with so many physical hardships. Their questions must have been how to influence things they could not directly control, was there any reason for hope and how could they relate to the Creator of it all?

A clue to the interest in this story can be found in the reaction to it for the next 3500 years. Unlike the pagan myths of the same period, this story took on a life of its own. It became the mainstay of Judeo-Christian culture. Genesis 1 explained why God formed these male and female people. They are to multiply, have dominion over the rest of what God made and subdue the earth. To accomplish this, God gave them every plant and animal for food. Furthermore, he made them in his own image. This meant that they were able to make decisions, able to choose what they wanted to do.

We are still asking these questions today with even more intensity. Richard Feynman, the Noble prize winning physicist, gave three lectures under the topic, "A Scientist Looks at Society" published under the title *The Meaning of it All*. It should not surprise us that a scientist is interested in the meaning of it all, including social relationships. Clearly, if we have not yet adequately formulated the answer to these questions, we should expect that every new attempt by individuals of different backgrounds can only help us draw our intermediate conclusions.

Common sense

We tend to believe that our explanations and conclusions are final rather than intermediate. If we have any sense of history we should see the flaw in this approach. We can only act on our current understandings but we should never rule out a better one down the road, one which may even drastically change our response. The history of every human study, theology as well as natural science, is filled with inadequate formulations and changes, maturing understandings. If this is true of our understanding of the natural world around us, why should it be any different with our understanding of God who should, by definition, be far more complex and difficult for humans to explain. Science has found that all space need not contain an ether to make action at a distance possible and theology has abandoned the need for a place of limbo for souls that were not baptized. Quantum mechanics allowed science to proceed beyond the point where Newtonian physics became inaccurate and theology has been able to improve its thinking about slavery, usury and sharing worship with people of different theological beliefs.

A problem we have when trying to understand the physical universe is that our common sense gets in the way, what G. K. Chesterton referred to as commonplace opinion. This happened at the time Genesis was being composed and it still happens today. Albert Einstein discovered that as you move faster, time slows down, you become more massive and you grow thinner in the direction in which you are traveling. None of that makes sense but it is true. Of course the speed you must travel has to be very fast before you notice it but it has been measured after long jet air travel using atomic clocks. Or consider a tree. Nearly 50% of the material forming the structure of that tree was formed out of air, not the ground it is growing in. Our common sense does not tell us this but the basic component of the tree is carbon. The photosynthesis which takes place in the leaves extracts the carbon from CO_2 in the air.

The science books I studied when young claimed that there were two laws of conservation. They stated that energy cannot be created or destroyed, nor can matter be created or destroyed. This certainly made good sense since matter, the stuff of the universe and energy, the ability to do work, are obviously two completely different things. The equation which everyone has seen, $E=MC^2$, equates Energy with Matter which implies that you can go from one to the other. The equal sign "=" is a symbolic substitute for the word "is". Thus if you say this equation in words it tells you that energy is matter. The frightening thing is that C, the speed of light, is a very big number, three hundred million meters per second. Since C is such a large number, you need only convert a very small amount of matter into energy and you end up with a huge energy release. The atomic bomb demonstrated this equation in a dramatic way.

Our powers of observation, and thus our common sense notions about things, are also affected by preconceived notions which may or may not be accurate. This is especially true concerning what we believe about the universe in which we live. To illustrate this, ask yourself which of the following statements are true and which are in error?
- Comet tails are always behind the comet.
- Comets are burning and giving off gas as their tail.
- The primary purpose of the front telescope lens is to magnify.

- The Sun shines by burning gas or from molten lava.
- The Sun is solid.
- The galaxy, the solar system and the universe are all the same thing.
- The Moon alone causes tides.
- Many stars rapidly change brightness (twinkle).

I hope you noticed that they are all false. If you, with your twenty-first century education, were in error about any of these, can you imagine the problem experienced in the time of Genesis? Neil F. Comins, a university lecturer in astronomy, discovered that his students came to his introductory lecturers with more than 1500 such erroneous notions about the universe, as documented in his interesting book, *Heavenly Errors*[3]. Of course, we survive these errors quite well. It is only when we try to draw practical conclusions that we risk ill effects. When we try to draw theological conclusions from such faulty notions, we just compound the error. In some 150,000 years of human existence on Earth, we have had science based on empirical, testable and repeatable observations only in the last 600 years. Before this there was experience and common sense. Experience, that is observation, was severely limited by a lack of technology. More often than not, common sense failed us as well. As Comins points out, "most of what our distant ancestors thought about the natural world was wrong."

What to make of it today

So what is our reaction to Genesis 1 today? It is a clever story. It has such a wonderfully primitive view of the universe. The writer seems not the least bit interested in the creation elements of the story. Instead, the point being made appears to be that everything in the universe is essentially good and humans are the caretakers. After all, this goodness is repeated six times in the account. While Genesis contains many elements in common with other ancient Near-Eastern culture myths, the goodness of the creation is unique to Genesis. Of course this claim of goodness immediately gives rise to another question. Why is there so much evil in the world? Lo and behold, Genesis tackles that question in chapter 2 but we shall save that for later.

Another point which separates the Genesis account from other ancient myths is that God created the nature around us and as a result nature itself is not godlike. This point is reinforced in Isaiah when God says, "Shall the potter be regarded as the clay?" (Is 29:16) The same image is found in Jeremiah 18:6. "Just like the clay in the potters hand, so are you in my hand, O house of Israel." Ancient people worshiped the Sun and moon as gods who had influence and control over their lives. Genesis objects that the Sun and moon were produced by God and thus are subordinate to him and under his control. This is not a trivial difference.

It is a nice touch that, as related in the beginning of Genesis 2, God needed a rest when it was all done. The creative God of Genesis adds a personal touch. This is a person doing these things and the most powerful person one can imagine. He organizes the chaos and makes safe places where plants can grow, birds can fly, fish can swim and lights can shine with wonderful and cyclic regularity. Into this he places the first human beings and then needs a well deserved rest. And even if he has to say so himself, he saw that what he had done was very good. It is also interesting to note that in describing the first six days, each ends with the statement, "There was evening and there was morning, the first day" etc. But on that seventh day when God rested there is no mention of a conclusion to it. Does this imply that this last day has not yet ended? This is a God that we humans can be comfortable with.

The Old Testament generations most likely took the details of the Genesis story as fact. They were a common sense albeit faulty description of how things looked. But those details only satisfied curiosity. They merely had entertainment value. They made the retelling of the story interesting and easy to remember. More recent generations have consumed their time still trying to reconcile the six days with, perhaps, six geological periods in history, or worse yet, take it blindly as six days of 24 hours each. It might be thought that no harm is done by literal interpretation but all too many people with scientific interests hear these views and conclude that our idea of God is clouded by myths and our eyes are closed to the obvious. The question we might ask is why so many in modern generations have got so distracted by the physical details of the story? These divert our attention from the purpose of the text and give precedence to the physical descriptions as if they were a newspaper account, or worse, a scientific account of what happened. The truly important aspects of the story were the ideas of goodness and stewardship.

To simply say that all things are essentially good does not of itself inspire enthusiasm or move us to repeat it to others. But the story of Genesis 1 does. Even if we maintain that the *Bible* was dictated word for word by God, we must not rule out the possibility that God would use a parable or take poetic license in expressing ideas which are too difficult for the intended audience or not directly related to his purpose. We should not deny God or the human author the right to use rhetorical devices such as exaggeration, metaphor or humor. If we miss the humor in the book of Jonah, for example, we will probably miss the revelation as well.

Should not this universal goodness and stewardship of the Creator's arrangement of things be enough to expect from a story of so few words and written so long ago? Why insist that it be a scientific history as well? We do not read Shakespeare's plays because the characters are real. We read them because his fictitious characters reflect the reality of human nature. We read Genesis 1, not because it is a realistic representation of what happened historically and physically but because it portrays why creation happened and it does it in a way that is attractive, memorable and charged with imagination and human interest.

Genesis 1 is like a snapshot of someone walking and they look off balance in mid-step. All previous movement has been eliminated and we don't see clearly where the next step will take them. Those who composed Genesis had no idea what creation was like or what followed. They only knew the present and that is what they give us in their picture. But Genesis does a great service by insisting that human beings are in the picture and have been written into nature. To modern eyes, however, the picture can lack focus.

The scientific view

Genesis is about observing and understanding the things that are, that exist in our experience, and not how they got that way. As knowledge of the universe matured, some churchmen thought that science was a threat to human dignity and humankind's position in the universe. They lost track of the divine revelation in Genesis. Some scientists on the other hand concluded that humanity has no significance other than what humans themselves invest in a human lifetime. They may have done this because the theologians were unable to convince them of the importance and validity of the revelation contained in Scripture or, worse, tried to teach science to the scientist through Genesis - an absurd idea.

Yet science is unable to address certain forms of reality. Science deals only with those things which are measurable, repeatable and thus predictable. As a result, using the tools of science, one cannot show that no other reality exists. For example, science has nothing to say about what makes creation good or how to determine the value of created things. Yet it is this kind of information we expect to find in the Scriptures. And while it is recognized that things such as value are subjective, that is to say, not universally shared by every person, they are, nevertheless, experienced.

They are real to those who can recognize them and that is another form of measurement.

Neither can science deal with the purpose of something. From the viewpoint of science, no physical thing can be said to have a purpose, not an electron, not gravity, not magnetism. Given that these things exist, science can only tell us what their effects are. That is not to conclude that nothing has purpose. This is simply a reality that is out of the realm of physical science. So when Genesis suggests that humanity was created with a purpose, to increase and multiply so that we could take responsibility for the stewardship of our Earth and the human society on it, we begin to understand better the character of both the Creator and the creature. Scientific evidence can no more claim that nothing but physical reality exists than Genesis can claim to be about the physical origin of the universe. For either to do so would mean that they were simply being dogmatic on a subject outside the scope of their investigation.

One advantage science has is that it is useful, that is, utilitarian. Sooner or later the most theoretical science yields practical results through technology, for example transistors or nuclear energy. While science only gives incomplete control over a limited part of the universe, this does give value beyond mere existence. Through the power of technology, a human can become a creator in the full Old Testament sense of the word. The chaotic arrangement of silicon atoms is organized into a crystal to form a transistor or a computer chip that drives our PCs. This sense of value is experienced by scientists and theologians alike but defies quantification except on the stock market.

We have meaningful control over our immediate environment to enhance it or destroy it. It is curious that science and technology is what helps us most today in exercising stewardship as well as destructive force over creation, at least locally. That is not a trivial capacity. Genesis sees this as the way nature was created. Science discovers the physical relationships of the stuff of the universe. Through Scripture we learn of the human relationships we have with each other and, by extension, with the Creator which seems to be why all the rest of the stuff of the universe is there in the first place. Those beautiful and imaginative tales of six days and Adam and Eve have captured the imagination of every generation since they were first handed down by word of mouth and then set into writing thousands of years ago. The first hearers of those words came away with a valid understanding of where they stood with respect to the world around them even though they might have had a faulty notion of how it happened and the shape and location of that world.

21

How creation happened is a matter of history in which there were no witnesses and that is not what the Scriptures are interested in. Modern science can now make a good case of what did happen in those first moments of creation. There resulted an extremely active material universe of galaxies, stars and planetary systems. Here and there, the development of life forms added a kaleidoscope of never-ending patterns of bright colors. Human life added understanding and creativity to what otherwise would have been a lock-step universe. The Genesis conclusion about the human purpose in the created world was profound and significant but we now know that humans arrived long after the original creative act.

An important thing to recognize about science is that we are the ones who practice it. Genesis is keenly aware of that. The first human person is later portrayed as naming the animals and having an interest in what was created. Science cannot dismiss humans as being irrelevant to creation. Genesis 1 is much about creation and nothing about days. It is all about the divine purpose, the mind of the Creator and nothing about the manner or method of creation, all about humanity and little about the physical world.

We have a curious relationship with physical nature. If we were to make the Earth uninhabitable for humanity through a nuclear event, that would have no implications for the physical universe. We would have brought it about locally through natural means. Even if we do not do this, the Earth will eventually be destroyed by natural means when our sun ages and expands and incinerates all organic material and evaporates all water from the Earth and then consumes the entire planet as it expands to engulf much of the solar system. Such events are visible to astronomers throughout the observable universe. This will be the fate of our planet Earth unless before this happens it is struck by an asteroid large enough to so disrupt the atmosphere and physical character of the surface of the Earth that survival of animal life becomes impossible. In fact, this has already happened partially in the Earth's past and caused the demise of much of the life on it. Nature makes human life possible and sustains that life. Human activity can affect only the physical and social environment in which we live but not the nature which produces that environment.

Even though those who first received the Genesis creation stories could not have used it in the way we can today, every generation can find a rich wisdom in it. Note the word "use" instead of "interpret". Interpretation implies that we are explaining the meaning of the words. When speaking of Sacred Scripture, we need to distinguish between interpreting the meaning which the divine author originally had in mind for the words versus the application of the words to meanings we can give them with our

22

understandings today. This latter use of the text is called accommodation. There is nothing wrong with accommodation so long as we recognize it for what it is and don't confuse it with what was necessarily meant either by the human author or intended by God as revelation. We can accommodate the creation stories in the same way we accommodate a parable. Those who composed Genesis did not have our concern for ecology in mind even though we can see it as a stewardship issue today. If the story helps us understand something better, then it should be used for that purpose.

Our world

What is the picture of our world as given us in Genesis 1? Beyond the obvious, that it is composed of land, water, sky, lights and living things, the picture lacks much detail. If we try to make a sketch of this world, it would be patches of dry land floating on water. These sections of land and water extend at least as far as we can see or have ever traveled. Over this is an inverted bowl holding back the water above the land. After all rain must come from somewhere. The bowl is filled with air. The lights of the heavens are attached to the bowl and it rotates around the land every 24 hours. We can derive this from the details of the story but there was no illustration included when Genesis was written. But then these details were meant to feed the imagination.[3]

If we had pressed the first readers of Genesis on the details of the Earth and suggested that it was flat, they would probably have agreed. After all, any other shape and the water would run away and it would all be dry land. Furthermore, any other shape and it would be dangerous to travel. One would run the risk of rolling off. If the bowl keeps rotating around this flat Earth, then the Earth must be a disk. This would make travel risky. One might step off the edge of the disk and then what? We have no way of knowing if anyone proposed these questions at the time but we can be certain that no one ever stepped off the edge.[4]

The truth is that the ancient Greeks knew that the Earth was round. Greece is a nation with many islands. As a result, they were excellent navigators. What is more, many of the islands which surround the mainland are mountainous. The sailors noticed that as they sailed away from one of these islands, they first lost sight of the beach but could still see the mountain. If, however, they climbed up the rigging, they could again see the beach for a longer time. Lastly, of course, they lost sight of the top of the mountain. The only explanation for this is that the Earth is a globe, it is round and not flat. We can rest assured that they did not keep this a secret.

During the forth and third centuries BCE, a number of astronomers worked on the problem of the Earth's dimensions. It was Eratosthenes (276-194 BCE), a philosopher and scientist of Alexandria, who made the first good calculations. By measuring the angle of the shadow formed by the sun in two different cities directly north and south of each other at noon on the same day and then measuring the distance between these cities, a bit of geometry gave him the radius of the Earth with only ½ a percent error.

When the Greeks concluded that the Earth was round, there was no need to go back and change the Genesis story. That question never comes up in the story. As is usually the case, a discovery always leads to more questions. If the Earth is round, then why do we not fall off? It is not as though we are stuck to it. We don't worry about this because we know that we haven't fallen off yet and so there is little chance that we will in future. But neither do we immediately coin the word gravity to explain it. If you think it appropriate that God explain to us just how he made the universe, doesn't it seem reasonable that he would also tell us why we do not fall off the Earth?

The philosophical answer at the time was that the Earth was the center of creation and the place to accommodate humanity. To Aristotle it was simply the heaviness of objects made of the stuff of the Earth. He saw no connection between earthly characteristics and those of heavenly objects. So whatever held everything to the Earth had no influence on what went on in the heavens. These theories of Aristotle were turned into dogmas which became difficult to resist. They were very much a matter of common sense and the danger in that was not appreciated. Why there is gravity still remains one of the scientific mysteries of our world.

In the mid-sixteenth century Nicholas Copernicus speculated on why the Earth was a globe and proposed a few possibilities that sounded reasonable to him. It could have been, as he wrote, "because this figure (shape) is the most perfect of all, as it is an integral whole and needs no joints; or because this figure is the one having the greatest volume and this is especially suitable for that which is going to comprehend and conserve all things."[5] He even went on to suggest it might be because everything in the world tends to this form such as a drop of a liquid when it falls free from any surface. While his explanation for the reasons behind his observations seem to us fanciful and almost mystical, still his observations were accurate.

His reasons do become more practical. He pointed out that if you move far enough north, you see that the stars in the north do not set as they rotate and you lose sight of the stars in the south. He also explained the experience of sailors mentioned above. This would only be true on a globe shaped Earth. It is clear that this was the general understanding at the time and even the Church raised no question concerning the Earth being a globe, even though it was not in the form described in Genesis 1. Yet a scientific explanation was over a hundred years forthcoming, when Isaac Newton quantified gravity and showed that it is a property of all material substances in the universe. Gravity is the reason the Earth is a sphere. It is the result of a central force.

From ancient times, the understanding of natural science and the natural universe was so limited that, even well into Christianity, the Old Testament image of God and the literal interpretation of the Genesis account of creation was a comfortable and satisfying one. We are now in the twenty-first century and most of us are no longer comfortable with this image. The remainder of this book traces the story of what happened to bring about this rethinking of our interpretation of Genesis and our approach to textual revelation. It also considers how our modern understanding of the natural world impacts our image of God and some of the implications of this new image.

We should not underestimate the importance of intuitive conclusions of the past. In fact, such intuitions served early humanity well and, in part, gave us Genesis 1. The reason we do not give them much thought on their own is that these conclusions became a part of the cultural assumptions which produced the sacred books which we believe contain divine revelation. Since these conclusions preceded the sacred texts and yet are incorporated into the thought contained in them, it would be helpful to look at them as a body of natural revelation, even though much of it was in error. They are an essential part of the evolution of the human understanding of God. Furthermore, they were the first recorded attempts to deal with the purpose of creation and thus, the nature of God. Today we can make the case that the natural sciences are now at such a new level that they can offer us new insights through natural revelation.

Notes

1. Although we don't know with certainty, as a name for a number, the term and symbol for zero in mathematics is not found until about 876 in India and in the thirteenth century in western Europe, some 3000 years after Genesis was first imagined.
2. It was not until the sixteenth century and Isaac Newton that we

began to get a handle on the nature of light. But we should not be too hard on Genesis and its view of things because even Newton's model did not last. Einstein and then quantum theory refined the model and raised a new set of questions – but more about that in another chapter.

3. Neil F. Comins (2001) *Heavenly Errors, Columbia University Press.*

4. Although neither the *Bible* nor Christian theologians ever taught that the Earth was flat, this accusation was made in the nineteenth century in books by Washington Irving, John Draper and Andrew Dickson and became fixed in popular imagination.

5. Nicolaus Copernicus (1995) *On the Revolution of Heavenly Spheres,* Prometheus Books.

3

The Arrival of Science

We have been considering the understanding of the universe which humanity had for more than 97% of its history. For most of the period for which we have a written account, from Genesis, the story was primitive and limited. It was the common sense view a person gets from observation of this world. But from what we know today about the universe and the processes at work in it, this picture is not so impressive. It can seem very much like someone building a lavish model train set. The only difference is that instead of going to the local shop and buying a set of model animals to graze in the make-believe field through which the tracks run, God could make them himself out of the material that was at hand. The whole thing ran like a clockwork model universe which God then wound up and watched with great interest. God was also ready to interfere at will or at the request of one of the human creatures he had placed in it. He could reach in and move the clouds or hold back the waters of a river or change the fate of a king and his armies.

Prior to the sixteenth century, we were not dealing with science as we understand it today. It was best called natural philosophy. It was a philosophy whose primary interest was not nature but humanity. Nature was seldom being studied in and of itself. But all that changed during the period we are to discuss in this chapter, the period from the theory of Copernicus (1473-1543) until the publication of the findings of Galileo (1564-1642). This period changed the way the western world would eventually see themselves, their view of the universe in which they lived and the way they investigated that universe. Since humanity had been considered to be at the centre of the universe, this was bound to have a profound impact on our perception of the position humanity occupied in that universe. This directly impacted religious thinking. Created things reflect in some way the Creator. But if nature is going to reveal anything to us about its Creator, we must first understand the workings of that nature.

Early theories

For some 150,000 years humanity struggled with nature in order to survive, understand it, tame it and use it to their advantage. Evidence of this is found in what we know as the stone, bronze and iron ages. They had also realized that everything was caused by something. It was natural to try to influence whoever had control over natural events, the gods. While the Genesis story recorded an account of the creator God who controls the universe, it is not a description of its physical reality.

The first serious attempt to explain the whole natural universe was made by Aristotle, the Greek philosopher and primitive scientist. While the philosophical contribution of Aristotle is the subject of study even today, his science is now no more than a museum display. But this obscures the influence his science had for more than 1500 years after its formulation. He had been a student of Plato who was a great philosopher but not an astronomer. It was Plato who insisted that the objects of the heavens must travel at constant speeds and in perfect circles. This was necessary since they were created by a perfect divine being. It was because Aristotle assumed this to be true that it became the basic dogma of astronomy until the end of the seventeenth century.

The model of the universe according to Aristotle was very logical, fitting and seemed to be confirmed by common sense. The Earth was at the center and was the most inferior part of the universe. It was here that change could be observed. Perfection, of course would not admit of change. Clearly, things move on Earth, are born and die. If you set something in motion it slows down due to friction. It also meant that the stuff of the Earth was unique and nothing like the stuff of the heavenly bodies which rotated around it. Nor were these bodies influenced in any way by the Earth.

The rest of the universe was composed of perfect spheres which were layered around the Earth like the layers of an onion. There were the spheres of the moon, the planets, the Sun and then the fixed stars. Significantly, the controller of all this was outside the last sphere which was the source of all perfection, the prime mover of the whole universe. While Aristotle was a pagan, notice how this image of the universe can confirm the image in the Genesis 1 story. It is little wonder that it was embraced by Christian theology as reality.

Greek mathematicians contributed much that was practical to western civilization. It had begun with the philosopher and mathematician Pythagoras (c 570–495 BCE). His geometry became the basic tool of astronomy. Being sailors, the Greeks quickly concluded that the Earth was a globe. Sailing required navigation and that required geometry and astronomy. Geometry was put to the service of navigation as well as architecture, computation of time and land survey. Geometry applications started with the Greek mathematician Hipparchus (c 190–120 BCE). His observations and methods were so accurate that he was able to determine the length of the year to within a few minutes of the accurate value. The measurement of the year was important to farmers in determining the seasons and the best time to plant and harvest. So there were many practical reasons to develop geometry and astronomy. Hipparchus also put together the first tabulation of the stars, the bible of the sailors, and the map of the constellations, those mythical figures which were outlined by the stars and marked the seasons.

Ptolemy, solutions and problems

Nearly three centuries later Aristotle's work was taken up by the mathematician and astronomer Ptolemy of Alexandria in the second century CE. He expanded the catalogue of the stars and set about to explain the motion of the planets in the solar system. He also was burdened by the Aristotelian assumption that the Earth was unmoved at the centre of the system. In fact, this view of the world was a comfortable one. How could the Earth be moving when you and I are standing on it and feel no movement? Furthermore, if it were not stationary, we would feel a constant wind as it rotated and that is not the case. Thus it is only common sense that all these luminaries are rotating around us on our stationary and central globe.

Another part of Ptolemy's logic was the accepted wisdom that all objects must fall to the centre of the universe. Our experience shows that all objects fall to Earth, so the conclusion was obvious. The Earth must be motionless since, if it rotated once every 24 hours, when you threw something up into the air it would not land in the same place from which it came. Even though this view misses the fact that the object you throw as well as the air are also rotating with the Earth, there is good insight in it.

Christianity went along with this because if we humans were the culmination of creation, the most important of God's works, then it was only fitting that the very ground we walked on must be at the center of it all. This was a philosophical conclusion, not a theological one. Under such persuasive reasoning, why would anyone question these traditional assumptions? To the ancient who traveled by foot, camel or sailboat, the size of the Earth seemed impressive when compared to the other heavenly bodies. Thus this model of the universe was accepted even into the sixteenth century.

There was still that nagging problem of the wandering stars we now call planets which did not hold their place against the fixed stars and even at times went backward across the sky. They did not quite fit the mechanical clockwork regularity of the rest of the heavenly activity. In order to explain the complex motion of the planets as seen from the Earth, Ptolemy built a complex clockwork system of circles whose centers were going around in larger circles. Thus, the planets were attached to the rim of wheels that rotated and the axle of the wheel rotated in a perfect circle around the Earth. In the end, he needed nearly forty wheels and yet the system still did not make consistently accurate predictions of the positions of the planets. In spite of this, his scheme remained the accepted model.

What made his model even more difficult to conform with observations was that he assumed that all the heavenly bodies moved in perfect circles. This idea had been proclaimed as dogma by Plato in the fourth century BCE. After all, the gods would not create anything that was not perfect and no curved path was higher in perfection than a circle. In spite of its complexity and inaccuracies, Ptolemy's scheme was so ingenious that it became the standard of natural philosophy in the West. Today, we would immediately view as suspect any theory which was so complex because we know from experience that this is not the way nature most often works.

The model was also one in which heavenly bodies had to be attached to something. We do not experience things floating freely without falling to Earth. Thus the luminaries of the heavens were attached to a transparent sphere which rotated around the Earth and the planets also had their own spheres holding them in place and turning at a different rate. Everything in this view seemed to fit not only common sense and basic observations but the revealed image of God as found in the *Old Testament*. Everyone, it seemed, was quite happy with it but there is no new insight and little original thinking in his model. While Ptolemy had arrived at a plausible explanation, over the long term it proved to be less than accurate and it was so very complicated. Furthermore, the tables which astronomers used to predict Easter were obviously not accurate enough. The date of Easter was drifting by almost a day every century. It was when an attempt to correct these inaccuracies was begun in the mid sixteenth century that the whole system started to unravel and Aristotle's science began to be questioned.

The stories found in Genesis are anonymous and we do not know much about the personal lives of those early mathematicians who influenced our understanding of the universe. But as we take up the story in the sixteenth century, all that changes and the history of our understanding of the universe becomes one filled with unique personalities and human adventures. The human drama can be as interesting and informative as the science involved.

G. K. Chesterton observed that there is a sense in which the past is living, not dead. To look at the past is to look at what people freely chose to do. This makes it a human story and not something as inevitable as leaves dropping in the autumn. If we found school history lifeless and dry, it was because our teachers left out the choices made in the heat of daily human life. We are about to look at a period which reversed both the traditional notions of the universe and our notions of Sacred Scripture, a turning point in western civilization. It happened because a few imaginative individuals chose to use new tools in a creative way. While the future can be seen in what is expected or imagination can conjure, as we rethink the past, we find it filled with things entirely unexpected. It is the past that is full of surprises as well as the future. Choice means free will and that means free imagination. What was about to happen in the history of human understanding can only be called a wild adventure.

Nicholas Copernicus

By the time we reach the sixteenth century, one thing was begging for a better explanation. What is the real description of the physical arrangement of the universe? Some astronomers were uneasy with the complexity and inaccuracies of the Ptolemaic system. Yet if you moved away from the long accepted explanation, you ran the risk of coming into conflict with the Old Testament account of the origin of the universe. Sooner or later, someone was bound to make the imaginative leap and consider the physical universe from a different perspective. The man with the curiosity and imagination to do that was Nicholas Copernicus. Attempts to explain the origin of the universe would have to wait until the age of modern science and, as we shall see, is still being worked on with great vigor and interest.

Genesis had enshrined the common sense view of the universe into an imaginative story about the Creator and the intellectual community held fast to the stationary and Earth-centered universe for almost 4000 years after the writing of Genesis. Nicholas Copernicus would cast doubt on that view. He was born in 1473 in Poland and both parents died when he was a boy. He was taken into the care of his uncle who was an influential Catholic bishop. Because the boy showed obvious talent, his uncle intended to groom him for a high place in the Church. He studied at the University of Cracow and later attended the University of Bologna in Italy. It was probably here that he acquired his first interest in astronomy. Upon returning to Poland in 1501, he was made a canon, a diocesan position attached to the Cathedral. Two years later he went to Padua to study medicine. As a result, he was well versed in law and medicine as well as conversant in Latin and Greek with a good head for mathematics.

It is known that in 1513 he built an astronomical observatory with instruments to measure the position of heavenly objects and an astrolabe to measure the angles between the stars. Observation, however, was not his strong point. He relied on the tables of Hipparchus compiled for the fixed stars and Ptolemy for the planets. It is clear that he was trying to derive a model of the universe which would give accurate predictions. But since his basic premise placed the Earth at the center, he failed.

The Copernican theory

This failure led him to reread the ancient philosophers to see if there were any dissenting voices concerning a stationary and central Earth. He found such in Cicero, Plutarch and others who wrote of the early recognition that the Sun controlled the motion of the planets. In fact the idea had been suggested as early as 270 BCE by Aristarchus. Yet in spite of this correct insight, it was never developed into a complete theory. Copernicus admitted that this idea seemed absurd even to him but it gave him the encouragement to attempt a new approach and by 1514 he had devised a credible model of a sun centered universe. In his model, not only was the Earth revolving around the Sun but it was also spinning on its axis every 24 hours.

As soon as Copernicus put the Sun at the centre, everything started to fall into place with a beautiful simplicity. And while it was no more accurate in predicting the position of the planets, at least it did not need all those complicated corrections and wheels of Ptolemy. This was its great appeal and yet could also explain why it had little initial acceptance. A rotating and revolving Earth violated all received wisdom and the traditional teaching of the academic community, not to mention common sense since we on Earth do not feel any motion.

For the next thirty years he attempted to improve his model to resolve the inaccuracies encountered by Ptolemy. But, so long as he kept to the idea that orbits were perfect circles, he would never quite succeed. It is strange how Copernicus was able to make the bold leap by putting the Sun at the centre of the universe but still held to the philosophical view of orbits necessarily being perfect circles since they were established by the perfect Creator, God. Even great thinkers are blindsided by first impressions and instructions. The Alexandrian and Greek astronomers and mathematicians were giants in their science and their data was used by Copernicus. Yet they never made the intellectual leap with which Copernicus arrived at the correct view of the solar system. We shall find

32

this evident also in other great figures of early science, men like Kepler and even Newton. It is evidence that philosophical convictions can be as demanding of our intellectual assent as physical evidence. It also leaves unexplained the workings of creative thinking which is necessary for bold, new ideas.

By about 1530 Copernicus had finished the manuscript in which he set out his theory under the title *De Revolutionibus Orbum Coelestium* or *On the Revolution of the Celestial Spheres*. It was no small work with modern editions containing over 330 pages. He demonstrated his conclusions by extensive use of geometry which conformed to tables of data concerning the position of the planets. The lack of accuracy in predicting the position of the planets was part of his reason not to publish his theory.

Another contributing factor for his hesitation was that it was contrary to the well established thinking of centuries of university scholarship. He could not prove either mathematically or physically that his theory was true. Since he was so well placed in the Church and his credentials were without question, he had no reason to fear anything from the Church concerning his theory. None of this involved any defined Church doctrine. His main concerns were in regard to the academic community but there was also the nagging problem of the Protestant Reformation. Martin Luther had published his ninety-five theses in 1517 and one had to be careful about ideas which involved disagreement with the Church. For its part, the Church had assimilated the traditional opinions of the natural philosophers since they agreed so well with the Genesis account of creation.

Finally, with the encouragement and assistance of friends, Copernicus allowed his understanding to be published. It is said that he saw a copy of his work on his deathbed before he died of a stroke in 1543. It went into a second printing in 1566 and even today there are over 600 copies of these in rare book collections around the world. Many of them have liberal annotations made by the original readers which gives evidence of the attention the book was given. Strangely, most of the annotations are on the mathematical sections and not on those which place the sun at the center of the solar system. Still, until hard evidence could be found, his scheme of the universe would remain in question and not a universally accepted fact.

On a personal level, Copernicus was shy with very few friends. He gave way under the strong influence of his uncle and others. In spite of this he developed an accurate basic model of the solar system which would eventually change all thinking about the physical universe. It is not known to whom or how many scholars he sent his manuscript for review but word of it began to circulate widely in spite of the fact that it had not been published. Even the book's publication was surrounded by the influences of not one but two individuals, Rheticus and Osiander. The latter not only added a letter to the reader at the beginning of the book but also did a bit of editing. These left the impression that the work was strictly theoretical and need not be taken as truth. It tended to turn the work into a mathematical description of orbital motion rather than the reality of the universe. The involvement of Osiander was only revealed in 1609 in a publication by Johannes Kepler. This made the true purpose of the work obvious as a physical description of the universe.

Copernicus' work initially received little attention from officials in the Catholic Church. One reason for this may have been that the Church had bigger things to contend with. Pope Paul III convened the Council of Trent in 1545 to deal with the Protestant Reformation and that was enough to completely occupy its attention. As we shall see later, it was the work of Galileo that brought the ideas of Copernicus to the full attention of the Church and in early 1616 it issued a decree condemning *De Revolutionibus* and, shortly after that, it was placed on the index of forbidden books.[1]

Observational proof of the Copernican theory would later be offered by Galileo. A convincing explanation of what is really happening in the heavens was not clearly and definitively understood until Isaac Newton was able to describe it mathematically with the laws of gravity and motion in his *Mathematical Principles of Natural Philosophy* published in 1687. Even then it was another century before this understanding was fully accepted by natural philosophers in many European countries.[2]

Tycho Brahe and new data

As a result of the publication of the theory of Copernicus, astronomers realized that, for the theory to be proven, the first step was to show through observational data how the Earth moved relative to the other heavenly bodies. This would require very accurate measurements. This task was taken up by Tycho Brahe, a Danish astronomer who was born in 1546, just three years after the death of Copernicus.

Tycho was born into a well-to-do family in Denmark and was abducted at an early age by a wealthy uncle. He was given the best opportunities for education into law. At the age of 14 he was astounded by a total eclipse of the sun which had been accurately predicted. It created in him a great and lasting interest in astronomy. Then just three years later

34

there occurred a conjunction, or coming together in the same place in the sky, of the planets Jupiter and Saturn. This time, however, he found that the Copernican tables were inaccurate by several days and he decided to make every effort to correct them.

After he inherited a small estate of his father, he built an observatory. In 1572, at the age of 26, he discovered a new star in the constellation Cassiopeia and this made his reputation. It also put him on the edge of controversy. Since the time of Aristotle, it was held that the heavens are constant and unchanging. Theologians agreed with this since God had created the universe and that was the way it would remain. This was a satisfying outlook which gave the feeling of constancy and stability to what might otherwise be a threatening and unpredictable world. The arrival of a new star cast doubt on this trusted opinion. This was, perhaps, the first incontestable observational reality which seriously shook a firmly believed idea about the physical universe. Remarkably, these observations were being made with the unaided eye as the telescope had not yet been invented.

Based on the reputation this discovery gave Tycho, King Frederic II, who was a patron of science and the arts, granted him the island of Ven, near Copenhagen, along with a stipend to fund and maintain an observatory there. By constructing larger and more accurate instruments, Tycho accomplished there the most accurate observations ever made of the stars and planets before the invention of the telescope.

He made a slight improvement on the system of Ptolemy by letting all the other planets rotate around the sun. He did, however, disagree with Copernicus. He kept the sun and the moon rotating around the Earth which was at the centre of it all. But this was not his big contribution to astronomy. What he accomplished was the most accurate mapping of the solar system, as well as some 700 stars. He did this work over a period of 20 years while living at his private island observatory.

Unfortunately, Frederic II's successor, Christian IV, decided to see where all the money was being spent. The State was under increased need for money. He visited the island to see Tycho who was an irascible man.[3] Tycho had acquired a taste for spending great sums of money while tending less to his civic duties on the island. Legend has it that during Christian's visit, as he opened the door to leave a room, Tycho's dog, which he called Lep the Oracle, blocked the doorway and the king kicked him out of the way. Tycho objected so strongly that the king removed his stipend and he had to leave the island.

In 1599 he settled into a new observatory in Prague under a new patron, Emperor Rudolf II. Fortuitously, Tycho's assistant in Prague was a German professor of mathematics and astronomy, Johannes Kepler. They worked together long enough for Kepler to acquire great respect for Tycho's observational accuracy. Unfortunately, Tycho no longer had the intellectual drive or the physical vigor that had sustained him at his island observatory. Yet, considered in their totality, his accomplishments were gigantic for the age in which he lived and the simple instruments he had to work with. Accurate data was now at hand for others to investigate. Tycho Brahe died in 1601 of a bladder infection after a session of drunkenness.

Johannes Kepler

Johannes Kepler was born in Germany in 1571 into a very troubled and turbulent family.[4] Johannes was obviously intelligent but also of very poor health. In his teens, he attended a theological seminary where his academic excellence made him unpopular with his peers. After graduation from university, although he intended to pursue his theological interests, he was offered the position of astronomer and mathematician at the university of Gratz. In spite of some hesitations, he accepted.

As was the practice since ancient times, Kepler's initial interest in astronomy was more mystical than academic. The heavens, it was believed, were populated by the outline of the gods who influenced the lives of those on Earth and astronomy was still linked to astrology. Kepler was pleased that part of his responsibilities in Gratz was to produce an astrological calendar. He seemed very confident in the validity of what he produced.

The foundation of mathematics was Pythagorean geometry and Kepler tried to demonstrate a relationship between the five regular Pythagorean solids and the motion of the five planets other than the Earth. The orbits of the planets were each contained in these solids which were sequentially nested one inside the other. He then attempted to show that the intervals which separated the time it took each planet to make one orbit, its period, matched the Pythagorean musical intervals. He saw this as a divinely created harmony of the spheres. While both of these ideas were in error, it gave him a sense of planetary motion which would lead him to his greatest contribution to science. It also brought him to the notice of Tycho Brahe whose assistant he became.

Kepler arrived at Tycho's Prague observatory early in the year 1600. It was the meeting of two completely opposite personalities. Tycho was noble and flamboyant while Kepler was humble and sickly. Tycho's passion was accurate observations while Kepler's was numbers and mathematical relationships. But the conjunction of the two so complemented each other that the result changed completely the understanding of the astronomical universe.

Kepler worked with him only a year and a half until Tycho's death but it was long enough to give him total confidence in any data Tycho had recorded. His first task under the master observer was to analyze the motion of the planet Mars. He used the long held assumption that the planets moved in perfect circles and at a constant speed. When he applied Tycho's data to the Earth-centered model of Ptolemy and the sun centered model of Copernicus, he found that the Copernican model was in much better agreement. There was, however, an error of 8 minutes of an arc between the theoretical calculation and the observed data. This is the angle formed by an object one inch high looked at from a distance of 286 feet. Because of his complete trust in Tycho's data, he placed the cause of the error in the model and not the data.

The first laws of nature

From the discovery of this discrepancy until 1605, Kepler worked on this problem and made two momentous discoveries. First, he could demonstrate that the planets were not moving in circular orbits but in an elliptical path, an elongated circle with two centers or foci. The sun was at one focus. He also calculated that the speed of travel around the sun changes with the planet going faster when close to the sun than when at the more distant end of the ellipse.

Being the number cruncher that he was, he also discovered that if one drew a line from the sun to the planet in its orbit, that radius line swept out equal areas in equal time intervals no matter where along the ellipse it was. Here was a mathematical explanation of why the speed changed. When the radius was longer, it must slow down to keep the area the same in equal time intervals. These findings were published in 1609 in the appropriately titled work, *Astronomia Nova* or *The New Astronomy Based on Causation* or *A Physics of the Sky*. He was quick to attribute these findings to the data of Tycho Brahe. These two discoveries became known as Kepler's first and second laws and were true for all the planets.

By 1618 he was able to add a third law. He discovered that if you took the radius of the orbit of a planet and cubed it, that is, multiplied it by itself twice, it turned out to be directly proportional to the square of the time it took the planet to orbit the sun. In fact the constant of proportionality came out to be the same value for all the planets including the Earth in orbit around the Sun. In other words, the number you got was a constant of nature, just like the mathematical constant π, which is the circumference of any circle divided by its diameter.

Historically, these three laws are also the first formulations to be considered laws of physical nature rather than mathematics. For a person of Kepler's character, finding these relationships was a thrill of a lifetime and more than enough reward for all his number juggling. It does, however, beg the questions - what made him try these combinations and how many other combinations did he try? What is more curious is that this relationship was discovered in context of looking for a relationship between musical harmonies which Pythagoras had described and the orbits of the planets.

In the case of the third law, there was good reason to pursue the relationship between the period of rotation and the distance of separation from the sun. Without it, the whole system would be arbitrary and meaningless. There had to be a connection and he found it. These laws were to become the basic assumption of astronomy. Modern science had begun by defining things in mathematical language.

Consider again the human dimension of what he had done. He had Tycho's tables of data concerning the position of the planets relative to the fixed stars in the background sky as seen from the Earth. But the Earth was not stationary. Rather, it was rotating on its axis as well as traveling in an elliptical orbit around the sun. Furthermore, no one could yet demonstrate if the Sun or the Earth was at the center of all this motion. Philosophically, everyone made the common sense assumption that the Earth was motionless at the center and Christianity was in agreement with that. Even common sense suggested the stable Earth model. Yet from this haze of erroneous assumptions and complex data, Kepler was able find the truth and express it in the irrefutable formulation of elliptical geometry and algebra. It was all done without a telescope, computer, slide rule or calculator. This was a momentous accomplishment.

Sadly, the significance of his accomplishment was not fully appreciated by those who knew him. Nor did he himself see the full significance of his discovery. It was left to Newton to use these three laws to produce a whole new science of physics. The remainder of Kepler's life was not happy. He saw the death of his daughter and wife and was caught up in many problems, family, financial and professional. Kepler died in 1630 of fever. But first another major character in the scientific drama came into Kepler's life.

Galileo Galilei

In 1564, twenty-one years after the death of Copernicus, Galileo

Galilei was born in Italy and became a natural philosopher, astronomer, and mathematician. In 1609 he heard of the Dutch invention of the telescope and after figuring out for himself how it must work, made one using lenses he obtained from a spectacle maker's shop. It had a magnifying power of only three. He was an inventive and practical man. After becoming skilled in lens grinding, he was able to built one with a power of eight and presented it to the Venetian Senate. He touted its usefulness in war. It would allow the Venetians to see any enemy ship approaching the harbor before they could be seen with the naked eye and give valuable advance warning and he was rewarded handsomely.

He proceeded to observe the heavens with instruments of magnification as high as 20. He reported what he observed in a small book called *Sidereus Nuntius* or *Messenger from the Stars*, which he published in 1610. Among other startling things he reported that the planet Jupiter had four moons orbiting around it. Here were celestial bodies, moons, orbiting something other than the Earth. These observations brought him scientific fame and he became more convinced of the Copernican system.

Kepler's sent a copy of his *New Astronomy* to Galileo for his review. In fact Kepler shared much of his thinking with Galileo in many letters and for his efforts only received two replies. They were both polite but none ever expressed an opinion about Kepler's views. Yet when Galileo sent Kepler a copy of *Sidereus Nuntius*, Kepler endorsed it fully and publicly. He also asked Galileo to send him a telescope so that he could see these things himself. Galileo never showed him the courtesy but did give telescopes to wealthy patrons instead.

Galileo proceeded to make many discoveries with his telescopes which fed his love of controversy. While none of them gave any kind of proof for the Copernican system, they undermined the traditional thinking in just about every conceivable way. Some of his contemporaries even refused to look through his telescope for they were certain that what he was describing was not possible. The images formed by his instruments were not of great quality and could be subject to question and many attempted to explain why they looked as Galileo described them but were not true in reality. In the end, however, Galileo was right about all his interpretations of what he saw.

The rise of controversy

Unfortunately, Galileo's physical arguments in support of the Copernican system were limited and not conclusive, if not totally wrong. He relied primarily on his explanation of tides being caused by the rotation of the Earth and an effect of the Sun. He could have obtained stronger arguments had he investigated the findings of Kepler but that was not to be. Then he turned to theology which was not his field, writing what is now known as the *Letter to Madam Christina*. In it he dealt with the problems of literal interpretation of the Scriptures. This brought him up against recent decrees of the Council of Trent concerning Biblical interpretation.

These were tumultuous times for western society. The Protestant Reformation had created political as well as theological and social unrest. The fifteenth and sixteenth centuries saw the introduction of printed books. Most books were devoted to the scriptures and other religious texts. In the sixteenth and seventeenth centuries information books were being produced as a result of the rise of European universities, especially in Italy. This simplified the widespread dissemination of ideas. Some Italian leaders, however, believed that the key to cultural stability lay in resistance to innovation and change. The Roman Inquisition, a tribunal which dealt with heresy, was established in 1542 by Pope Paul III in response to the Protestant Reformation. The Index of Forbidden Books was established by Pope Paul IV in 1557 and Copernicus' *De Revolutionibus* was added to the list in 1616. In response to the Reformation, the Church had called the council of Trent which decreed in 1546 that:

> No one [should be allowed to] distort the sense of Sacred Scripture according to his own opinions ... contrary to that sense which is being held by our Holy Mother Church whose duty it is to judge the true science and interpretation of the Holy Scriptures or even contrary to the unanimous consent of the Fathers.[5]

While the decree of 1546 does not mention anything about a literal sense of Scripture, it does confirm the continued interpretation of the Church and the consensus of the Fathers, the writers of the early church, as having what amounted to undeniable authority. But in fact literal interpretation was never far from their mind. After all, Jesus had said, "This is my body", and Protestant reformers refused to take that literally as the Catholic Church most certainly did.

While the creation story of Genesis seemed to describe a world in which the Earth was at its centre, it did not specifically teach it as scientific fact. But there were other passages which presented the notion of a stationary Earth. For example we read, "He established the Earth upon its foundations, so that it will not totter forever and ever." (Psalm 104:5) Since the psalms are poems, it seems a strange format in which to seek scientific facts. "Tremble before Him, all the Earth; indeed, the world is firmly established, it will not be moved." (1 Chronicles 16:30.) This is written in poetic format as well so one would question how literally it should be taken. "He stretches out the north over empty space, and hangs the Earth on nothing." (Job 26:7). Also, "The sun rises and the sun sets; and hastening to its place it rises there again." (Ecclesiastes 1:5). Finally, "So the sun stood still, and the moon stopped, until the nation avenged themselves of their enemies. Is it not written in the book of Jashar? And the sun stopped in the middle of the sky, and did not hasten to go down for about a whole day." (Joshua 10:13). Surely all these simply describe what the sky looks like from the Earth and were not meant to be astronomical facts.

In his *Letter*, Galileo sought to fortify his position by quoting the great Latin theologian, Tertullian (c. 160–c. 220). "God is known first through Nature and then, again, more particularly by doctrine: by Nature in His works, and by doctrine in His revealed word." It seems that both Galileo and Tertullian were aware of and advocating what we have been calling natural revelation.

What followed can only be described as an attempt to discredit Galileo personally. In 1615 the Holy Office of the Vatican began an investigation of the matter and on 24 February 1616 presented two propositions before a panel of theological experts. These "quailfactores" took only one week to reach their conclusion. Galileo's *Letter to Madam Christina*, in spite of its shortcomings, had demonstrated that there was no contradiction between the Book of Nature and the Book of the Word. Both had the same author. This argument was not adopted in the case and Galileo himself was never asked to testify. The decision reached after no real scientific investigation was that the Copernican system was condemned and Galileo was admonished not to hold or defend either in words or in writing any movement of the Earth.

He was, however, given mixed messages from different individuals in the Vatican and he left convinced that his scientific understandings were not in question. This was not the feeling of his detractors and they awaited their chance to do further damage. It came in 1632 with the publication of his *Dialogo*. The title came from the format of the work, a style popular at the time, written as a discussion over four days between three characters who compared the cosmologies of Ptolemy and Copernicus. Its conclusions were obviously in support of the Copernican system and some of the treatment of the Ptolemaic arguments were seen as offensive.

41

Galileo was recalled to Rome.

He arrived there in 1633 and after a number of hearings, his *Dialogo* was prohibited, he was found guilty of holding the Copernican system as true and so was held suspect of heresy, ordered to be imprisoned and given a penance. The sentence was then immediately commuted.[6] Many of those who already had copies of the book scrambled to hide them from the authorities of the Inquisition before they were confiscated. After spending some time at the grand houses of influential friends, he returned to his home in Florence where he remained for the rest of his life.

Copies of the *Dialogo* were smuggled to a publisher in the more religiously tolerant Netherlands where it could be printed without fear of the Church in Rome. It must be said that, in spite of his tendency to court controversy and the bluntness of his writing, Galileo always maintained his belief and loyalty to the Church. His last years were filled with poor health, possibly malaria, and he died on 8 January 1642 at the age of 77.[7]

Today the Galileo affair has been put to rest by the Catholic Church. But with the final process being so hesitant and confused, one wonders if its lessons have been learned. Biblical inerrancy had nothing to do with it. It was all about authority and saving face. The Church had gone along with the natural philosophers so completely and so publicly that to change their view might call their authority into question. It was much about human intrigue, little about theology and even less about science.

Impact of Galileo

The effect of what Galileo did was to free scientific investigation from the stifling restrictions caused by philosophical and theological interference. He demonstrated that scientists could not allow what had been said by previous scholars to limit further investigation leading to a better understanding of the universe. A valid understanding of the universe is far more important than being at the centre of it. Far more exciting and useful is to discover the truth.

So what is the natural revelation which sprang from this period? Does astronomy reveal anything to us about the Creator God? Not directly, but it certainly equips us to think about such a God. Astronomy gives us a proper sense of scale. This was one of the major things missing in the pre-Copernican model. God did not create a small but luxurious model of a universe that he could put on his coffee table and admire, a flat base with a glass dome from which were hung the celestial bodies. Rather, while the real universe is so immense that it exceeds our imagination, still, we are the ones who are capable of investigating it and understanding it. We are also the ones who, with each generation, continue to conclude that there must be a reason for all this beyond its own existence.

If the physical size of the universe makes us feel insignificant, all we need do is read those first two chapters of Genesis. They spell out our importance and that is no small service. At the present, we are the culmination of creation on Earth, not chronologically but evolutionarily. But, as we shall see later, this does not mean that we are necessarily the last step in this evolution. We are also the stewards of what was created. It could have been put no more beautifully than by saying, as Genesis does, "The Lord God took the man and put him in the garden of Eden to till it and keep it." (Gen 2:15)

Then God brought all living creatures before the man "to see what he would call them." Ever since, we have been doing just that with countless scientific names and terms. In Old Testament culture, to name something meant that you had power over it and responsibility for it. Science can say nothing about responsibility. It is only when we combine the scientific notions of the complexity and immensity of the universe and the revealed notions of humanity's position and purpose in that universe that we can arrive at a truly useful picture of who and where we are.

Galileo's contribution was not limited to the motion in the solar system. He did much groundbreaking work concerning the motion of physical bodies and worked out the mathematical relationships between acceleration, velocity, distances and lapsed time in his famous inclined plane experiments. This gave direction to scientific experimentation and created the atmosphere in which Isaac Newton could develop the science of physics.

Copernicus, Brahe, Kepler and Galileo were men of their time, geniuses with flaws, They were not quite scientists in the modern mold but were willing to reconsider some traditional ideas. This was necessary for the arrival of modern science. From the time of Aristotle to Copernicus, the academic world and the Catholic Church were more interested in philosophy and spirituality than physical science as we understand it today. They drew many wrong conclusions about humanity and the Earth because they knew more about a personal God who loves and is concerned for us than they did about the nature God created to sustain their existence. But just as Aristotle set the pattern of thought for 2000 years, Copernicus, Kepler and Galileo prepared the way for the next intellectual landmark in human understanding by starting true observational science and the formulation of natural laws expressed in mathematical terms and not philosophical language. And just as the previous 2000 years are best described as Aristotelian, the new era would be Newtonian.

What then was the long-term effect of the Copernicus/Galileo era? As natural philosophy evolved into a mathematical and experimental science, the Copernican model found wide acceptance. As for the Catholic Church, the twentieth century philosopher George Santayana put it well:

> Later the system of Copernicus, incompatible at heart with the anthropocentric and moralistic view of the world which Christianity implies, was accepted by the church with some lame attempt to render it innocuous; but it remains an alien and hostile element, like a spent bullet lodged in the flesh.[8]

Perhaps the best indication of how alien and hostile this was is seen in how long it took the Church to officially admit their error concerning Galileo. What was needed by both the natural philosophers and the churchmen was a period of enlightenment and that is exactly what happened in the centuries after Galileo. While the Church wrestled with a perceived loss of authority, science made a great leap forward through the methods acquired in the Enlightenment and through the genius of Isaac Newton. He was able to reduce the theory of a heliocentric solar system to mathematical equations and make the acceptance of the idea unavoidable. In doing so, he established the foundation of the science of physics.

Notes

1. Before banning it, the Church used data from *De Revolutionibus*. In 1582 Pope Gregory XIII established the Vatican Observatory in Rome to produce a revision of the calendar of Julius Caesar. The Julian calendar had the year lasting 11 minutes and 14 seconds too long and the corrected Gregorian Calendar is what is used today. In 1925 the Vatican observatory was moved out of Rome to Castel Gandolfo southeast of Rome because the city lights obscured the night sky. Its library contains a collection of the original works of all the men discussed in this chapter and astronomers associated with the Vatican Observatory continue to contribute to science today with a sister observatory in the State of Arizona.

2. On a personal note, it was thought that Copernicus was buried in Frombork Cathedral but four attempts to find his remains starting in 1802 failed to find them. Then, after using x ray scanning of the floor of the cathedral, a body was found which was thought to be

Copernicus. The skull had evidence of identifying characteristics but the conclusive evidence came through DNA testing. The DNA of the skull matched that of a hair which had been found in a book which had been owned by Copernicus. Modern science had come to his rescue. Fittingly, he was formally reburied with full church ceremony in the cathedral on 22 May 2010 and fittingly marked by a stone depicting his model of the solar system.

3. The bridge of Tycho's nose had been cut off in a duel and he fashioned a number of false noses which he wore to be more socially acceptable.

4. His father was a mercenary soldier. His mother had emotional problems and was accused of witchcraft, an accusation encouraged by her behavior. Only the intervention of Johannes who by that time was influential, saved her from prosecution.

5. Denzinger (2007) *Encridion Symbolorum,* Loreto Publications.

6. Curiously, his daughter, who was a Carmelite nun, was permitted to recite this penance for her father.

7. In 1979 Pope John Paul II called for an investigation into the Galileo affair but the process was not an example of openness and clarity it might have been. Only one member, the director of the Vatican Observatory, had any expertise in the history of astronomy. The others were chosen by virtue of their names and positions. After 1983, there were no more meetings of the commission. Finally, in 1992, Cardinal Paul Poupard ceremoniously made a statement purporting to declare the findings of the commission. The Vatican astronomer on the commission knew nothing about the official statement and some of the information contained in it was not historically accurate. In 2002 a conference of scholars was called at Notre Dame University in the United States and its report can serve as the example of what the Vatican commission should have produced.

8. George Santayana (1913) W*inds of Doctrine*, J. M. Dent & Sons.

4

The Enlightenment

The development of natural science in the sixteenth century raised new interest in how to investigate and understand things. The Greeks had advised that an intelligent person could reason to most conclusions about the truth of things. In the thirteenth century the scholastics or schoolmen, under the influence of Thomas Aquinas (1225–1274), organized and codified the process of rational investigation so that it was a tool for investigating what could be known about God through philosophy.

In spite of his interest in theology, Aquinas was very much a rationalist at heart. The arguments in his *Summa Theologica* pick clean every scrap of evidence that reason and logic can find to support an idea. In spite of this, some institutions today hesitate to see scholasticism as a true philosophical system. They dismiss it as philosophical meandering on theological subjects rather than the highpoint of medieval rational investigation.

In the sixteenth century, two contemporaries of Galileo saw the need to rethink the process of human reasoning. They were Francis Bacon and René Descartes. Although they differed in their approach, they did focus minds on the new reality of a developing natural science. They demonstrated that this new science required rethinking many old assumptions. That conclusion was to become the spirit of a new age, the Age of Enlightenment. We will consider here only three individuals who contributed substantially to science and the spirit of the Enlightenment.

Francis Bacon

Francis Bacon (1562–1626) was a Londoner with many talents. He was a lawyer, member of Parliament, essayist, philosopher, attorney-general and Lord Chancellor. But it was his writing in which he set out his philosophical approach to learning which had the most lasting effect on science. He championed reason which worked on the observation of nature. He was an empiricist in opposition to both Aristotle and the scholastics. For him, truth was to be found through experience, through engaging with nature, not the exercise of authority. His true feelings toward scholasticism is perhaps best seen in his comment in an essay on studies. He suggests that if a man's "wit be not apt to distinguish or find differences, let him study the schoolmen; for they are cynimi sectores."

The Latin expression literally means "dividers of cumin seed." Today we would say hair-splitters. Such was his attitude to the schoolmen that in the introduction of an1819 edition of his essays we read;

> By his two great works, *On the Advancement of Learning* and *The New Organ of the Sciences*, ... did this mighty genius first break the shackles of that scholastic philosophy, which long had crushed the human intellect; and diverting the attention from words to things, from theory to experiment, demonstrate the road to that height of science on which the moderns are now seated, and which the ancients were unable to reach. (London, published by John Sharpe)

In spite of this exaggeration for effect, in this period thinking became empirical, reliant more on investigation and physical evidence than theory and philosophical deliberations. Bacon advocated a new way to advance learning and reform the scientific methods used to understand the physical world.

It must be added, however, that it was Bacon's experimental curiosity which may have been his undoing. While riding in a carriage in North London one cold March day, he became curious about the ability of cold to slow down the spoiling of meat. He stopped the carriage, purchased a chicken and proceeded to stuff it with snow. He came down with a chill and in the beginning of April died of bronchitis.

René Descartes

René Descartes (1596–1650) influenced Western thought in philosophy, human affairs, science and mathematics and was ultimately thought of as the father of modern philosophy. Born in France, he was educated at a Jesuit college and then studied law. After graduation he entered the military, primarily to travel and make contact with the intellectuals of the day. This brought him to Germany, Italy and finally Holland where he decided to remain and where he did most of his writing. In 1649 he went to Stockholm at the invitation of the queen to tutor her in philosophy. He contracted pneumonia while there and died in 1650.

Descartes was a good counterbalance to Bacon's empiricism. For Descartes reason and mathematics were the tools for determining truth and he began with a systematic doubt of everything. He explained this principle in his *Discourse on the Method of Rightly Conducting the Reason and Seeking Truth in the Sciences* published in 1637. His first philosophical principle is, "That in order to seek truth, it is necessary once in the course of our life to doubt, as far as possible, of all things." His seventh principle, however, is, "That we cannot doubt our own existence while we doubt, and that this is the first knowledge we acquire when we philosophize in order." He explained that it is repugnant to "conceive that what thinks does not exist at the very time when it thinks." In other words, to doubt requires the existence of a doubter. This is the origin of his widely known expression of this idea, " Cogito ergo sum" or "I think therefore I am."

He was not implying that everyone should reinvent this logical wheel for themselves. He did mean that for him it was necessary. He proceeded to work his way through the fundamentals of reason and the existence of things so that it could be seen to be grounded on a firm foundation and could no longer be challenged. Although he did not have the experimental interests of Brahe, Copernicus, Galileo or Bacon, he did much to establish the theoretical basis for modern science. This was to be so even though many of the physical theories he concluded in this process of resolving doubts were later to be proven in error by the very science he promoted.

It is sometimes overlooked that the cogito statement is also a profession of rational individualism. Such thinking ultimately moved other Enlightenment thinkers to define human rights, the liberty of individuals and the rejection of arbitrary authority such as that exercised by royalty or ecclesiastical hierarchy. It was thought that moral authority originates within the individual and individualism became a hallmark of Western culture, the foundation of the concept of democracy. This may remove the restraints which society in general can exert on the individual and for some that is a problem. It can deprive them of the support they need even for their own happiness and demand more maturity than they have acquired. Respect for and the value of the individual certainly had its origin in Christianity but it was given a new and broader justification by the empirical rationalism of Descartes.

Descartes was also one of the most prominent mathematicians of his time. He developed his mathematical principles as an appendix to his *Discourse on Method*. In it he set out the relationship between algebra and geometry. The notation he used is what we use today, even to the use of letters at the beginning of the alphabet for parameters or constant values and those at the end for the unknowns. We still call the coordinates of our graphs Cartesian coordinates. In spite of this, his greatest interest was in science and philosophy.

His systematic doubt could have brought him in conflict with the

Catholic Church but that was not acceptable to him. His *Discourse on Method* deals at length with the existence of God and how we deal with revealed truths as well as truths discovered by scientific means. His religious faith never wavered and he even suppressed his agreement with Copernicus because of the controversy raging in the Church at the time and the trial of Galileo over his support of the Copernican system. His method of doubt did contribute in no small way to the general intellectual atmosphere of the Enlightenment and his mathematics facilitated the work of the next great figure of that movement.

Isaac Newton

The same year Galileo died and only 12 year after Johannes Kepler died, Isaac Newton (1642–1727) was born. He was a very complex character and very much a loner. He could also be a very unpleasant and defensive man. His time as president of the Royal Society in London brought much esteem to that institution but he also abused his power, especially in his treatment of Robert Hooke, in part over disagreement about the nature of light. This period of his career can make uncomfortable reading.

He was a closet alchemist and managed to keep this a secret until just before his death. His search for the philosopher's stone was not from a wish to turn base metal into gold and become rich, but to understand God's creative process. All these men of genius were not only so very right about some things but so very wrong about others. Most often, the things they were wrong about were assumptions they accepted from tradition and did not question. Perhaps there is a lesson in that.

Newton was both a physicist and a mathematician who built extensively on the work of Descartes. The mathematical expressions he derived to describe and define the motion of physical objects were so fundamental that the system became known as Newtonian physics. What Newton demonstrated was that the physical world was mathematically predictable at all times. Newton's principles are still valid today although, with the ability to work with objects going at speeds approaching the speed of light, it was found that these expressions had to be modified, as shall be seen in Chapter 8.

When Newton was a professor of mathematics at Cambridge University, it was expected that he would take holy orders but with the help of influential friends he managed to avoid it. While he was fiercely anti-Catholic, he also had a few bones to pick with the Church of England, especially concerning the doctrine of the Trinity. This he kept hidden along with his alchemy until his deathbed when he refused the last rites. In spite of this, Newton wrote far more words on the interpretation of Scripture than he did about science.

Newton turned his attention to the third law of Kepler which, as we saw in Chapter 3, was the relationship between the planet's distance from the Sun and the period of time it took to orbit the Sun. By using it in his equation for orbital motion, he could express the movement of planets in terms of the following parameters: the centripetal force that caused the planets to orbit around the sun, the mass of the sun and the planet and finally the distance between them. He had defined the force of gravity between any two objects, be it the Earth to the sun or an apple to the ground. This was the mathematical explanation for why the Earth and other planets were in orbit around the sun. To see the connection between orbiting planets and objects dropping to the ground was a profound insight. It was the ultimate confirmation of the ideas of Copernicus and Galileo. Philosophically speaking, this was action at a distance with no connection in between. Many of his contemporaries questioned how a force could be exerted through empty space. Yet the reason for gravity would have to remain one of the mysteries of science even today.

What Newton described in the language of mathematics was how this force of gravity acts but not why it exists in the first place. He realized that the one thing the Sun, planets and apples had in common was their matter, the stuff they were made of. This was why Kepler's third law was the same constant number for all the planets of the sun. They are all made of the same stuff, matter. It also proved that Aristotle was wrong in thinking that the heavenly bodies and the Earth had nothing in common since stars were sources of light and the Earth was not. This had been another failure of common sense. Newton, more than anyone, gave credence to the ability of enlightened thinking to explain the truths of nature. Science and reason became the method of choice.

Questioning everything

With Newtonian physics, science took on a whole new character. Because his definition of gravity conclusively threw over the assumptions of the past, it created a new atmosphere in science. Scientists no longer felt bound by tradition. In fact, the attitude grew that everything was open to question, investigation and experimentation. This was the only way to have certainty about things. It placed its reliance on experimentation and mathematics which gave a certainty far beyond any authority or tradition and left the subject open to peer review and confirmation. Experiments had to be repeatable.

This feeling of freedom to question extended to much more than science. It found application in social institutions, government, philosophy, economics and religion. For the Enlightenment, mathematics, experimentation and human reason were to be the measure of all things and all things needed to be looked at again in this scientifically enlightened way.

The Enlightenment is considered to have ended with the French revolution in 1789. This social upheaval was an enlightened class struggle against the clergy as well as the nobility. The stage was set for it by many great philosophical thinkers of the period such as Voltaire, Diderot, Pascal, Spinoza, Leibniz, Rousseau and Hume as well as Benjamin Franklin and Thomas Jefferson who were the leaders in structuring the declaration of independence of the North American colonies. Many enlightened spokesmen did not just challenge Christian tradition. Rather, they put it to the test and concluded that it was wanting. But these were heady times and we can understand why this new culture of intellectual freedom was unsure how it could proceed in a constructive and meaningful way.

Nor did the Catholic Church quite understand how to respond. Even in recent times, some Christian have been content to encourage a devotional culture at the cost of a culture of understanding. This approach is often advanced under the disguise of preserving the mystery in religious belief and practice. To fall back on tradition and authority was certainly not going to be effective in this new culture of Enlightenment, and some would add, not then nor any time since then. It was the freedom found in the Reformation which opened the way to progress in the study of Sacred Scripture. Perhaps because of this beginning, the Catholic Church was loath to accept the new methods.

As late as 1893 Pope Leo XIII issued the encyclical *Providentissimus Deus* on the study of Scripture. This was followed by Pius X who issued the *Syllabus Condemning the Errors of the Modernists* and *The Oath Against Modernism* in 1907. These were such negative and cautionary expressions concerning any critical approach to the *Bible* as to discourage Catholic scholarship. The language used is such that it can remind us of the famous line from Hamlet, "The lady doth protest too much, methinks" which implies a loss of credibility. In spite of this language, many Scripture scholars realized the reasonableness of the new approach but could not express this opinion in public. The sacred texts of the *Bible*, however, were considered the ultimate authority. The problem was to understand to what things that authority applied.

One of the hallmarks of the more scientific approach to the Scriptures was textual criticism. It involved linguistics as well as historical methods of research. The ancient modes of writing had to be understood. What did they mean by history? What was the purpose of their poetry? Scientific scholarship could help separate physical errors from spiritual meanings. This was not a quick process and continues in our twenty-first century. But we should recognize that such a scientific approach found its inspiration in the Enlightenment. While there were those in the Catholic Church who resisted such a disciplined investigation of Scripture, the encyclical *Divino Afflante Spiritu* of Pope Pius XII promulgated in 1943 was considered to be the Magna Carta for Catholic Scripture scholarship. Catholic scholars were now encouraged to use all the modern tools of hermeneutics.

The Scriptures were recognized as a library of books. The human authors of these books used their own language and experience and were the recipients of divine inspiration and not divine dictation. They were informed by the history and cultural atmosphere of their own time. They were moved to express their understandings in words of their own choosing. They wrote in all the various literary forms. The *Bible* contains many types of literature: history, fiction, poetry and the like. Furthermore, these books were written over a span of some 2000 years. It is not adequate to approach this library as simply the word of God. New tools of textual research needed to be devised.

The people to whom the revealed texts are given are human just as the scientists are human with all the complications that implies. Copernicus could not free himself from the idea that heavenly orbits were perfect circles. Brahe was an irascible perfectionist. Kepler was mystical about numbers. Galileo could deny his scientific belief in an ecclesiastical court and Newton was a closet alchemist. It should not surprise us that the *Bible* suffered from too much respect as "the word of God." Should we not expect that these revealed texts contain much that is human and that human preconceptions would influence what was written?

While it has to be said that the response of some churchmen was to fall back on tradition and authority, the Catholic Church is wrongly accused of being against science and reason in the period before and during the Enlightenment. The Greeks had made gods out of astronomy with astrology but Christianity condemned it. This was not an anti-science gesture. The time immediately before the Enlightenment has been called the dark ages but that is certainly not an accurate description. The academic institutions which trained the scientists were, for the most part, ecclesiastical. Throughout the history of Christianity, scholarship and ordination were strongly associated.

In the Catholic Church, there were monks and popes who made admirable accomplishments in mathematics and astronomy. The Vatican Observatory is one of the oldest astronomical institutions and astronomical research has continued under the auspices of the Vatican Observatory even to this day. Yet the reality is that popes have been a mixed lot. While some were at home with science and do not attract our notice, others were most certainly not. Professing to be open to science is easy to say but can be difficult in reality. The most distressing thing is that, as in the Galileo affair, in most cases there was no dogma involved in the controversy; rather, the conflict stemmed from efforts to maintain ecclesiastical authority.

Impact of the Enlightenment

The word science comes from the Latin word for knowledge. If the Age of Enlightenment was anything, it was an explosion of knowledge which was driven by new ways of discovering what things are and how they function. In turn, this new understanding of nature and society led to an atmosphere of imagination, curiosity and invention. It is little wonder that this made possible the industrial revolution. The 1700s produced the electric telegraph, lightening rod and battery. Navigation benefited from the invention of the sextant and the marine chronometer as well as the use of steam engines in boats and canal systems transported good and raw materials in great quantities. Agriculture saw the development of the seed drill and the threshing machine. Machines such as steel rollers, metal lathes and the spinning jenny made factories an industrial and social reality. In the social context, we might also mention the invention of the guillotine.

Machines for making sheet paper and lithography increased the potential to disseminate knowledge aided by the publication of the first English dictionary by Samuel Johnson. Every segment of society was affected by these changes. A general interest and wonderment concerning the things of nature found expression in cabinets of curiosities as conversation pieces to collect, even in the home, small wonders from sea shells to preserved specimens in jars. So much interest was found in these things that artists painted pictures of these collections. Music made a great step forward with the development of the Baroque style with its increased complexity and ornamentation. Many of our best known composers are from this period: Bach, Handel, Vivaldi and Scarlatti to name a few.

The science of dissection which came into its own in the latter half of the 1600s began the ascent of biology and the first questions concerning the process of reproduction and the matter of spontaneous generation of living organisms so that by the mid 1700s the term "reproduction" was replacing "generation." All of this was made possible by the development of the microscope. This century also witnessed the development of a vaccine against smallpox which was a global killer at the time and has since been eliminated from the Earth.

The Age of Enlightenment was an extremely busy hundred years and would probably never be surpassed until our own age of the computer and the internet. The Enlightenment impacted every aspect of human life, medically, socially and politically. It should not surprise us that it impacted religion as well. We have seen how better understanding of our astronomical universe forced a rethinking of what Genesis 1 was telling us about creation and ultimately resulted in clear principles for interpreting the Scriptures using literary tools.

This learning process in theology, however, lagged behind the progress which science was making. To a certain extent this is understandable. Science depends on observation and measurement. Theology is one of the humanities and its tools are reason aided by logic and revelation. The one element science and theology both should have in common is reasonableness. Those first scientists were as keen to preserve their faith in God as they were their trust in the new science. At times the theologian did not make it easy for them. In our day, many scientists have lost patience with the theologian and dismissed their reasoning all together. This gulf was widened by the next momentous scientific insight.

► 5 ◄

Approaching Evolution

Up to this point we have been considering what natural revelation can tell us about the God who created our universe. We must now investigate what that creation can tell us about ourselves, in other words, the origin and nature of Homo sapiens. As we did in chapter 1, we should first look at the preconceived notions we may bring to the subject. In our western culture, those notions come to us primarily from the second chapter of Genesis.

Genesis again

The first time we read Genesis 2:4 it may have startled us. In chapter 1 we were intrigued by the story of the six days of creation. In it, the first human was made out of the dust of the ground, given stewardship of all creation and told to increase and multiply. Suddenly, in Genesis 2:4 we read; "These are the generations of the heavens and the Earth when they were created. In the day that the Lord God made the Earth and the heavens…" and what follows is a second story of creation which does not match the first.

This second story is even more interesting than the first. It has a magnificent garden which gives rise to four rivers. It contains every type of tree to both please the eye and yield fruit that is good to eat. All this is for the delight of the two first humans who enjoy nakedness. There is an animal that talks and they are visited by God who walks with them in the garden. Clearly humanity is the central subject of this chapter and much blessed by their maker. In the account, we learn about human sexuality, a man and a woman becoming one flesh. They are necessary helpmates to each other. We learn why childbirth is accompanied by pain, why nakedness is a cause of shame and why the snake must crawl legless on the ground. It is in fact a study of the central concerns of every person during a lifetime on Earth; the presence of evil in the world and the ultimate evil, death. Genesis 2-3 is a profound study of good and evil, life and death, heaven and Earth, man and women, knowledge and ignorance.

So why is human life on Earth such a struggle? The answer Genesis 2-3 gives is that our first parents were driven out of the garden because of disobedience and left to toil by the sweat of their brow. Life is a series of choices. Our first parents made a bad choice and we are stuck with it. But all is not hopeless. In Genesis 3:21 we are told, "And the Lord God made garments of skins for the man and for his wife, and clothed them." The banishment from the garden did not mean abandonment. God still provides for their needs in spite of their disobedience. When all is said and done, this is a healthy attitude for a primitive people, those for whom the story was originally devised. And while the details of this story do not come up again in the rest of the *Old Testament*, this theme of suffering the consequences of our choices is central to all the Scriptures. The answers offered may not be supportable by archeological evidence but they were most probably adequate for their immediate audience over 4000 years ago and, in so far as they describe a relationship between us and our Creator and not physical details, adequate for us today.

Such matters as these are not trivial. They address things which are at the heart of being human: life in the real world, hope in spite of difficulties, the importance of relationships both to human partners and to the God who walks with us. Should we not think that this is enough to expect from a text composed a couple of millennia before the birth of Christ? Yet if we take the details of the story as historically accurate, a fundamentalist point of view, we risk descending into pure fantasy. We will most certainly find ourselves surrounded by logical constructs and we will be hard pressed to prove their existence or show their usefulness. If we are curious about the origin of humanity, would it not be better to seek the answer from observed evidence rather than from philosophical conclusions drawn from ancient stories which were never intended to explain physical history or give scientific proofs?

The story in Genesis 2-3 is an early and beautiful attempt to explain the existence of evil in the world and we do well to resign ourselves to that fact. St. Paul approached the subject with the same resignation when he said, "For I do not do the good I want, but the evil I do not want is what I do." (Rom 7:19) Shakespeare had Portia in *The Merchant of Venice* say, "If to do were as easy as to know what were good to do, chapels had been churches and poor men's cottages princes palaces." These are adequate statements of fact but not speculative explanations. If we need explanations today, we might turn to genetics and study the existence of an altruistic gene or one which appears to control our tendency to violence. These are studies being conducted by scientists offering natural revelations about our human nature and if we want answers with evidence, we should not ignore their work.

When I was a child, time was spent in religious instruction classes describing what the world was like before the fall of Adam and Eve. They enjoyed the praeternatural gifts, also called the state of original justice, which meant, among other things, that they would never die and explained why they could walk naked and not feel shame. They had complete control over their appetites and were in harmony with all their surroundings. But what does it say about God to the twenty-first century mind that he arranged that Adam's soul could so master his flesh as to prevent the occurrence of death but make it contingent upon obedience to such an arbitrary prohibition as not to eat the fruit of a particular tree?[1]

While I enjoyed those lessons about the praeternatural gifts which we were given with such conviction by a dedicated catechist in the 1940s, I wondered where on Earth we would all fit had they not eaten the apple and no one died since the creation of Adam and Eve. Anthropological evidence today leads us to believe that Homo sapiens originated in Africa and not the Euphrates valley as Genesis implies. But all this literary creativity in the Divine Word is of no consequence when compared to its assurance that our Creator is concerned about us and walking with us.

We have seen that from the first recorded thoughts on the subject of the universe until the sixteenth century, the focus of attention was always on the Earth and on humankind who inhabits it. After Copernicus and Galileo, the focus changed. The Earth and its inhabitants were not the center of the universe but only a part of it and that universe was proving to be much bigger than ever expected. With the advancement of natural science as opposed to natural philosophy, some began to fear a cosmological blow against the dignity of humankind.

Eventually, modern physics revealed the stuff of the universe to be filled with mysteries and uncertainties. Astronomy made our Earth seem to recede into insignificance. But it also meant that its Creator was more powerful than we could ever have imagined before this natural revelation. To people of faith, it meant that we who inhabit the Earth are no less significant. The significance, of course, comes from the possession of what are perceived as spiritual capabilities, a soul.

The evolution debate

If the demotion of our Earth by astronomy to an insignificant globe in an almost infinite universe of stuff weren't enough, along came Darwin and his theory of evolution. Some regarded this theory as a biological blow against human dignity. Some interpreted it as meaning that we were simply a continuous and natural development from apes. Objections to the idea of evolution take a narrow focus concentrated on humanity and in the context of an Old Testament story rather than a broad focus on all creation. A narrow focus is what caused the predecessors of Copernicus and Galileo to remain in error for centuries. Those who find the concept of evolution disturbing also suffer from a narrow focus. The surprising thing is that now, in the twenty-first century, legions of people still have a very serious problem with this concept. Let us begin by looking into the current debate.

Why is evolution such an emotive word for so many people today? The reason is simple, it appears to leave God out. And while our Earth may not be at the center of the universe, in faith experience we are still the most important thing God created and that makes us different from everything else in the universe. If we come to this conclusion from the whole of written revelation and not simply from the Genesis stories, then so far so good. Unfortunately, at this point, the logic takes a false turn. It maintains that God somehow physically had to make humans separately from the rest of creation and by a method completely different from all other living beings. To some it seems necessary to maintain that physically we could not have come from any other life form on Earth in spite of the fact that chemically and genetically we have so much in common with other life forms. In Genesis terms, suddenly there was Adam and Eve, the progenitors of all humankind. Those who hold this idea today seem to do so as tenaciously as those who thought that it was necessary for the Earth to be the center of the universe.

But wait a minute. How is Homo sapiens unique in its creation? To a person of faith, we are different because we are destined toward a life after physical death. We have an immortal soul though one that is extremely difficult to define. It had a beginning but will have no end. But where did that term soul come from? While the word is found throughout the *Bible*, it has variable meanings and none quite like the understanding we give it today. In fact, some of our theological ideas about soul come from the Greek philosophers Plato and Aristotle. To Aristotle the soul meant a principle of life and admits of many grades of life. He recognized how different living and non-living beings were but did not know that this was the result of organic complexity and could explain it only as a new type of being existing in a duality. Even plants have an Aristotelian soul. Of course, the human soul is quite different.

It was Thomas Aquinas in the thirteenth century who took Aristotle's concept and gave it a Christian meaning. He taught that the principle we call the mind or the intellect has an operation apart from the body. It is something without bodily substance and does not depend on the body for its existence, is incorruptible and produced by God. Yet the human being is not a soul only, but composed of soul and body.

We need to understand better the nature of humankind and explore further the concept of soul and immortality. We need to investigate the interface between the biological life in the human body and the human as a person, as a unique individual. To do this requires that we turn to the highest level of the biological and neurological sciences. One wonders why in religious circles there is such a preoccupation with the biological origin of the human body rather than these pressing questions about the human soul. We do have Scriptural references to the origin of the body but little about the soul except that it is made in God's image but not how or when. We will never adequately determine the exact physical origin of that first human being. The evidence has little chance of being uncovered. For the soul, the only thing we can do is philosophize? The sciences, however, are making great advances in organic chemistry, genetics and neurology to explain the human body so let's use this and then philosophize.

The next question for people of faith is, where did any individual human endowed with a soul come from? In Genesis terms we know that the first one came from the dust of the Earth formed by the Creator and into which he breathed the breath of life. But after that, the rest of us come from the biological act of reproduction. And since that is a purely physical act, logically, philosophically it can only produce a physical result. This seems to imply that God also acts at some moment and endows this new biological life with an immortal soul, that is, something which will persist after biological death. He again breaths life into them unless, of course, our concept of soul cannot yet accommodate the true nature of the human soul.

In the case of human beings, even our language supports a separate creative act and we call the process procreation rather than simple reproduction. Upon death, the body will return to the dust from which it came and the soul, that breath of life, to its maker. To be sure, we well understand the physical process concerning the dissolution of the body but how clearly do we understand what happens to the soul?

The point to be made here is that evolution is a continuous process while creationism represents and requires that God inject new entities at will or else they will not exist at all. This latter view is thought to be supported by the Genesis account while the evolutionary view is overwhelmingly supported by physical observations. This discontinuity will require our close examination. But to do this, we need to include details of the latest science, including concepts from quantum physics. As a result we will delay this discussion until subsequent chapters.

Where evolution is happening

Evolution is not just a biological concept. The planet Earth and the stuff it is made of also evolved. It seems to be the way of natural things. What has only recently come to our attention is that while the evolution of the planet has had a great effect on biological evolution, more surprisingly, the evolution of life has impacted that of the planet. Geologists are turning to the biologist to explain why certain things happened to the Earth, such as the presence of free oxygen in the atmosphere.

With very convincing arguments, the Big Bang theory tells us that very quickly after the Bang a condensation, or should we say evolution, of the elements of matter, the stuff of the universe, began to take place. Gravitational and other forces caused the formation of galaxies of stars which were born out of the material of the universe left by the Big Bang. But we are interested in one particular star, our Sun. Around it swirled all manner of stuff that had not yet been pulled into the Sun by its large force of gravity. Solar wind, subatomic particles blown away from the nuclear reaction producing the Sun's great heat, as well as gravitational and electrical forces pushed and pulled together particles of dust and eventually formed large and small chunks of matter which increasingly collected together to form the beginning of planets. These chunks of matter began to collect and grow in size by accretion. Finally, about 4.5 billion years ago, they formed four masses closest to the Sun so large that their own gravity pulled them into spherical shape. Their orbital motion kept them from falling into the Sun. Others formed further out but were somewhat different in composition.

We call these closest four planets Mercury, Venus, Earth and Mars. Our interest is Earth. It just so happened that it was at a unique distance from the Sun which gave it special characteristics. Eventually it would be not too hot and not too cold on the surface, an ideal environment for biological activity. At first, massive collisions with all the debris it was collecting caused Earth to be extremely hot, in fact molten. This heat was increased by the decay of radioactive isotopes as well as gravitational energy released as heavy metals, mostly iron and sulfur, sank into its core. This core became surrounded by a molten mantel, the surface of which cooled and hardened into a crust.

Great cells of convection currents formed in the liquid mantle and caused fissures in the crust through which the gasses, including steam trapped in the mantle, were released. Eventually the whole surface of the Earth was covered by a shallow sea of water with volcanic islands protruding above the surface pouring out even more steam as well as solid material which thickened the crust. The whole thing was enveloped by an atmosphere of carbon dioxide which had been dissolved in the mantel. With each eruption of lava through the crust this CO_2 atmosphere was deepened. Eventually these volcanic eruptions succeeded in forming a large continent. This process took some 700 million years after the formation of the initial mass of the Earth. The determination of this process is not the product of speculation. The oldest rocks found on the surface of the Earth are between 3.8 and 4.28 billion years old. But this is the age since they solidified as rock from molten lava. Some of the material which originally formed the Earth is still drifting around in space and, at times, is captured by the Earth's gravity and falls as meteorites. These are pieces of the original material out of which our solar system was formed. The age of these rocks has been determined to be 4.6 billion years.

The convections of the underlying magma caused the initial continent to fragment and drift apart. The North and South American continents were at one time connected to Europe and Africa. To this day they are still getting father apart at the rate of about 2 centimeters a year. A trench along the centre of the Atlantic Ocean continuously opens and allows molten lava to fill the gap. The collisions caused by the drift of the continental plates have produced mountain ranges by uplifting the ground masses. The collision of the continents of Indian and Asia caused the uplift of the Tibetan Plateau and formed the Himalayas. These changes altered the climate by changing air currents and the circulation of moisture and thus global temperature. At times these continental plates are pushed under the adjacent plate. Often the stresses generated by this are suddenly released producing a rapid uplifting of the edge of the plate. When this happens under the sea, it can produce a tsunami.

The age of the Earth and the determination of the history of changes that have occurred on its surface is the study of geology. One of the main characters who established this as a science was a man whose name is seldom mentioned, Niels Stensen. He was born in Denmark in 1638 where he began his studies in medicine. He moved to The Netherlands where he became well known for his work in anatomy and his skill in dissection. He then went to Florence where his name was Latinized to Nicholas Steno. There he enjoyed the patronage of Duke Ferdinand. In October of 1666 some fishermen caught a large white shark and the Duke ordered that the head be sent to Steno for dissection. When he examined the teeth, he was struck by their similarity to stones which were found in rock in many of the hills in the area and were so common that they were thought to have fallen from the sky.[2]

Steno was inquisitive enough to wonder how shark's teeth had been turned into rock and how they came to be found on hills. The second question was easy to answer. These hills were originally the seabed where the sharks had lost the teeth and it had eventually been pushed up by the movement of the Earth's surface, through earthquakes. He argued that over a period of time such objects underwent the exchange of some of the material they were made of with minerals in the sediment. He published his findings in the curiously named *Dissertation Concerning Solids Naturally Contained in Solids* (1669). He had explained the formation of fossils.

The brilliant insight which resulted from his findings was that as material fell to the bottom of the sea, it formed strata or layers. These could be easily seen on cliffs and the sides of caves. The youngest layers were on the top. As a result, the position of fossils in these strata were an indication of their age. This was the true beginning of geology. By this time, Steno had converted to Catholicism and was aware that his proposal not only contradicted Aristotle, but might also run afoul of the Church. As did Galileo during his tribulations, Steno offered this as a proposal but did not exclude other explanations.[3]

As a result of all this, it can be seen that our Earth is not a static and solid ground upon which we can carry on our human trades. It is a partly fluid foundation and atmosphere which slowly but constantly changes our environment. Each time we hear of a volcanic eruption, we are reminded that underneath us is a molten sea of magma upon which our continent drifts. Each time there is an earthquake, we are reminded that these continents are still drifting and colliding along fault lines. The natural sciences are constantly improving our understanding of how the Earth works but because of its size and the timescales needed to bring about change, there is little we can do to control it although we can affect it, especially the atmosphere. Nevertheless, this is our home. Understanding the place we inhabit can help us understand what that creator had in mind for us. But first we address the question: how did we humans get to this place?

Appearance of living things

The world of inert matter exhibits a universal characteristic. It is constantly running down. Things naturally go from hot to cold, high energy states to lower energy states, complex arrangements to simple ones. Radioactive elements decay to more stable states. All this has to do with what is defined in physics as entropy. Strictly speaking entropy is the measure of the randomness in a system. Consider the heat shield of a space capsule. It appears to be a hard and stable material fixed to the leading surface of the capsule. At the level of the molecules of the material it is made of, it has the very orderly arrangement similar to a crystal. Because of the capsule's high speed, the shield has very high kinetic energy of motion.

But when it falls back into the atmosphere it encounters the air friction which causes the temperature to rise and the material of the shield gets so hot that much of it vaporizes in a glowing flash which imparts a high kinetic energy to the atoms of the material which disperse into the atmosphere in every direction. Thus the orderly motion of the hard shield is transferred into the chaotic motion of individual atoms of the atmosphere and the capsule slows down. It is robbed of that energy of motion. The energy of the orderly motion of the capsule has been reduced by increasing the randomness of the motion of the atmosphere into which it fell. Kinetic energy of the capsule's movement runs down and entropy, or randomness, increases.

Material substances, however, have a capacity to work against this trend to run down, at least for a finite period of time. When it does, we find ourselves in the realm of organic chemistry and living things, biology. Organic chemistry describes how materials absorb energy and organize substances into larger, not smaller molecules. These become the building blocks of amino acids, proteins, and on into such things as DNA and all other components of the living cell. They lock away the energy of the sun. For example, when wood burns, that energy is returned to the atmosphere as heat.

The early Earth was covered by a sea of water in which the organic process had begun to build up larger and larger molecules producing a nutritious soup. Energy for this came from the Sun's radiation, lightening strikes in the atmosphere and the interior heat of the planet. This global ocean churned and flowed through a wide range of temperatures and was exposed to differing levels of sunlight. At some moment somewhere the molecular structure reached a critical point at which it became a cell, the basic unit of life. The molecules had reached a size and complexity through which it could close in on itself and become a unit of living substance. By living we imply a degree of self-movement. A high school biology student can observe this movement through a microscope in a whole range of single cell organisms. Classically, the definition of a living organism became one which exhibited the capacities of growth, repair and reproduction.

Whether this happened at more than one location is a moot question for all it had to do is happen once. From that moment on, the cell drew from the surrounding fertile soup and grew to a critical size. At that point, it divided and in the process replicated itself into another cell. It is only with the arrival of the cell that we can truly speak of a living organism. That first living organism on Earth was most probably in the form of single-celled bacteria. They may have originally formed around thermal vents in the sea bottom where hot water with high concentrations of minerals pours out from near the mantle. They are found on the deep seabed even today.

Bacteria have been found trapped in water droplets in salt crystals 200 million years old and yet still able to reproduce when put into a proper medium. Their genes were very similar to that found today in bacteria. Fossils of bacteria have been found in western Australia in rocks 3.5 billion years old. We conclude that it took a billion years for just the right environment to occur in the primordial soup of the early sea for the first primitive bacteria to form. But so stable and hardy are the laws which govern organic molecular chemistry that, once formed, there was an explosion of this bacterial population.

That first life could not have been a one-off. It could not have remained a static life-form like an inorganic rock formation or the shape of a continent. By its very nature, it was a dynamic event which could not have been stopped no matter how extreme the environment became. There is evidence of bacteria metabolizing at temperatures as low as -80C and perhaps even -196C, the temperature of liquid nitrogen. As for longevity, living bacteria have been found 3 kilometers deep in the Greenland ice sheet which makes them 200,000 years old. In truth, what had been started was a biosphere, an activity which would, in evolutionary terms, quickly envelope the entire globe.

We are accustomed to say that living organisms adapt themselves to their environment. It sounds like they are making decisions which promote their survival. In fact it is the survival mechanism of natural selection which is at work. Those bacteria in the Greenland ice sheet survive by clinging to microscopic grains of clay inside a film of liquid water only three molecules thick which covers the clay. While their only food source is iron molecules in the clay, it is estimated that this might be enough food to last a million years. Even more startling, as gravity pulls water into every available cavity and crevice of its container, the mechanism of the biosphere, natural selection, would eventually exploit every possible design for living organisms.

Because the process is based on a mechanism, it is not adequate to refer to it as a process of chance. It is more like a groping, a process which ends up trying every possibility. Teilhard de Chardin, whom we shall discuss in the next chapter, referred to this groping as "directed chance." It demonstrates amazing ingenuity which seems to focus totally on the future possibilities of the biosphere as if it were a single organism which contained the planet within itself. No sample of dirt or rock, water or air can be taken which does not show evidence of life. To isolate an inert sample from life forms, we must take extraordinary steps at filtering and sterilization. This has given us the sometimes bizarre array of living plants, insects and animals both macroscopic and microscopic which we find on the planet today as well as those we find only in fossil form. It should not escape our notice that this same mechanism has also produced socialization as one of its aids to survival.

There is a broad evolutionary process at work. First the proto-material of the big bang evolved into the basic units of material substances, the atom. The atom, with all its apparent simplicity as a fundamental building block, has in modern times begun to reveal its inner complexity. Then these atoms, controlled by the laws of organic chemistry, formed monstrously large molecules which evolved into cells of living substance, a new and higher level of complexity. These cells were very successful in their liquid environment. Soon cells multiplied in prodigious numbers and new complexity. Just as inert atoms reacted with each other to form stable combinations of atoms, i.e. molecules, so cells did the same and formed multi-cellular organisms. This was an advance to the next level of complexity and finally led to the differentiation of cells to perform different functions necessary for a colony of cells working in harmony to form different organs. This differentiation is one of the effects of genetic mutation.

Early successors of those first single celled organisms can still be found in the form of stromatolites. These are large colonies of cyanobacteria which look much like rocks and form in the very salty water of Hamlin Pool in Shark Bay Western Australia. The curious thing is that these organisms played a role in changing the whole atmosphere of the Earth. They have the ability to carry on photosynthesis. In the presence of sun light, they take carbon dioxide and water and produce the carbohydrates out of which they are formed. This process releases free oxygen. At first, most of this oxygen was released into the water which supported the bacteria. The ancient sea water contained little free oxygen. As a result it had a high concentration of iron which, with no oxygen, remains dissolved in solution. As soon as the oxygen was released by the bacteria, it combined with the iron and formed iron oxide or what we recognize as rust. This settled in the sediment and can now be seen in layers of red earth in the archeological strata in the hills of Australia and elsewhere around the world.

Eventually enough oxygen was released into the sea to permit an explosion of marine life forms in the oceans some 570 million years ago. Oxygen was also released into the atmosphere in such quantities that marine life was eventually able to migrate out of the sea and become land organisms. For such a volume of oxygen to have been released, there must have been a very high concentration of these bacteria. If you find it difficult to imagine microscopic bacteria changing the atmosphere of the Earth, remember that they had some three billion years to accomplish the task. The reason we do not find such great concentrations of these organisms today is because, as new higher life forms developed, they used the bacteria as food and became their natural enemies. The reason that they are still found in Hamlin Pool is because the shape of the pool traps the sea water and evaporation produces such a high concentration of salt that the natural enemies of the bacteria cannot survive while the bacteria can.

Unlike the oxygen in the sea water which became bonded to iron atoms and settled to the bottom and formed red mud, the oxygen in the atmosphere had nothing to use it up, that is until plant and animal life evolved. Over time, the biosphere was capable of taking over dry land and eventually even the air with insects and birds. The rest of the biosphere's history was directed by both the mechanism of biological evolution which forces living organisms to explore every possible path and form and by global geological events on our planet. While we are impressed by the number of living species that inhabit the Earth today, we must remember that there have been mass extinctions because of global and local geological events. In the last 3.5 billion years, more species have gone extinct than are still extant today. But many of these extinctions must be considered not as dead-end excursions in the proliferation of living things, but as necessary links to the next step of evolution toward more and more complex organisms. You and I populate the biosphere today as one of its most recent and most complex arrivals.

Hopefully, a new picture is coming into view. In it the Creator is not hanging lights on the dome of the sky to illuminate his creation and then separating dry land from water and populating the air, water and ground with individual species, including humanity. Instead the creator has produced something so full of potential and stability that it stretches our imagination and understanding beyond our ability to explain it to our satisfaction either theologically or scientifically. But that very fact makes us even more determined to try to understand it. Only those who have lost the desire to understand creation prefer the ancient and static picture.

Before the theory

No theory arises in a vacuum and so it was with the concept of evolution. The first appearance of the word evolution in a biological sense is in the late 1600s but it is used there as the process of developing from an early to a mature specimen of an individual organism. It did not envision the development of a new species. Today we understand the word evolution to mean a process by which species of plants and animals develop from earlier forms. In fact, all living species on Earth may have had one common origin. It seems a simple enough idea. So why was it the mid nineteenth century before the idea took root? The simple answer is that a lot of ignorance had to be eliminated before that could happen. In the first place, no one ever questioned where species came from. Genesis had said that God made all the animals and plants so what was there to question? Even pagan myths had gods making these things. Everyone knew that plants came from seeds, although you could also get some of them from cuttings. But the animals were a whole different source of confusion.

The animal question was not where did individual species come from. They too were each created by God. As strange as it may sound, the real question was where did the individual animal come from, especially each human person? There were conflicting theories but in reality, no one had a clue. As we might have expected, after Genesis came Aristotle. For him there were lower animals and higher ones. For the lower ones, spontaneous generation was the logical answer. Insects grew out of dirt and maggots were generated by rotting meat. As late as the mid-seventeenth century there were formulas on how to produce mice from dirty clothing and wheat grains kept in a warm, dark place for a certain time. Even the Royal Society supported the idea of spontaneous generation into the late seventeenth century.

Aristotle taught that what animated all living things was a soul and there could be a succession of souls as an organism developed. For humans, he thought that the succession of soul development could be anywhere from six weeks for boys to twelve weeks for girls with the development of the embryo. Such accuracy without the least bit of physical evidence astounds us today. Thomas Aquinas Christianized the Aristotelian

67

concept of the soul. He even thought that the human ensoulment did not take place until the organism was developed enough to take on human potentiality and agreed with Aristotle's timetable. Christian scholars were predisposed to accept the concept and only much later changed the moment of ensoulment to the moment of conception. Of course at the time of Aquinas, conception was not understood. The change in thinking was based not on evidence but the pure logic that the effect must be proportional to the cause. It also meant that "ensoulment" was the proper word since for a time at least there was a biological entity which was not human and then it became human.

There was precious little understanding of the process of human reproduction. Because of the time delay between cause and effect, the connection between copulation and pregnancy is not an immediately obvious one. The Old Testament idea of the man planting his seed persisted into the seventeenth century but there was little understanding of the contribution of the woman in the process of conception. For some, she was simply a fertile environment in which the man's seed could develop. But then why did the offspring favor the mother at times? Even this use of the word seed is incorrect. A seed is the result of the merging of both the male (pollen) and female (stamen) plant sexual components. But lacking physical evidence, the man seemed to be sowing seed in the woman who provided a fertile environment for the development of the child that resulted.

Women suffered greatly from the almost total ignorance of how to promote their reproductive health and childbirth was a dangerous thing. Aristotle considered women as incomplete men. It wasn't until the beginning of the eighteenth century and interest in anatomy that there was any attempt to explain the relationship between the male sperm and the female egg. It was during this time that the word reproduction began to be used with regard to humans rather than the term generation. Only in the nineteenth century could women expect that their physician knew much about the function of the female body.

Some maintained that the male component contained all that was necessary for full development of the child. All the constituents of the anatomy were thought to pre-exist in the seed. This was the theory of Preformation and as late as the end of the seventeenth century, it was thought that if you had a powerful enough microscope to view the "spermatic animal", one would see a very tiny but fully formed human being. Others thought that it was the mother that contained the egg which had the fully formed human and something about the male sperm caused it to develop, turned it on as it were. Some even referred to this process as fermentation. In this atmosphere, how could there be any concern about the origin of species when there was so little known about the origin of individuals within a species? The mechanism of evolution is embedded in the process of reproduction. With such ignorance about the reproductive process, little wonder no one hit upon the idea of evolution.

Biological science

Just as the sixteenth century saw massive change in our understanding of the physical universe and the methods by which we arrive at that new understanding, so the seventeenth century brought about intensive investigation into the biology of living organisms and how they are generated and develop. That investigation was motivated by the new scientific spirit of the sixteenth century. Theories about animal generation abounded. It was time for experimentation and physical investigation to determine the facts, not theories. Science was the process of investigating the things you can see and not speculating on the things you cannot see.

There were numerous personalities involved in this seventeenth century revolution in thinking concerning animal generation and many of them were associated with the University of Leiden in the Netherlands. The history of the period is a fascinating one. One person who stands out is Nicholas Steno who, as seen previously, developed fundamental principles of geological stratification. Earlier in his career, while at the university in Leiden, he acquired great respect for his skill in anatomical dissection. At the same time medicine, his field of interest, was seeking better understanding of the human body and its functions. The topic changed from a discussion of the body "humors" to the function of the individual organs of the body and dissection was the starting point.

This effort naturally led to the dissection of the genital organs of animals and eventually human corpses. As usual, theories abounded but eventually evidence pointed to the possibility that the woman contained eggs in what at the time were referred to as the testicles of the woman, that is, the ovary. The question became how the egg managed to travel to the uterus where the fetus developed. The question of who was the first to proclaim the egg theory became a bone of contention and in 1673 the Royal Society was, in effect, asked to adjudicate the matter. Of the four claimants as being the first to see and describe eggs in the female, the society declared that Steno was the first and had reported it in 1667.[3]

Clearly, dissection was not enough to advance the science much further. What was needed was new technology. Just as the telescope in the hands of Galileo allowed cosmology to make a quantum leap in understanding, so too another optical invention proved the turning point for biology. While the microscope appeared in the Netherlands at the beginning of the seventeenth century, it was seen as of no real value. Drawings made from viewing insects through an early microscope were made in Italy around 1625 but did not arouse much interest. The potential of microscopic studies was finally realized in the great work of Robert Hooke (1635-1703). He was tasked with the regular presentation to the Royal Society in London of the results of experiments. In 1664 he published a large book of his drawings called *Micrographia*. It contained detailed drawings of everything from the point of a needle to the body of a flea and amazed everyone who saw it.

At roughly the same time as Hooke announced his discoveries, biological advancements using the microscope were being made by a Dutchman, Antoni Leeuwenhoek (1632-1723). Curiously, Leeuwenhoek had never gone to university and, unlike all other academics of the day, spoke only Dutch. He was a cloth merchant in the city of Delft. It may have been an interest in investigating the minute structure of cloth that initiated his interest in the microscope. Leeuwenhoek fabricated his lens by drawing a heated glass rod out to a thin strand and then letting a small bead of glass form at the tip. This sphere became a single lens microscope. The magnification was 150 times and more. His clever innovation was to position the lens on a metal plate which was equipped with a mounting system to hold the sample in place and could be adjusted by turning a screw. He began regular correspondence with the Royal Society concerning his observations. The society was slow to accept the accuracy of Leeuwenhoek's drawings until Hooke was able to confirm them with his own observations.

Leeuwenhoek's real breakthrough came when he devised a way to observe liquids and discovered that some samples of water were full of tiny animals which were constantly moving. He even observed bacteria which were far smaller. The Society had suggested that he make observations of bodily fluids. In 1677 he observed human semen and was astonished to find an unbelievable number of "animalcules" with thrashing tails. He then went on to find these same types of creatures in the semen of an assortment of animals. All this caused him to conclude that it was this living male semen that developed into the fetus in the environment of the female.

While he was wrong in this conclusion, the discovery changed the whole character of the debate and investigation into animal reproduction began to make progress. It wasn't until the nineteenth century that it was concluded with certainty that a single sperm united with a single egg to produce the embryo which developed into an adult. Embryology would come into its own only after technological advances in optics and the invention of the compound microscope which used a magnifying eyepiece to examine the image formed by the front lens. All of these events and discoveries provided the background which made the idea of evolution possible.

Notes

1. Of course, when is the last time you heard anyone talking about the praeternatural gifts? There is constant reference to our fallen nature but seldom discussion of how things were before the fall. It is almost one of those speculations that died of non-relevance. It seems that Limbo may do the same thing. Limbo is that state of natural happiness into which anyone who has not reached the age of reason and not been baptized is sent after death. In 2006 The International Theological Commission was asked by the Vatican to consider whether limbo is a reality. The idea had evolved in response to Augustine who thought that non-baptized children went to hell since they did not have sanctifying grace. The offensive nature of this opinion was eliminated by inventing a place of natural happiness called limbo. This idea remained until the Second Vatican Council where the idea seemed to be dropped since it was nothing more than a theological hypothesis with no biblical foundation. But the root of the issue is not trivial. If limbo goes, what is the effect on the teaching of Original Sin? Speculative theology can weave a complex web.
2. As a young boy who walked the beaches of the Gulf coast of Florida, I have picked up many of these black objects which we knew were petrified sharks teeth.
3. It can be added that after Steno became a Catholic, he set science to the side, was ordained a priest and then bishop and died at the age of 48 while working with the poor in Northern Germany. In 1987 he was beatified by the Church, the first step to being declared a saint.

6

The Theory of Evolution

Seldom is the name of a person so strongly associated with an idea as the name Darwin is to the term evolution. The reason is simple. No idea since the Copernican theory of a heliocentric universe has had the potential to upset traditional thinking about the nature of human beings. Scientific discoveries about the universe drastically changed our understanding of the place humanity inhabits. But evolution directly challenges our understanding of humanity. Today we feel quite at home with the idea proposed by Copernicus and Galileo.

In spite of all the weight science has been able to bring to bear in making evolution a well established theory, many today find no comfort in it. As the twenty-first century barely begins, evolution has been the concern of the White House and the Vatican, the subject of a court trial in Dover Pennsylvania and the focus of an institute funding millions of dollars of research for the purpose of discrediting it. Evolution has had a direct impact on the religious thinking of the past and has much to say about all living things, including ourselves. It was Charles Darwin who first helped us codify what nature was revealing about the process leading to human life and why it has been so successful in surviving on our planet.

Darwin, the person

Charles Darwin was born in 1809, the son and grandson of English physicians. This explains why he started his studies in medicine but after two years he switched to Cambridge University and began studies to become a clergyman. It seems, however, he acquired a keen interest in natural history and shortly after graduation in 1831, he acquired the position as a naturalist on the now famous ship Beagle and spent five years sailing around the world. At the numerous ports of call he was able to study fossils and the local species. This caused him to raise the question of how species developed. It was not until 1859 that he published his conclusions in the book *On the Origin of Species by Means of Natural Selection*. In 1871 he extended his idea of natural selection to humans in *The Descent of Man and Selection in Relation to Sex*.

Eventually his scientific work began to undermine his faith but it is thought that the final blow came with the death at the age of 10 of his daughter Annie in 1851. He was extremely devoted to her and when she died, he was crushed. What kind of God would allow this to happen? As is so often the case, it is when a question becomes personal that we begin to see more implications. In April, 1882, he died, an apparent outsider to religious faith. What is this theory which so impacted his own life and has caused so much consternation in our society even to the present?

The theory of evolution

The two volumes by Darwin on natural selection and the descent of man were seen by many as a biological blow against human dignity. One could conclude that God had no necessary part in the arrival of humanity on Earth. It could all be explained by physical natural laws. Evolution is a natural process by which organisms can adapt to an environment and increase in complexity. It is both a survival mechanism as environments change as well as a way to improve the capabilities of an organism within a stable environment. The evolutionary mechanism by which this happens is called natural selection. Do not be misled by the term selection. It is not a matter of choice.

The reproductive process of living organisms is extremely stable and consistent. Throughout history we have taken advantage of this in animal and plant breading even without knowing the mechanism by which it happens. But changes, variations within a species, can occur for a number of reasons. When this happens, it can have an effect on the survivability of the offspring. Survivability can be affected by such things as mating success, fertility and rate of development. If the change promotes survivability, then the change is more likely to be preserved into future generations. If it decreases survivability, it is unlikely to be perpetuated very far and eventually the last surviving example of it dies and the variant becomes extinct. Natural selection is not an efficient designer and produces many bad results which eventually disappear.

How these variations happened was not understood at the time of Darwin nor by the monk Gregor Mendel (1822-1884), Darwin's contemporary, who derived the mathematical regularity of inherited traits through successive generations. Unfortunately, Mendel did not get the notice of the scientific community which his discovery deserved and this slowed progress toward a science of genetics. Nor, perhaps, did either of them adequately appreciate one very necessary controlling element, time. You and I may look at the proliferation of so many species with such great differences in form and capability, such bizarre colors and habits, their ability to live under water, on land or even fly, and think it impossible that this mechanism of natural selection could ever have produced them all.

What we are not appreciating is the length of time nature has had to work its magic. Much diversification is possible in 3.5 billion years, that is, the passing of a million years, 3,500 times, during which living beings have flourished on Earth. It would certainly be impossible if the Earth were only 6000 years old as many thought until rather recently but surely our perspective has improved.

The contribution of genetics

A quick clarification of terminology might be helpful here. The genetic code which determines all the characteristics of a living cell and thus the organism which those cells form is carried by huge molecules called DNA. In the DNA molecules, the segments which carry the information for a particular characteristic, are called genes. Within each cell, the DNA is organized into structures called chromosomes. The human cell contains 23 chromosomes, each of which can be made up of as many as 220 million pairs of base molecules.

Since the beginning of the twentieth century the science of genetics has begun to understand the particular genes which determine each characteristic of the whole organism. The composition of genes is extremely stable but they can be altered by a number of things. This can happen spontaneously through accidents in the process of being replicated during cell division. They are also subject to external influences such as radiation or the presence of certain chemicals. Any change causes what are called mutations in the organism.

When these mutations happen in the egg or sperm cells in animals or the pistil and stamen in plants, they are also passed on and change the offspring. These causes of genetic change are obviously random and pure chance although it is now possible to bring about genetic modifications directly for desired characteristics. The effect each change will have is often catastrophic to the organism but it can also be beneficial. At the risk of getting too technical, it may help to appreciate the mechanisms of genes and the number of places where the change can happen.

The complete set of genetic material in each cell of an organism is called the genome. Every living cell has a region called the nucleus. By the late 1800's this nucleus was discovered to contain threadlike structures which when subjected to certain dyes can be seen through a microscope. Thus they were given the name chromosomes (Greek, meaning "color body"). When a cell is about to divide, these chromosomes line up and copy themselves and each copy moves to a different part of the cell. Thus, when the cell divides, there is a complete copy of the genetic material in the nucleus of each resulting cell.

Genes are coding material. They are long chain molecules which lie on the chromosomes. They are composed of two types of material, deoxyribonucleic acid (DNA) and ribonucleic acid (RNA). It was James Watson and Francis Crick who discovered in 1953 that the structure of the DNA molecule is a double helix. This explained how, by the unwinding of the two strands, they could duplicate themselves exactly, thus the great stability of genetic material.

RNA, on the other hand contains only one strand and is present both in the nucleus and the rest of the cell interior. It turns out that while the DNA contained the genetic coding, the RNA is used as a molecular transportation system. The DNA passes on a template of a protein to the RNA in the nucleus. The RNA moves out of the nucleus into the cell material and synthesizes the needed protein. This is the process carried on in all living organisms and produces proper growth of the organism as well as stable reproduction.

But this is not the end of the adventure. In science, each discovery raises new questions. It was noticed that all animals had about 20,000 genes for protein codes no matter how complex the organism: a brainless worm, cats or people. Yet you and I are a far more complex organism than a worm or even a cat. The human genome is made up of about 100,000 different proteins necessary for making all the tissues of the body. This implies that there should be about 90 million DNA bases strung along the 23 human chromosomes. But in the process of sequencing the human genome, that number turned out to be about 3 billion. The question is, why all the extra DNA?

Recently discovered evidence is growing to indicate that the function of RNA has not been fully appreciated. DNA, it seems, is not only the depository of genetic codes but is also an RNA factory and the more complex the organism, the more complex the RNA system turns out to be. As a result evolution may not only be a function of genes for proteins but genes which produce RNA and these RNA in turn regulate some of the coding DNA. This adds another element to the evolutionary mechanism.

There is one other fascinating possibility. Since RNA is a component of the interior material of the cell around the nucleus and not attached to the chromosomes, it can be passed down inside the sex cells, egg or sperm, during division and not as part of the formal genetic material. The fact that RNA can be modified by environmental influences raises a startling possibility which would add to the mechanism to evolution. It would mean that characteristics which were acquired during the lifetime of an individual could be passed on as well as genetic mutations. It is another element in natural selection. If this turns out to be the case, the whole evolutionary mechanism becomes much bigger than we thought.

The uncovering of this process underlines the danger of ever thinking that we now know it all and deciding that the complex physical human organism could not be the result of purely natural processes. The change needed for the evolution of an organism need be in only one gene – or perhaps one RNA. As a result the target area is large even in the simplest organisms and, again, living organisms have had 3.5 billion years of opportunities to bring about mutations. To be complete then we should say that the mechanism of evolution is natural selection, time and the stability as well as mutability of organic compounds.

Scientists have been able to overcome partially the requirement of long time periods when observing genetic changes. In the 1920's they began to use organisms with very short generation periods. The fruit fly was the first to be used. It has a mere two-week lifespan. While bacteria do not reproduce through egg and sperm, the genes are replicated in each generation which can be as short as fifteen minutes to an hour. This rapid generation time in bacteria is why they can quickly become immune to antibiotics and become superbugs and also makes it possible to observe not only the transfer of inherited characteristics but chance mutations as well.

Mass extinctions caused by drastic changes in the physical environment on Earth raise an interesting question about evolution. Can it work in reverse or must we think of it as always pushing forward in the direction of greater complexity? Could conditions change such that the return of a primitive characteristic, which was lost because it was no longer useful for survival, would be advantageous? It was originally thought that evolution could not revert back to some previous state, a process called atavism, and that this was confirmed by fossil evidence, or rather the absence of any evidence of having done so. This principle was proposed in 1890 by the paleontologist Louis Dollo and became known as Dollo's Law. A better understanding of genetics, however, brings the principle into doubt. Yet, if the evolutionary change was caused by the loss of a gene, then the chance of the characteristic reappearing is extremely slight.

It is now known that there are mechanisms which simply switch off a gene even though the gene may remain present in the species for millions of years after being switched off. This means that something could also occur which turns the gene back on. In evolutionary terms, this could be beneficial. It means that previous characteristics are held in reserve in case conditions should arise which might benefit from their return. Even within humanity, the occasional birth of people with an extra finger on each hand or webbed toes may be a remnant of the primitive amphibian origins of animal species. The mechanism of evolution is extremely effective in guaranteeing the survival of living things.

Chance and chaos are not dirty words

In scientific literature, words have specific, almost clinical, meanings that may differ somewhat from the common, colloquial expression of those same words. Words like random, chance, chaos and arbitrary are not dirty words, even when applied to the physical origin of Homo sapiens but can be very emotive. Anything which happens in the physical world does so by following the laws of physical nature. As a result, while we may describe something as having happened by chance or at random, no law was broken in the process or any external intervention needed. The reason we could not predict what happened was because of the complexity of the circumstances and not because someone was rolling dice with the possibilities. In fact, even the outcome of rolling dice could be predicted if only we knew and controlled all the initial conditions at the time the dice left our hand.

In the study of chance and chaos, one principle is described as a sensitive dependence on initial conditions. A very slight change of initial conditions can bring about a drastic and unpredictable result which is difficult to foresee. Yet at each step, all the laws of nature are followed. This is why it is so difficult to predict the weather very far ahead as well as the roll of dice. In fact, the exaggerated example of this principle is that today's weather was influenced by a butterfly that flapped its wings in the South American rain forest four days ago.

Some believers see a universe whose outcome has been completely determined by the Creator. So how do we reconcile this with what we see around us as the result of chance, as random and unpredictable? The fact that it is unpredictable does not mean that we must demand the intervention of the Creator. This principle tells us that the reason for the unpredictability comes from its complexity and sensitive dependence on initial conditions which we cannot adequately determine. It is not because someone is interfering in natural events. Because we cannot know or determine all the initial conditions when we roll dice, we conclude that the number that comes up does so by chance and is completely random. Yet each step along the way, the movement in the hand and the final tumbling along a surface are all determined by understandable laws. We just can't measure nor can we easily control all the factors involved.

The situation is the same with the mechanisms of evolution. Given a worldwide ocean of atoms and a billion years, the time it took for primitive life to be formed on Earth after the conditions became right, you end up with more opportunities for unique combinations than the human mind can imagine or write the number for. What was needed for primitive life was the formation of particular organic compounds and the rest was automatic according to the physical laws of organic chemistry. When we honestly consider this situation we cannot say that there is no way a living thing could happen by itself. This is like saying that when I throw a ball, it cannot drop by itself. Furthermore, how can we expect a scientist today to duplicate this life generating process in the laboratory during a single human lifetime and so prove that it is possible? For those who understand the concepts of organic chemistry, it is more reasonable to assume that it is possible.

It gives the wrong impression to say that evolution is dependent on undetermined or purposeless things like chance and random events. It depends rather on the result of natural laws which exploit opportunities that occur unpredictably. As surely as we climb a mountain because it is there, natural selection will eventually take life along every path open to it. Even to our experienced eyes, some of the results seem most improbable and yet turn out to be quite successful. Witness the strange 40 day gestation of the kangaroo embryo. Because it lacks a placenta through which to be nourished by the mother, it must crawl wormlike in its early state of growth from the womb to the pouch in order to be suckled and mature for another six months. As difficult as that sounds, it works. Just as artists investigate every possible format and style, evolution explores every shape, color and size.

Examples of human creativity are not imitating natural evolution but rather participating in it. Our individuality is determined by how we think. Our social environment is determined by how society in general thinks. Again, our social nature is part of the survival mechanism of our species and some of the genes which contribute to our social nature have been identified.

The heavenly watchmaker argument

In 1802, the English clergyman William Paley published a book entitled *Natural Theology*, an exposition of what created nature can tell us about God. In it he used what became a classic analogy. When we observe a watch, we see in it purpose and function which only an intelligent designer could have produced. But living organisms are far more complicated than any watch and so they too must have had a designer and that designer is God. The logic is simple and forceful but is the analogy valid?

Metal needs the application of external forces to create the exact shapes necessary to be parts of a watch. The watch is most probably made of brass which is an alloy of copper and zinc. Nothing about these metals, no law of physical matter, can cause a single gear, much less a watch, to happen spontaneously. The component parts of living organisms can assemble themselves following the laws of organic chemistry. Once the watchmaker produces a watch, it can never duplicate itself. In living organisms the molecules which form a living cell begin by replicating themselves until all the basic parts of another cell are present. Then the cell divides into two cells which are duplicates of the original. This process can be watched through a microscope. If that cell which just duplicated itself was an embryo, the cell of a newly fertilized egg, then it will not only continue to duplicate billions of times but differentiate as well into all the unique and specialized cells needed to make the organs of the body. All this will be accomplished without the need for any outside help.

This happens because the laws which govern matter when configured in what we call organic structure provide this natural capacity. This is why forensic biologists can take the molecules of DNA from a few individual human cells left at a crime scene and cause them to replicate themselves until a large enough sample is had to identify their unique structure, and thus identify the person they came from. That capability to replicate has been designed into the nature of carbon, oxygen and all the other elements involved in organic structures. The result is as predictable as when you raise the temperature of carbon in the presence of oxygen. The carbon will burn every time producing carbon dioxide gas. The divine watchmaker/cellmaker did not do his work at the time the cell came into being. All the designing was done long before matter took form. Every molecular configuration which that matter could subsequently assume was a result of the laws designed into it. It was simply a matter of enough time and the right environment to permit it to take on that form. This process makes Paley's pocket watch insignificant by comparison.

From consciousness to reflection

We all recognize that the transition which is most difficult to imagine as a natural result of evolution is the arrival of intelligence or human consciousness and reflection. Anatomically, the difference simply involves the size and organization of the brain. As in every genetic modification, the physical change in the gene may be slight but the evolutionary result gigantic. The gene involved is known as ASPM or the beta-catenin protein. It was identified when investigating the inherited condition microcephaly which causes small brain size and mental retardation. While the process is not completely understood yet, in those with this condition the mutation of this gene produced a smaller version of the gene's normal protein and resulted in smaller brain development.[1]

We are genetically very similar to the apes with which we share 99% of our genes. It is thought that as long ago as 6 million years our evolution parted company with the ape. It was all up to a gene which greatly increased the size and complexity of our brain. That new complexity increased our intelligence. We devised language and could communicate with greater accuracy and detail. We became problem solvers and developed stronger social skills. Of course this also meant that we were able to lie and cheat as well as love and care for others. We were capable of reflection and could place value and priorities on things and relationships. We could do things out of reason rather than simple instinct.

All this did not happen in one simple genetic change but the result we see today is light years ahead of the apes which developed parallel with us from a common ancestor. It does beg the question, when did the human species appear on Earth? If the Creator was required to make humanity in a unique act, he certainly hid the event by sneaking us into a succession of fossil remains which evolved prior to our arrival. It appears that we suddenly stepped into the head of an evolutionary parade wearing a uniform only slightly different from those behind us to indicate that we were the leaders. Or perhaps we should say that we had no uniform at all – being without body hair and requiring clothing made of the skins of those species that did. The point is that the parade was not interrupted in the least and was noticed only by ourselves. Physically there was little that was remarkable about our arrival.

The sciences of genetics and biochemistry are complex in the extreme but they are progressing with breathtaking speed. It is the greatest folly to think that we can call this progress into question based on philosophical conclusions drawn from ancient texts which were never intended to teach science or natural history. Material substances work according to natural laws which are capable of generating living organisms and even evolving into intelligent beings. This does not necessarily lead to the conclusion that we are only material beings. Natural science cannot deal well with that issue. It does say, however, that people of faith cannot neglect to take our physical nature into account when considering what human nature is.

How to determine God's plan

There is much more that could be said about the process of the evolution of planet Earth and the life forms on it. There are the questions of the global changes which have caused repeated mass extinctions affecting, at times, the majority of living species. Numerous ice ages have cyclically disrupted the migration and survival of living beings. Plagues, droughts, the impacts of gigantic meteorites and cyclic rising and falling of sea levels caused by the ice age cycles have constantly changed the inhabitability of the surface of the planet. Many of these events have taken place since humanity became the intelligent creature we are now. It is up to the theologian, not the scientist, to explain how these events fit into God's plan.

In spite of the things which natural revelation can suggest to us about God, strictly speaking the tools of the theologian are faith, revelation and correct philosophical reasoning. Only the last of these tools is shared with the scientist. The theologian does not have the observational technology which can confirm the cosmological theories of the physicists. Theologians lack the mathematical language which so adequately describes the working of natural law. As a result science has the clearer arguments and the stronger proofs. When scientists are speaking within their field, the theologian must take great care when the implications of science appear to be in conflict with theological conclusions.

Starting from mathematical expressions of known natural laws, mathematics can derive new statements of natural law. Science describes how nature works. Philosophy can ensure the reasonableness of conclusions. Theology searches for divinely revealed confirmation of that reasonableness and its relationship to the spiritual nature of humanity. These are obviously not mutually exclusive tools or methods. Rather, in the hands of someone who understands the capabilities and limitations of each, they work well together. In unison, they can enable us to experience more fully the intellectual satisfaction and fittingness of certain ideas. They can combine physical, logical and metaphysical reality in one embrace.

Good science and good theology will not clash. The Earth has been shown not to be at the centre of the universe. If we had concluded otherwise from reading textual revelation, the assumption must be that we have be misreading that revelation. If science demonstrates that the Earth is 4.5 billion years old and not 6000 years old, we must learn to live with that fact and ask why we misinterpreted the *Old Testament* and what that implies about the purpose of the Creator and our status on Earth. It also offers us an important lesson about what we can legitimately expect to find in the sacred text. When the overwhelming conclusion of science is that, given such a long period as 3.5 billion years, living organisms can evolve into the complex and marvelous organism which is the physical reality of Homo sapiens, then it is true folly for the theologian to seek scientific reasons why that cannot be so. Unfortunately, this is exactly what a large number of people are attempting to do in the twenty-first century.

Why evolution is problematic

Globally, the number of Christian fundamentalists who believe in creationism, that humankind was created separately and uniquely without reference to other forms of life, is relatively small. Yet recent surveys have shown that more than 40% of North Americans are creationists. Their militancy may be causing us to exaggerate their number and making it difficult to decide if they are growing or decreasing in number. So why are we concerned about their presence? While the vast majority of religious people have shed the fundamentalist view of creationism, many of these have held fast to the image of God which fundamentalism generates.

Science and logic may have made it easy for us to abandon the image of a God who is required to separate oceans and continents on our Earth. He may no longer be required to create separately every individual species of living creature. But what about God's relationship with us in our daily lives or events which affect the general human population? The fundamentalists see God as controlling everything even here and now. They are not indulging in a cliché when they say, "God willing, it won't rain tomorrow." But what do the non-fundamentalist mean when they say that? This is the rub. If we concede too many things to the natural course of events and not the intervention of God, is there a danger that we will lose the image of God all together? On the other hand, if we attribute everything that happens to the will of God, is there a danger that we are exaggerating his involvement? Are we carrying a good thing to an absurd extreme? The solution is not to hold on to what very often is a Bronze Age *Old Testament* image of God in spite of our better understanding of nature. The better solution would be to update our image of God and our spirituality in light of what we now understand about the reality of human nature and its environment. We will address this specifically in the last chapter.

At this point in our consideration we need to appreciate the reasonableness of science and understand the significance of the theory of evolution. Fundamentalists reject ideas of great importance which we will investigate further in the next chapter. The first and most obvious thing about us is that we are of the same stuff as the environment in which we live, physically, biologically and, to a certain extent, socially. The idea of evolution assumes that natural laws produced our nature. Since we see a glaringly obvious evolutionary process at work in that nature, it is reasonable to assume that we are included in it. The objections which creationists raise concerning evolution are not scientific ones. Instead, they create a science fiction account of the origin of the universe in order to conform to a literal reading of a story composed by a Bronze Age civilization.

One of the uniquely human characteristic is our capacity and instinctive drive to understand ourselves and our environment. Part of the process of understanding is the formulation of a theory which suggests investigation into observable facts. Whether investigation proves the theory to be right, wrong or in need of modification, this process often suggests a new theory and the whole process becomes cyclical. Theories propose questions and the human intellect finds some of its greatest satisfaction in discovering the answers. Creationism is an intellectual dead end. With respect to the human intellect, it is unnatural, a deus ex machina. This may have worked in Greek drama where a god was needed to resolve the plot and so one was lowered in a basket to the middle of the stage to do the job. It has no place in serious thinking.

It is imaginative and poetic to talk about God forming Adam from the dust of the earth and breathing life into him and there was the adult Adam fully formed and standing in the garden. Then while he slept God removed a rib from his side and formed Eve to be his helpmate. But recognize it for what it is. It is all so clinically sterile, so tidy, so polite and civilized. But it is another thing to include the details of evolution. These are messy, including perhaps false starts and extinctions. It all seems so tentative because of the long periods of time involved. It can seem so indecisive since the actual place or time of the arrival of the first man will never be known with certainty.

This is very much like the difference between a poetic account of the birth of a child which sings of hopes and loves, and the earthy reality of birth which is preceded by the act of sexual intercourse, months of morning sickness and discomfort leading up to hours of labor pains and the messy transit of the baby from the womb into the light of day. If religious faith is to exist in the real world, it cannot escape the physical realities of that world.

Notes

1. Tragically, the characteristic is passed on when two carriers procreate. It is frequently found in Pakistan where some 60% of marriages are between first cousins.

7

The Reaction to the Theory of Evolution

Seeing the big picture

Evolution is not a phenomenon of living things alone but of the physical universe as a whole as well as our planet Earth in particular. Look at what has been happening to our perception of that universe and that planet. Prior to the sixteenth century, we lived on a stationary Earth which was confined at the center of a sphere upon which were hung luminaries of the day and night and which had nothing in common with the stuff of our Earth. If you have visited a planetarium, you get the same sensation. When the lights are on as you enter, you are very much aware that you are in an hemispherical room of no grand scale. Yet when the lights are dimmed and you begin to see the projection of the night sky, you realize that it looks exactly like the real thing. It is not a three dimensional image any more than the real night sky is to our eyes. The lights in it are fixed with respect to each other and rotate around us in unison and at a fixed distance.

Galileo and his telescope change that view forever. The lights revealed a dynamism of their own and, with the development of technology, the heavens became for us a universe so large and extensive that distances had to be measured in terms of time. These luminaries were thousands and millions of light years away. The only way we can get our imagination around the distances involved is to compare them to the distance light would travel in a year moving 186,000 miles each second. Whenever we look to the heavens, what we see happening is never happening as we watch. It is always what happened in the past. It may have happened millions of years ago and its image took that long to reach us. This is the way we must measure the real world which people of faith believe is the result of a creative action of God. The understanding of size and sequence of events since that creative act is an important contribution to our image of God.

In the seventeenth and eighteenth centuries attention turned to the time scale of our Earth. Again, we started with a world created as a fixed and finished entity in the time of six days as described in the sacred text. But when the reality of strata and fossils was discovered and an interest in natural history grew, our concepts of space and time became more realistic as well as more interesting. In spite of the long time periods involved, what began to impress us was the dynamism of it all. Our earth was not a static place but had a dynamic history which was still unfolding. What is more, our earth is part of a continuum with the space-time dimensions of the universe.

This maturing of our vision of the universe made it possible for the great conclusion drawn in the nineteenth century that living organisms also evolve in time through the mechanism of natural selection and that there is no reason to think that humankind is not included in that process. No matter how many stages of evolution we want to identify, all life came from one source and humanity is physically part of that progression and not a separate creation. We can say that all life depends on DNA. Genetics shows the similarity and not the dissimilarity of living things. We are not spectators of natural history but participants in it. We are not standing on the sideline watching a grand parade go by. We are part of the parade, but a very unique part of it. For we are the ones who know it is happening. We are the ones who, in the words of Genesis, are naming all the animals. As Julian Huxley, the twentieth century evolutionary biologist, put it, humanity is evolution become conscious of itself. The conclusion from this natural revelation is that the new understanding of space and time includes humankind.

Is it theory or fact?

The objection is sometimes raised that evolution is only a theory. The emphasis here is on the word "only" as if that made it something far from fact and with very diminished certainty. When scientists investigate something, they are not like tourists walking through a new city seeing what they can see. They are usually looking for something specific. The exercise usually starts with an hypothesis. This takes the form of a proposition, a conjecture derived simply from reason or logic as a starting point for further investigation. The hypothesis is formulated as a possible explanation of what may be the reason for certain observations. It is the product of assumption, a what if, not evidence or proof. At this point it is much like an educated guess.

The formulated hypothesis gives direction to further investigation. Even when an hypothesis is disproved, that contributes to our understanding. The scientist asks what observations might prove or disprove the hypothesis and either result is equally important. Once enough evidence is accumulated indicating the truth of the hypothesis and no evidence makes it an impossibility, it becomes a theory. It becomes a tool for understanding an aspect of nature. When the theory is a very broad one, such as evolution which involves time periods of billions of years and diversity of billions of species, most of which no longer exist, and a mechanism which produces results we cannot easily predict, then there is always room for objections to certain details. This is why evolution is still classed as a theory and not a law. The theory may, however, involve many laws, for example, biochemistry and genetics. Today physical evidence overwhelmingly confirms the theory of evolution. As a theory, it means that there are still discoveries to be made.

One of the great values of a theory is that it suggests directions for investigation without necessarily expecting a definitive answer which leads to a new law of nature. When Einstein proposed his theory of relativity, it was formulated mathematically. Physicists around the world set about devising experiments to prove or disprove it. Today it is still called the theory of relativity but in reality it is more like a fact of engineering. There are situations in which, if you do not take into consideration relativistic motion, your device will not work. Fortunately for most of us, these devices are things like particle accelerators where speeds approach the speed of light and not the more leisurely speeds of automobiles. Classing evolution as a theory marks it out as a wealth of possibilities for further investigation and not an idea with tenuous science merit.

The theory of evolution is also predictive. Since life began in the sea, we can predict that there must have been animal species which marked the transition from sea creatures to land creatures. Since this transition should have taken place some 400 million years ago, what needed to be found was the location of geological strata from that period. Such strata were found in the Canadian arctic and a recent investigation found well preserved remains of just such a species which was give an Inuit name, Tiktaalik. Tiktaalik may not be a missing link, but it is certainly a transitional species.

The future of evolution, Teilhard de Chardin

We have been proposing that our outlook is often too narrow. If the evolution of living beings has been going on for 3.5 billion years, it would be folly to think that it has now stopped. We know that the physical universe as well as our planet and all living organisms are evolving as we observe them. So what is the future of human evolution? If we think evolution has come to an end, we are overlooking the process by which we got here. It is a curious thought but true that only in the last 500 years have we begun to appreciate the true size of the universe in which we live and the duration of time during which it has existed. Nothing written before the mid-sixteenth century benefited from that knowledge. It is now time to consider the future of human evolution.

One person stands out as a leading thinker on this subject, Pierre Teilhard de Chardin. A French philosopher and Jesuit priest, he became a well recognized palaeontologist who travelled extensively and was involved in much productive archaeological research, especially in China. He was an extremely creative thinker and this brought him into conflict with Catholic Church officials.

To the point at hand, one of his major works was *The Phenomenon of Man* which he finished writing in 1940. Because of a prohibition issued by the Church against its publication, it did not appear until 1958, three years after his death published by friends with whom he had left the manuscript. While the warnings issued by the Church concerning his writings are still in force, Teilhard's work is enjoying renewed interest today and with good reason. I will only treat here his visionary understanding of the process of evolution and what this has to say about the future evolution of mankind. This, however, is in no way the limit of his broad range of thinking.

Does human nature continue to evolve?

Humanity shares consciousness with the rest of the animal kingdom. What makes the difference in a human is the capacity of reflection. It is the ability of the mind to turn our thoughts back on ourselves. It is the ability to deal with ideas by abstraction from physical sensations and perceptions. Teilhard saw this power of reflection as a change in state in the human evolutionary line. But it was a change in state of far greater substance than water changing from the state of a solid to liquid or from a liquid to a gas. This change meant that humanity could rely on inventiveness rather than merely success by chance. The forces attracting or repelling us were not only physical but were the affective forces of sympathy and antipathy. Humans could look to the future for ultimate survival. This made humanity functionally superior to all other life forms.

The future is central to Teilhard's view because in humankind, evolution depends on things like hope and the perception of value and purpose. Without these, there is only the animal instinct to survive, reproduce and fulfill immediate short term needs.

Teilhard projects natural revelation into the future prospects of humanity. These are speculations, but so is all futurism. Yet these speculations are based on past evolutionary events which, prior to their fulfillment, could not have been predicted by any except the most informed and most imaginative. Teilhard was just such a person. It would be a pity if the Church which gave substance and guidance to his spiritual life ended up ignoring the insights which his firm grasp of science as well as his strong religious faith and obedience generated. Like Galileo, will it take 400 years for Teilhard's thought to be rehabilitated by the official Church?

Evolution has brought space and time alive. What is more, it has generated such an advanced level of consciousness in humanity that we can understand and contemplate the process which brought us into existence as well as be aware of ourselves as participants in the process. It is obvious that evolution was relentlessly working its way in the direction of reflection and we are the ones most eminently capable of it. Now that our current level of reflection has been achieved, evolution is able to continue into a higher level.

In each step of evolutionary development, the new functions or characteristics which resulted are nothing more than what the laws of nature are already capable of. All the properties of an organism can be preserved and passed on through the molecules of DNA. Cells can be directed to differentiate into muscles or nerves. These developments took long periods of time and many genetic mutations to coax them out of the pool of all physical possibilities. But once intelligence reached the level enjoyed by the human species, criticism, consultation with others and judgement were possible and this accelerated the pace at which desirable and successful innovations were produced in society. Even before the mechanism was understood, plant and animal breeding was carried out by our predecessors to encourage certain desirable characteristics. We are now beginning to eliminate diseases caused by genetic flaws.

Natural selection means that changes which bring about increased survivability are the ones preserved in subsequent generations. The next step in the evolutionary process in the conscious and reflecting human species is socialization. An example of the process of social evolution is the various forms of government which have been tried for the benefit of society. While we cannot determine with any accuracy what percentage of this characteristic is genetically based and how much is the result of logical reasoning, few would deny that both are involved and both are the result of an evolutionary process. We recognize this most when a desirable characteristic is absent in an individual such as in cases of autism, a tendency to violence or the absence of a motherly instinct in an individual. These characteristics are not simply matters of nurture but are recognized as physically based and even inheritable characteristics.

Social development within the various populations of the world is as much the result of evolution as the varieties of life species. And as is always the case in evolution, we find it trying out different possibilities but with a difference. Foresight means that we recognize in advance paths which will not be acceptable. Driving it all is an almost overpowering curiosity and the satisfaction that comes from discovering what we did not know. Humankind may not be at the center of the universe but we are much more We can understand the present and plan the future.

The last few centuries more than any other period of human existence have demonstrated that reflective life is full of energy and evolving at an accelerating rate. These few centuries, by comparison to all other zoological periods which lasted millions of years, are but an instant in evolutionary time. This offers a small bit of solace to those impatient for the arrival of a global period of human concern, civility and stewardship, a greater flourishing of charity and honesty, responsibility and gentleness.

Technology has generated an explosion of knowledge and ways to share it. The human spirit is having a difficult time keeping up with it. Perhaps this is an indication that religion itself has been hindered by its hesitation to embrace this new scientific environment. Religion must demonstrate how a sense of the spiritual and its value system can enrich this new, informed society. Yet only by relating these to our physical reality and our natural origin can the moral values and social responsibilities which religion champions become as stable, forceful and self-perpetuating as the characteristics dictated by our genes. This is the essence of the future of human evolution.

Turning points in human evolution

Teilhard de Chardin suggested some turning points in human evolution. The first change was in economics. Even into the seventeenth century society and the state were measured by the extent of their boundaries and produce of the land. Relentlessly, however, money became an impersonal and fluid basis of wealth and commerce which recognized no boundaries. In the West especially economic growth was a large contributor to its success.

Energy was the next turning point. Until the eighteenth century, we used only two sources of energy, fire and muscle. Science promoted engineering and that produced an industrial revolution which brought about not only great social changes but eventually oil, electricity and nuclear energy. It made possible means of transport which effectively changed the size of our planet.

Because Teilhard died in 1955, he never saw the most recent turning point, the computer. I refer not only to the advances in science and

90

commerce which the computer made possible by its ability to quickly and accurately process mountains of data. It is only because of computers that satellites were possible and the communication highways they made possible. They have brought us the internet and put a vast store of information at our disposal. It is not only a library on our personal desk that grows immeasurably each day. It also provides powerful search engines to find the information we need. The internet has made possible globalization of information as well as commerce.

All these things have changed the way we think, communicate, socialize and do business with one another on a global scale. Biological evolution resulted in a brain of sufficient size and complexity to allow us to discover and understand the universe in which we live. Through technological evolution the computer has evolved into a device of sufficient capacity and complexity that its network of communication lines, not neurons, allows each of us to search and gain access almost instantaneously to the vast bulk of this knowledge in our intellectual universe. Our capacity to reflect on these things means that we can set priorities and place value on them. When we do these things, we are out of the realm of science and in the realm of the human spirit.

Transportation, globalization and the internet have created a new human environment as radically different as when 3.5 billion years ago, oxygen-producing bacteria changed the Earth's atmosphere and made life on dry land possible. The bacteria took almost a billion years to accomplish their magic. The internet has made its mark in less than a century. The lesson of the evolutionary past is this - adapt or become extinct. Yet there are forces today which want to suck the new oxygen out of our atmosphere and pretend that adaptation is not necessary and can be dangerous. This is why twenty-first century Western societies should be concerned about the intention of extreme fundamentalists to remake whole societies based on their interpretation of ancient religious laws.

Islamic fundamentalists wish to impose Sharia law which is based on seventh century revelations and their derivations. These laws attempt to govern every aspect of life from politics to banking, social issues to business law, and for every individual in that society, but always based on a point of view of millennia twice removed from our own and with little reference to how human knowledge and society has changed in the interim. Perhaps worse, it does this without any central clearinghouse to attempt a baseline of belief and practice. Or they may be Christian fundamentalists who believe that we can learn nothing from the way the natural law functions without first passing it thorough the filter of the literal interpretation of the 4000 year old revealed texts. While no one would say that adaptation is easy, still it is the only way to open new possibilities which will not exist without it.

The new environment has not changed our bodies except those changes brought about by better nourishment as well as the burden of new opportunities for excess. Science contributed much to the cultural and economic growth of Western society. Christianity also made its contribution to this growth by encouraging individual responsibility. The period of Enlightenment promoted a fertile liberalism which encouraged new ideas. We are new creatures, far more aware than any generation before us, of the relentless evolution which is sweeping us along and of the possibilities this offers us.

Science discovers new remedies for disease. Travel and communications makes us aware of where these remedies are most needed and globalization makes it possible to supply those in need. Populations in poverty or suffering from injustice are no longer distant and hidden. They have faces we can watch in our living rooms. Is not the evolution of this awareness one which can serve the intentions of the creating God who made us stewards of our physical as well as social environment? Our individual world extends far beyond our house, family, field and country. Why should anyone not feel comfortable with this perspective of evolution? This is the kind of design one would expect from a truly intelligent creator. This design becomes more surprising and inspiring, and turns our naturally selfish urges, our survival instincts, on thteir head. It pushes us outward as participants in an evolution which is not purely biological, but no less procreative.

Creationism awakes

In reaction to the eventual general acceptance among scientists of Darwin's theory, the term creationism began to be used in reference to those who opposed Darwinism. But the term eventually became the subject to ridicule. A law in Tennessee forbade the teaching of the theory of evolution in public schools. In 1925 John T. Scopes, a high school teacher in Dayton, was convicted and fined $100 in what became known as the Scopes monkey trials. The verdict was later reversed on technical grounds by the state supreme court. The fact that the law remained on the books until 1967 gives testimony to how strong feelings and convictions about Genesis can be.

The term was rehabilitated by being changed to Scientific Creationism by Henry Morris in a book by that name published in 1974.

Morris was a "Young Earth" creationist which meant that he followed James Usher's seventeenth century determination that the Earth was 6000 years old. Perhaps unconsciously creationists find it easier to believe that God created the first human 6000 years ago rather than accept that we appeared 150,000 years ago and yet God waited until some 4000 ago to begin revealing himself in written revelation. In 1970 Morris founded an organization called The Institute for Creation Research as part of Christian Heritage College in California. The purpose of the institute was to defend Christianity from the Godless dogma of evolutionary humanism. In 1972 it became an independent organization.

It may be because Morris was also a hydraulic engineer that the flood story became central to his evidence of a young Earth. All the archeological evidence of great age such as numerous layers of strata and the formation of the Grand Canyon which exposed the strata had to be explainable by rapid events rather than long periods of geological time. It was explained that the sedimentary rock accumulated rapidly during the catastrophic, global flood, perhaps taking no longer than a year. Today you can go to the institute web site and read the answers to such pressing scientific questions as: was the Genesis day twenty-four hours long (yes), how did Noah cope with all those animals in the ark (part of the answer is due to hibernation)? You can also obtain a masters degree from the institute in such studies online.

The great advances which science has made during the last century seemed to conspire against the fundamentalist view of creation and especially the nature of the human species. More and more creationists found the scientific explanation very compelling. One solution would be to find some way to base their beliefs on a scientific foundation. They could tolerate relinquishing the details of the six days of creation but astronomy and geology relegated the details in Genesis to the status of a parable instead of history. Creationists were determined to salvage in some way a special creation of humanity. Biological evolution became the place to draw the line. Those preparing for battle were mostly North American Christian fundamentalists.

The invention of Intelligent Design

In 1991 a much more formidable organization entered the fray, the Discovery Institute. It is funded by millions of dollars from conservative Christian donors. Its mission is very broad but one aspect which has been central is the issue of evolution. It became such a central part of their effort that they established a separate Center for the Renewal of Science and

Culture to deal with evolution. One thing which has characterized all their efforts is their sophisticated sensitivity to public relations and the use of the media. Although they agree with most of the ideas of Scientific Creationism, they do not use the term and will disavow any real understanding of it. Instead they use the term Intelligent Design (ID).

The term was probably first used by the British Philosopher Ferdinand Schiller in his 1903 book, *Humanism*. In it he said, "It will not be possible to rule out the supposition that the process of evolution may be guided by an intelligent design." The title fit the need to escape the term creationism. In the hands of the Discovery Institute, ID is the idea that Darwin cannot explain all the aspects of the living world and this suggests a design in nature by an intelligent agent. They are clever enough not to name the agent but surround the idea with as much scientific terminology and reasoning as possible. They actively participate in legal moves to require that ID be included in the biology curriculum of public schools by framing the idea as a scientific alternative to evolution. They attempt to drive a wedge into the idea of evolution with pseudo-scientific arguments in order to foster religious conservatism.

Most educators have seen through this ploy and resisted the effort. At best, ID can have a place in a history, religion or philosophy class but has no place in a science classroom. If living organisms are physical, then the physical sciences must deal with them using physical laws and experimental methods. If theists think that there is more, they must prove their point but not by faulting scientists for refusing to delve into the supernatural. A hallmark of science is that it deals with things which can be observed and predicted. ID is trying to introduce an undefined source of an unpredictable influence on natural things. Whatever that attempt is, it is not science.

The scientist has a very practical mindset. Even if an idea is not what you would like or expect, if a thing works, you use it. An idea can be tested by the constant accumulation of evidence, which is the case with evolution. An idea is dropped the moment it can be falsified which has not happened with evolution. By its very nature, ID cannot be either tested or falsified. In order to reach a conclusion, science proposes hypotheses which can be tested. How does one test the hypothesis proposed by ID? At best, it might be considered a method of detecting the presence of design by some intelligent cause. The problem then is deciding at what point another separate design is executed: with each cell, each organ, each organism, the first of the type? And how can you decide and where is the evidence? The beauty of the theory of evolution is not that it completely answers all questions. It is a model that fits very well the information we have. Best of all, it gives scientists reason to refine our understanding by seeking more data. ID is a scientific and intellectual dead end.

The millions of dollars spent by the Discovery Institute funding scholars to find ways to discredit the theory of evolution would be better spent funding creative minds who could locate human evolution in the spirituality of faith. This would be a far more productive and beneficial course to pursue. It also avoids the pitfall of becoming year after year increasingly out of step with scientific advances.

When ID enters the public legal and political forum, it becomes a free for all. Critics maintain that if ID is taught in classrooms of the United States, it violates the First Amendment by promoting religion. But its proponents counter that ID is science, not religion. Promoters of ID maintain that it is their right of free speech that permits them to teach it in the classroom. Opponents counter that free speech does not mean that you can say anything you want wherever you want. And on and on it goes. When we clear away the smoke, we can see that this whole situation is caused by a fundamentalist approach to religion and divine revelation. We must not lose that insight. What drives the fundamentalist to seek scientific evidence of their religious beliefs is perversely a fundamental lack of faith. For this reason, it is fruitless to deal with individual arguments proposed by ID devotees. Instead, we need to address this issue of faith. This can be done using their own theological assumptions.

It is a problem of faith

In its simplest form, supernatural faith means having the disposition to accept what God has revealed because it is God who revealed it. This assumes that God has, in fact, revealed things to us and that we can freely accept them, or not, as having been given to us by him. This also assumes that we have at least some reasonable although perhaps not provable grounds for our assent. These grounds come in the form of experience and not logical proofs. Even if a person is not raised in a religious family, the cumulative experience of life may dispose the individual to query what others of faith call divine revelation and can lead to acceptance of its divine origin. Strong experiences in life can do the same. For those who were raised in a faith atmosphere the constant experiences in life can make them feel more secure in the practice of their religion and this is a response to faith. Of course, others may well have experiences which have the opposite effect such as the death of a child or being confronted by extremely evil events which cause them to seriously question their faith, their disposition to believe.

By definition, faith is a mystery, something which cannot be fully understood. This does not mean that we cannot understand anything about it. That would imply that we cannot even talk about it since we would have nothing to say. The mystery here is how God freely reveals these things to us and then how we are free to accept these or not. This is why Christian theology teaches that faith, this disposition to believe, is a gift freely given by God. Some use the term grace to describe such a gift. The idea that it is a gift comes from the *New Testament.* "For by grace you have been saved through faith, and this is not your own doing; it is the gift of God, not the result of works so that no one may boast." (Eph 2:8)

We also assume that the divine motive behind the gift is so that we can establish a personal relationship with God. The whole of the Scriptures is a testament to the relationship between the human person and God who is a person. This is not a relationship as the chemical relationship between sodium and chlorine which combine to form table salt. The interaction of these two chemical elements always happen under certain defined conditions. The relationship we are talking about requires a relationship between two persons. A person is a being who can freely act of its own accord. And if God wants to establish a relationship with us, God must be a person. You can appreciate that the deeper we go in this journey of reason, the farther removed our theology becomes from physical or psychological science. It also means that science has nothing to do with faith nor can it directly contribute anything to it. The theory of evolution can neither confirm nor discredit faith any more than the theory of relativity can.

So why does faith look for some physical necessity of God's activity when it comes to the body of a human being? We are not discussing the soul here. Intelligence is not necessarily evidence of a soul. Most people have about 100 billion nerve cells in their brain. The roundworm is able to carry on its life activities with only 302 neurons. Our intelligence, inventiveness and curiosity is brain-based and not soul-based. This is why it can be the product of physical evolution and presents no problem to faith or theology.

Yet the soul is central to religion. How can an intervention of an Intelligent Designer, which we cannot prove or disprove, help understand our non-physical, supernatural nature? Our attention should be on the nature of the God we believe created us, not on how he is required to intervene in physical things we do not scientifically understand. To repeat the words of George Santayana, science is thinking God's thoughts after him. What natural science reveals to us about God is how he thinks, what his physical priorities are or the true magnitude of what he created. Notice how we are referring to him as a person. Faith and its companion, theology, seeks to discover what God thinks, his motives and the relationship between himself and his creation.

There will never be physical evidence of the moment a soul comes into being and so we do not bother trying to find it. We will never find physical evidence that it was necessary for God to specifically interrupt the physical evolution of material things on the Earth in order to bring fully evolved humanity into existence. To insist that this did happen is to invoke what has been called god of the gaps. When primitive humanity could not explain the weather, the motions in the heavens or the reason for victory or defeat in battle, they presumed that a god had been involved, in other words, giving ignorance another name. The accusation of a god of the gaps is often used to discredit believers by those who find religion unnecessary.

The God I believe in is not the god of the gaps but rather the God of the things I understand. The person of faith is willing to accept that all the physical things we understand well had a cause and a designer. What is not very well understood is at which point the divine creative act was required. The fact that the physical reality of something is understood does not remove the need for an ultimate designer or creator. Yet it seems that when some people today lack enough faith to trust God's ability to create a nature with the potential of accomplishing on its own all the things we see around us, they seek the support of physical signs wherever they can find them.

Evaluating Intelligent Design

In essence, the Intelligent Design theory describes not a physical reality but the lack of natural continuity, an interruption in the physical evolution of things on Earth because the designer intervenes. As a result, it is the lack of a physical sign that gives them assurance that God must have acted independently of all the rest of physical evolution. This is a risky choice. For most people, the reasonableness of the theory of evolution is enough. The long time durations of evolution mean that it is wholly unreasonable to expect to find any physical evidence of the moment or location where any key step along the way happened. Throughout history natural science has continuously replaced a god of the gap with clear physical explanations. In fact, it is constantly giving explanations for the latest ID arguments regarding things being too complex to have been the result of evolution.

In ID, the focus of attention is on hypothetical events in the history of our world through which certain complex organisms were designed, including the special creation of the human species. No intelligent person can deny the role of natural selection in the development of the great variety of species on Earth. Yet it works by producing and then eliminating huge numbers of bad results. What kind of design is that? ID contributes little or nothing to our understanding either of ourselves or God that we don't already know from basic observations.

Everyone agrees that living organisms are complex but what can ID add to that insight? No element of ID is provable nor able to be demonstrated physically. So what purpose does it serve? At best, if we are honest, it simply fills a need to bolster a weak faith. At worst, it distracts us from the difficult task of trying to better understand the implications of a personal God and our relationship with that God. Perhaps unconsciously there is the fear that if we discover too many physical, biological causes for the faculties of human nature we might not need God at all. Again, this is the result of intellectual insecurity and we should see it for what it is.

For someone insecure about religious beliefs, the necessity of an intelligent designer is a way to strengthen the idea of a personal God. Yet, as we shall see in chapter 9, the concept of God is able to stand on its own. There is no need to use questionable demonstrations that physical nature requires such an intrusive God to explain the things we observe. The idea of a personal God is as difficult to comprehend as the realities we find in the physical world? What fascinates the physicist are the mysteries that confront them and which drive them to new levels of inquiry. Among these is the quantum behavior of all atomic objects, electrons, neutrons etc., and even light which can act like a particle at one moment and a wave in the next depending on how you try to observe it. Or there is the event which started the whole universe which we descriptively call the Big Bang. From it all matter naturally evolved into a universe of billions of galaxies and each containing billions of stars. Around one of those stars, a planet formed on which evolved uncountable living species of great complexity. Finally one of those species developed the ability to observe and understand this whole process. Yet this insight is not something out of divine revelation nor science fiction but science fact.

By attempting to use science to show the necessity of an intelligent designer, fundamentalists convince only themselves. Their arguments are flimsy at best and scientifically unprovable and unnecessary. For example, the ID argument that some things such as the flagella of bacteria are too complex to have evolved naturally is trivial and irrelevant. Can there be anything more complex than the process by which a single fertilized egg cell in the womb of an animal, humans include, keeps on dividing billions of times while differentiating into every various cell type of the body from nerves of the brain to muscles and bones as well as all the internal organs with all their interconnections? Yet this is accomplished naturally and automatically in all animals including us with no intervention from an intelligent manipulator. Creationism needs not only an intelligent designer but an intelligent manipulator acting here and now. Biology shows this to be unnecessary.

One could also point out that after birth, this process of growth must eventually be stopped. There is an optimal size for every organ in the body. Geneticists are just now discovering what it may be that shuts off the genes which cause growth by continuous cell division. After all, when cells suddenly restart uncontrolled division we call it cancer.

So what does ID buy its proponents? The fundamentalist requires signs even outside the Scriptures showing that God is personally interested in us. By saying that our nature requires that God made us in a special act implies just such a personal God but in an obtuse way. The effect of this on the scientists is counterproductive. They do not see a special creation as necessary and so for scientists this interfering God serves to discredit the notion of a personal God.

The specific intervention of an intelligent designer in evolution is required only if we must accept biblical creationism. Supporters of ID don't like to use the word creationism but they certainly start out with it as a basic premise. Otherwise why defend an idea which is contradicted by science when it is not necessary or essential to the concept of a personal God? If a personal God does exist, then that God could have created nature with the potential to produce humanity through evolution just as easily as by special act outside evolution.

Not to see this possibility is to miss the point about the true nature of creation and reduce God to the role of a watchmaker who must design, fabricate and assemble every part of every watch. When he has finished this one, he must set about making the next one. Evolution, on the other hand, tells of a watchmaker who has devised a method of mass production to make the process more efficient – the laws of organic chemistry which allow the replication and complexity of giant molecules. This divine watchmaker also devised a method whereby whole watches were able to duplicate themselves – reproduction. Finally, these watches were also able to produce new, more useful, beautiful and long lasting models on their own – natural selection. Now that is a clever and powerful watchmaker! This is a greater designer than we could ever imagine or desire. To those with faith, this is what happened and we need nothing but good science to reveal it to us. This is a valuable natural revelation.

Faith, reason and science

The more fully science understands the physical universe, the more we are forced to reconcile our notion of God with the universe we believe God's design made possible. It is a difficult but necessary task. At its most difficult, evolution will not shake our faith in God. Rather, it will expose the incomplete status and shortcomings of our understanding of God and that is a good thing. At its best, it can indicate the directions our theology needs to go in order to understand more clearly the point at which physical knowledge ends and faith begins. It is a task we will never make progress in if we are determined to hold world views formulated in the Old Testament period of history. Precisely because we now understand our world better than they did 4000 years ago, God can now expect different things from us than he did from Old Testament society.

There are scientists who declare that the human is simply the result of chance physical events in a universe which has no purpose. This conclusion, however, is not a scientific conclusion but a philosophical one about science. Scientists who think this way are just as much fundamentalists about science as religious fundamentalists are about the *Bible*. They are reading literally the book of nature. They think that only those things which can be expressed mathematically can express truth. For the scientist, the nature and workings of the natural laws are exciting and richly rewarding in themselves. To a believer, along with the wonders of the natural world, the existence of a personal God is a truly exciting vision of the universe.

The problem here is Scriptural fundamentalism, the literal interpretation of the words of the *Bible* because they are the word of God. But what is being overlooked is the involvement of the human author of those words. If God decides to use human writers to communicate to us things he wants to reveal about himself or us, then he is going to be limited to the experience and verbal ability of the inspired person doing the writing. How could a human being write intelligently about things he knows nothing about and does not have the vocabulary to express? What he would be writing would be gibberish. This is why Genesis 1 is not a true representation of the creation of the universe. It served the purpose at the time it was written and still does now, so long as we are not looking for science. That was not possible at the time it was written. Scriptural Fundamentalism will ultimately repel those who find the understanding of the physical universe exciting.

People of faith do not believe a revealed truth through the light of reason. They believe revealed truth because of the authority of God who revealed it and God gives them the disposition to do that. The obvious problem here is "it", the revealed truth. It is reasonable to assume that the "it" does not refer to things we can well determine ourselves through scientific investigation using the abilities our evolution ultimately gave us as human beings. This principle eliminates many issues of biblical interpretation, for example the factual history contained, or not, in Genesis 1. But that still leaves an imposing number of very tricky questions which go to the heart of religious faith, the arrival of human individuals with non-physical souls for example in Genesis 2-3. Genesis, of course, does not speak in terms of souls but from what we infer from later revelations, we can. Stated this way, we are assuming that there is a moment when an individual acquires the characteristics we attribute to a soul. There may well be a number of scenarios which lead to immortal human individuality which can also accommodate the natural process of evolution and result in the existence of an immortal person.

This does not imply that faith abandons reason. Faith is a God-gifted willingness to accept the reality of something in the absence of physical or historic evidence because of the presence of a clear statement of its reality in the revealed text. Since textual clarity is a subjective judgment, there is not a universal agreement on what that reality is. It is evident that the problem is not whether God can reveal something but whether in fact he did clearly state a particular thing to be so. The problem is not with the principle of revelation but in the details. If, as fundamentalists do, you presume as revealed anything the words of the *Bible* literally imply, then the details will bury you in all kinds of contradictions and logical dilemmas. Oddly enough, the advice given as an escape from these contradictions is simply to have faith in God who will not deceive us. That is fair enough. But if that is the answer, then one does not need science to confirm anything so why involve science at any point as ID attempts to do?

Reason can aid faith. We should expect that the God who recognizes us as reasoning beings couches his revelations in evidence which makes the revealed truth reasonable. People of faith find these indications in such things as miracles, both biblical and those recognized as happening in our own time. They are seen in the messages of the prophets, people in biblical times who are regarded as speaking for God. Most especially, revelations are seen as coming from the hand of God as a result of the way God has intervened in the history of Old Testament people and ultimately guided us to these conclusions.

This begs the question, how does the reality of the physical evolution of humanity affect the evidence of the hand of God in directing human history? For a person who assents to the gift of faith, it should have no effect. After all, the evolution leading to humanity preceded human history. The revelations contained in the *Old Testament* are to be found in the constant direction given to Israel through the events of their history and the words of the prophets, none of which concern the specific physical human origin, not even, as we have seen, in the first three chapters of Genesis.

Evolution encounters faith at the point of immortality and so we should deal with it at that level. Without immortality, we are dealing with an Aristotelian soul operating a biological entity and at the dissolution of that biological structure, there is nothing that the principal of life can operate through. What forces us to say that Homo sapiens must be the result of a special creative act and not natural evolution? God could still be concerned about and thus influence our lives without having created us in a special act counter to the evolution of all other life on our planet. The creationist/ID mentality tries to be very scientific about everything except when humanity encounters God. This approach is not necessarily driven by a literal interpretation of sacred Scripture. It can also arises from the need to feel close to God and a groping for security.

This fundamentalist phenomenon, this reaction to a globalized society is occurring in Islam as well as Hinduism and orthodox Judaism. In Islam, of course, it has become politicized by extremists and sadly mixed with the ultimate expression of faith, that of becoming a martyr, distorting the whole idea of martyrdom and using the term for what is essentially mass murder of innocent people in a suicide bombing. The cause is insecurity, fragility, uncertainty and the conviction that they are being victimized. The failures of science and modernism can give the impression that we are caught in a global system too large to control and alien to the dignity of the individual. Modernity has made it possible for the greedy, the dishonest and the embezzler to work on a global scale. All we have to do is have a connection to the internet and we soon become target of those who would steal our identity and the money in our bank accounts or sell us a bogus product.

The Great Recession and economic failure on a global scale will only increase the tendency to retreat into this contradictory mindset in which the solution is a personal God heavily involved in our daily lives. The contradiction is that if God is so close and involved to make us feel secure, why do so many fall victim of natural and human initiated calamities, even when we pray to be spared? What we have is a complex confusion of ideas. Communications and travel have made us a global society. Our groceries have moved from the corner shop and local farms to the multinational megastore. Our economy is backed by financial instruments which are global in scope. Home mortgages are ultimately owned by foreign banks and nations. All have become too large to fully measure their intrinsic value or regulate. Little wonder then that there is a tendency to retreat into the protective embrace of a personal God who includes us in his care and is willing to control the circumstances, surroundings and outcomes of everything we do. The disposition of faith makes proofs of this divine involvement unnecessary.

But the question still remains, has this situation arisen, at least in part, because of the inability of pastoral theology to keep up with scientific discovery? Has the tenacious grasp of perceived tradition prevented Christianity from taking on modern scientific understandings of anthropology? Is there a way for Christianity to discover the contribution it can make to that anthropology with its rich concept of the spiritual nature of humanity, a pastoral anthropology if you will?

Dealing with opposition to evolution

So how are we to deal with the creationists or those who insist on the interference of an intelligent designer as opposed to the natural evolution of living things? Perhaps the best advice is that we can't. We are dealing with people whose religious faith is heavily invested in a literal interpretation of the words of the *Bible* and a whole industry has been established to support them in that notion. Part of that industry now tries to wrap the fundamentalist idea in the language of science which serves to counteract any lack of faith caused by the scientific culture in which they live. It is rather rich to accuse science of not being able to adequately support the theory of evolution with evidence when, in fact, there is no scientific evidence, nor can there ever be, for their notion of Intelligent Design. In a culture which respects individual conscience and religious pluralism, we can only wish them well. But what we must not do is concede any ground in their attempt to burden the science classroom with this non-scientific distraction.

Much the same advice can be given concerning religious fundamentalism of any form. Fundamentalism is not a monolith. It takes on all manner of degree and kind. In chapter 9 we shall introduce a contemporary form of religious fundamentalism which has nothing to do with the Scriptures. Fundamentalism can be very dangerous. It often trivializes God by making him seem obsessed with arbitrary requirements, contradictory statements and what can come across as inhuman cruelty and vengefulness. It can make us blind to natural revelation. But we must not let fundamentalism obscure the human evolution which has brought us to our present state. Fundamentalists today approach the question of evolution as if it were a minefield which must be approached with great fear and care or, better still, should be avoided altogether. The fact is that evolution is what makes sense of our presence on Earth.

While we can see gross examples of the misuse of our physical and social environment, never before have so many people had the power to do so much good for so many, all of which was brought about by science and technology. Yet never before has there been a system of thought like religious fundamentalism which has the potential to do so much intellectual violence to both science and religion at the same time, not to mention the social violence we have witnessed in recent times. So long as we can keep advocates of intelligent design from interfering with our education systems, then they only impose limitations on themselves. The real danger arises when fundamentalist thinking spills over into the political arena and imposes extreme ends to be accomplished and extreme means to bring them about. In the hands of extremists, this is what produces suicide bombers and intolerant states which bring to a halt any hope of social evolution for the good of humanity. It is for this reason that we should constantly assert ourselves against fundamentalist interpretation of divine revelation while at the same time be sensitive to the sense of the sacred which is deeply imbedded in most cultures.

The human is the only species that is capable of causing its own extinction. With the evolution of the human level of understanding, reflection and choice came the ability to direct or even end that evolution. If we were to end it, it would only be the end of our species, not every living species on Earth and not the created universe. Nature would continue relentlessly and, in a few billion years, most likely arrive at a similar evolutionary point, if not on our planet, since our Sun will have died by that time, then in some solar system somewhere else in our universe. The creator God could continue to be recognized by conscious, rational beings as he is by us, that is if there is not such a species already in existence somewhere else in the universe. This view of evolution has much to teach us about ourselves and the involvement of a creative God. This is the genuine longterm thinking of theology. There is not just the eternity of the immortal human soul but the physical durability (for eternity?) of nature and the laws which govern it.

Theologians should be as enthusiastic and determined about increasing our understanding of God as the scientists are to increase our understanding of the natural universe. All should recognize that they are both digging deeply into what are at present mysteries to us. Attempting to do this while tenaciously holding a death grip on every traditional notion of God will prevent any progress into a greater understanding of God. Where would we be today if scientists refused to let go of the view of the universe which was traditionally held from the time of Aristotle until the sixteenth century? And do we understand the nature of this personal God very well? Very probably not. But Christian theologians have been able to discover much using the revealed texts and the words and actions of Jesus Christ in the *New Testament*. If approached correctly, the recent advances of science should be able to contribute to a better understanding of the Creator God. Clearly, not only is God a mystery to us, but the things he created hold mysteries for us as well. Modern science has only begun to expose these mysteries.

8

Modern Science

Advances in science have been made by those who were capable of creative thinking and could feel the excitement of imaginative discovery. Fortunately, most scientific discoveries have not been accompanied by the somewhat credible account of the joy experienced by Archimedes, the Greek mathematician and engineer, around 200 BCE. When he watched the water being displaced as he lowered himself into the public bath, he suddenly saw the solution to the problem of determining the purity of the gold in an object. His excitement was so great that he ran through the town naked shouting "Eureka", I found it. But there is excitement in discovery, in suddenly understanding something better by making an association between things previously thought to be unrelated. The results can be thought of as a revelation.

If twentieth century science has done anything, it has certainly clarified the inseparable bond between the physical human nature and the characteristics of being human. Some theologians might be uncomfortable with this but the relationship cannot be denied. The discomfort is caused by the feeling that we are headed toward a physical explanation for everything that the human is capable of doing or experiencing. Some fear this would make God and religion unnecessary. The laws of the chemical nature of matter which were forged in the Big Bang make possible the organic molecules of living organisms. The full potential of these molecules when formed into genes had not been appreciated until this century.

The discomfort is influenced by an incomplete understanding of the limits of both science and theology. The instruments of science can be extremely impressive. The Large Hadron Collider in Switzerland is 17 miles in circumference. It is poised to discover what the stuff of the Big Bang was like. Orbiting telescopes and planetary landers are investigating the solar system and roving the surface of the planets taking photos and samples. Impressive computer power is being concentrated on the determination of the human genome and identifying which genes influence what part of human nature. Magnetic Resonance Imaging (MRI) scanners can show which parts of the brain are being activated by thought processes such as decision making. I suspect that the elephant in the theologian's parlor is instrument envy.

But there is another viewpoint. All the work done by these wonders of science and engineering is public knowledge. One of the strongest principles of science is peer review and should not some of these peers be theologians? The best scientific thinking of the day can be a revelation not only to scientists but theologians as well. These instruments may well give us great insight into the nature of things but they cannot tell us anything about their value or purpose. Such things are a value judgement of the human observer. Science may be able to show the physical implications of the strength of gravity but it cannot tell us anything about human relationships even though it is that gravitational strength which makes us physically possible in the first place. There is plenty of room for the theologian in the intellectual landscape.

My intention in this chapter is not to indulge in what can be called gee-whiz science. This type of science is thought to justify religious journals in stating that they have no problem with science and are willing to report on it. This is the type of science reporting after which one is moved to say, "Wow, isn't God great!" The type of science they find hard to deal with is that which might require us to rethink some longstanding religious opinion or theory or rephrase a theological formulation. We should make no mistake, most religious dogma is theory, philosophically logical but not demonstrable to the exclusion of any subsequent reformulation. It is this kind of challenging science which stands to offer the theologian natural revelation which was not possible to know in the past. We here consider two general fields of science: physics and biology.

The scientific method

Before any of the sciences can be appreciated, the methods they use must be understood. Scientists have devised a progressive pattern of logic and experimentation which has proved successful. It would be useful to consider this method in general and then look at how this might be accommodated by theology.

The first step is to identify or define as clearly as possible the question or subject we want to understand. At this stage there are usually more questions than answers and may involve a certain amount of observation and measurement. The next step is to form an hypothesis or theoretical explanation for what we have observed but derived from the incomplete data at hand. This is not a hunch which is based on intuition but rather suggested by sketchy data. This serves to focus the question more clearly and eliminate side issues. The hypothesis must then be tested by predicting what should happen according to our hypothesis under well defined circumstances.

This is the meaning of an experiment and should give us new data regarding the question. The experiment should also be of such a nature that others can repeat it to confirm that they get the same results. Finally, the data is analyzed and either confirms our hypothesis or suggests fine tuning the original theory and a new experiment is run. One counter example, however, refutes the whole hypothesis. Still, even when the theory is proven wrong, we have learned something and advanced understanding. Knowing what something is not can be nearly as important as knowing what it is. When a final conclusion is reached, the structure of the experiment and all the data must be offered for peer review.

Let us apply this method to a question which has direct theological implications. A scientist can be convinced that there is more to being a human being than those things which can be explained by the purely physical human characteristics. They must still ask the question; how has our species come to be what it is? As a scientist, this means that only physical data can be used without any recourse to ancient writings or traditions. As part of the effort to clarify the question in the first step of the scientific method, it is recognized that recent developments in instrumentation have shown that some human functions previously thought to be non-physical, involving decision making, emotions and the ability to relate to others for example, can be shown to have a physical basis and so are not excluded from scientific consideration.

It is reasonable to hypothesize at this point that humans share the same origin as all other members of the animal kingdom. To test this hypothesis we need to investigate how many physical characteristics humanity shares with the rest of the animals and ask if this level of similarity is convincing. Upon analyzing the data, we discover that the similarities are overpowering. Every aspect, from metabolism, circulation and neurology to genetic composition and method of reproduction display an essential likeness. We can only conclude that our hypothesis is correct. For the sake of this example as a process, it is not necessary to go into detail and justify our data.

But this conclusion exposes a basic question; what explains the great difference between us and the rest of the animal kingdom? This means that our original hypothesis did not address the origin of all the uniquely human characteristics. This requires that we form another hypothesis and investigate further. Our process demands another iteration. The new hypothesis could be that increased brain size explains any human characteristics not found in other animal species. Current data convinces us that this is the case and has even identified the protein which controls brain size. We touched on this in chapter 6. We are thus free to conclude that the most likely cause of the physical human species is the same natural processes which produced the rest of the animal kingdom. Since we do not know what discoveries will be made in the future and we know that we were not able to investigate thoroughly every aspect of human physiology, it does not eliminate the possibility that we did not uncover an existing contrary example that would negate our hypothesis. This is why I used the words "most likely" in the conclusion. This is a satisfactory conclusion for the scientist since the understanding seems likely but is always open to new discoveries.

But here the theologian raises a question. What about our ability to make value judgements concerning our art, music, creativity, individuality, appetite for improving the social environment of our species and making provisions for future generations, our sense of purpose and almost universal conviction that there is more to human life than what our physical senses can detect and that we can experience in a physical lifetime? There are at least two possible responses: either there is a physical basis for these capabilities as well but we just have not discovered them yet, or there might be a non-physical basis for them in which case the physical scientist cannot deal with that. This is the point at which the theologians can begin their work. But they must not lose sight of where this point is. To hypothesize that the human species had a different beginning which was not based on physical evolution as was the rest of the animal kingdom means the abandonment of the natural and logical explanation which science was able to work out and demonstrate quite convincingly in the previous hypothesis. There must be overpowering evidence that evolution was not the cause before the scientists, even the ones who accept that humanity is different from the rest of the animal kingdom, will ever take any other explanation seriously. We will develop this in more detail in chapter 12.

One final point must be added concerning the scientific method. In spite of the fact that science has the clearest and most demonstrable proofs, the good scientists knows that what they are looking for are the best possible understandings of partial truths. In other words, behind most proofs are a set of assumptions. The scientist constantly questions assumptions. If we think we have arrived, then we stop searching and thus we discover nothing and do not advance understanding. Science is always a work in progress. Should not this be the approach of theology as well?

Physics

The changes in theological thinking which we mapped in chapters 3 and 4 were brought about in the earliest days of physics. Although experimental science was only in its formative years, the theological implications were momentous. The earth was displaced from the center of creation and, for most people, the way we read the first chapter of the book of Genesis was altered forever. Isn't that enough of an accomplishment to ask of physics? Modern physics is not going to prove the existence of a Divine Creator but for those already disposed toward such belief, the concept of Creator is carried to a new dimension by modern physics. That should not enrage the scientist but the believer who has little scientific background may be a bit envious of science which advances with ever increasing pace and seems to leave theology in its wake. Science should motivate the spiritual writer to investigate the possibilities which such understanding can open even for the ordinary believers if they are properly guided.

One of the characteristics of physics in the last hundred years or so has been its ability to draw together what seemed to be unrelated topics into a few root concepts. Newton's laws of motion seemed to be just one topic in a grand physical set which included heat, sound, light, gravity, electricity and magnetism. But then it was discovered that both heat and sound can be explained by the motion of atoms and agree with Newton's laws. Toward the end of the nineteenth century James Maxwell proposed that light was electromagnetic radiation which unified three phenomena. This left only gravity standing by itself where it still stands today.

This reduction process is a satisfying one. It leads to clarity of thought and efficiency in experimentation by providing different angles from which to approach a subject. It reminds us of Ockham's razor which dictates that one must not multiply entities beyond necessity.[1] Physics has easily taken Ockham's principle to heart and in recent times even speculated on a single Theory of Everything. When a theory becomes extremely complex and the equations which express it big and cumbersome, then it is looked upon with suspicion. One wonders if theology could benefit from such clear focus on root concepts. One might suggest that among them would be the Trinity, i.e. the nature of God, the Incarnation as the evidence of the nature of the human soul and grace as the reason for human existence.

Two concepts have dominated and inspired the age of modern physics. They are relativity and quantum. These are usually referred to as theories yet many things in physics cannot be explained if these two

110

concepts are ignored. Relativity is a fact of engineering and not some mysterious hunch which has not and probably will not ever be proven. Both topics started out as theories and because quantum, for example, suggests such strangeness in physical nature, it is difficult to understand and some aspects are still not understood and much debated.[2] What can be of great value to the theologian is the approach taken by physicists when confronted by strange or mysterious ideas and phenomena which stretch credibility as well as our ability to understand them. The parallels in theology can be striking.

Relativity and strange time

Say the word relativity and everyone immediately thinks of the name Einstein. In fact Galileo was the first to explain relativity. He did it as part of his argument that the sun and not the Earth was at the center of our solar system. The argument was raised against him that we should feel the wind and motion if we are traveling so fast as to orbit the sun once a year. His defense was that all motion is relative to some fixed reference point. If everything around us on this Earth is moving along with us as well, we cannot detect that we are moving. I will leave the convincing logic of this argument for you to work out but you might imagine riding in an airplane. How can you tell you are moving while cruising at 30,000 feet?

We call it Einstein's theory of relativity today because he was the one who took the idea to new heights and found some amazing implications. Best of all, he did it using a brilliant experiment completely in his mind. He was only 16 when he did it in an attempt to prove that ether did not exist.[3] The accepted theory of the day was that there was a substance called ether which was at rest and occupying every place in space and that light travelled at 300 million meters per second (mps) through the ether. This young lad proposed the situation in which he was traveling at the speed of light and holding a mirror in front of himself. If the theory of ether were true then the light would never make it to the mirror because he and the mirror were moving at the speed of light. Thus, he would not be able to see himself in the mirror. In using such a train of logic, Einstein was doing what is called a thought experiment, the kind of experimentation which is open to theologians.

While he was not able to confirm this by physically doing the experiment, he knew that something was wrong because the conclusion contradicted Galileo's idea of relative motion. When traveling at a constant rate, we cannot detect that we are moving – the airplane again. But if he could not see his reflection, he would know he was moving. He decided that his experiment was wrong because it only worked if ether existed so he concluded that it did not exist. This eventually led Einstein to ask, if the speed of light was 300 million mps, what was that speed relative to? Against what do you measure it? The answer he concluded was that, no matter what our situation or how we are moving, we always discover that the speed of light is that same constant value. In other words, light always travels 300 million mps relative to the one observing it.

As if this were not strange enough, things were to become even stranger. One of the conclusions of his special theory of relativity was that, relative to someone at rest, for a moving object, the faster it moves, the slower time runs. This is not just mental gymnastics. The equations which Einstein derived to explain it are used to make very mundane things work properly. If the mathematics used to determine your position on Earth using the orbiting Global Positioning System satellites were not relativistic equations, you would not be in the right place. In ordinary circumstances, we do not notice this effect because the speeds must be extremely fast to make the slowing measurable. The whole situation inspired someone to pen the following limerick. I suspect that the anonymous author must have been a physicist because it has the correct insight and the humor of a good scientist enjoying the strangeness of nature.

Relativity
There was a young lady named Bright,
Who traveled much faster than light,
    She started one day
    In a relative way,
And returned on the previous night.[4]

No matter how far you decide to pursue the subject of relativity for yourself, it is a fascinating and curious journey with many more surprises than just the property of time. What relativity had done was save physics from the limitations of classical Newtonian physics which ran into problems when speeds were high, especially when approaching the speed of light. Relativity also revealed a new approach to what became called the space-time continuum. We will not investigate here this view of physical reality. In effect, relativity said that absolute space and time do not exist and that space-time was curved and not linear.

In the very early 1900s, it was determined that the atom was composed of electrons in orbit around a nucleus. The mass and charge of the electron were determined in 1909 by R. A. Millikan. An attempt to use the Newtonian laws of orbital motion to explain the motion of the electron proved a complete failure and relativity was only a slight improvement. Descartes developed the relationship of algebra to geometry which allowed us to visualize not just equations but the way things behaved in the physical world. The algebraic Newtonian laws of physics told us how these physical things moved and where they were at any time. Everything seemed so tidy, determined and fixed. It was all very comforting. Einstein's relativity introduced an element of weirdness concerning time and gravity but at least its mathematical expressions were understandable and experimental demonstrations made it all real. But then along came quantum physics and the strangeness began to challenge our concept of reality.

Quantum and strange behavior

A word of caution is needed before we proceed into this section. In the next few paragraphs, we will be dealing with the topic of quantum physics. Please do not skip this section as irrelevant or beyond understanding. I will make no attempt to explain quantum physics to you. That would require that I understood it and I don't. What I will attempt to do here is tell you of some of the conclusions and implications which the best practitioners of quantum physics have arrived at. Once we have seen this, we can then ask if any similar situations exist in theology.

In 1900 Max Plank postulated his quantum hypothesis which proposed that the energy levels of a physical system could only exist in discrete quantities and not in every value in between. This was followed shortly by Einstein's proposal that light existed in individual quanta or particles which were later called photons. There followed in the 1920s a series of disputes and discoveries involving great minds and interesting characters.[5] Quantum mechanics became a staple of physics when dealing with the atom and its particles where Newtonian laws do not work. We will briefly pursue just one application of quantum mechanics.

Absolute truth is to be found in mathematics. It begs the question, is it a physical truth or an ideal one? You know quite well what a perfect sphere is but could you ever fabricate one in the physical world? Every physical example would only be an approximation. The concept of a sphere, however, is a very simple one excluding all complications. Its geometric surface is all the points in three dimensional space equidistant from a fixed point called the center and remember, points have no dimensions. That statement is a mathematical model of a sphere. It sidesteps the question about what a surface is in the real world.

If we could fabricate a perfect glass spherical lens, we know that its surface is not a continuous entity. It is composed of individual atoms spaced a finite distance apart. The atoms themselves are not solid but mostly empty space. In fact, if the nucleus of a hydrogen atom, the simplest of all atoms, were the size of a tennis ball, the radius of orbit for the single electron orbiting that nucleus would be close to a quarter of a mile away from the nucleus. The space inside that radius up to the nucleus would be empty. Further more, electrons orbit a nucleus in what turns out to be a cloud of probability rather than a nice planetary system. So how can we describe the way light behaves when focused by a lens or why some of the light that hits the surface reflects off and does not continue through to the image formed by the lens?

It might be tempting to say that we don't need to know. We see what it does and can write a mathematical equation to determine the point of focus and make lenses so what more do we need? Let's preserve some of the mystery in science. But scientists never stop asking questions. When the surface of the glass is looked at as an array of atoms, quantum electrodynamics is the most adequate way to explain the observed tendency that some of the light is reflected back. Further investigation of this characteristic of light yields a way to eliminate that surface reflection which makes the image brighter.

It may be that we do not understand why quantum electrodynamics is a reality any more than we understand why mathematical truths are a reality but we use what works. Pure science eventually generates technology and a brighter image is a desirable thing. A mathematical representation of what happens in surface reflection was devised in the mid twentieth century by Richard Feynman and colleagues. It was eventually called the Feynman diagram and involves, by his own description, little arrows and a hypothetical stopwatch. Feynman once said, "I feel more dignified when I say we are "computing the probability amplitude of an event."

Physics explains how the natural world behaves. Although the electron does not obey Newtonian laws in its behavior at the atomic level, quantum electrodynamics does give a fundamental picture that is usable and, while being extremely peculiar, it is satisfying as well. But do not ask the embarrassing question, what is an electron or why does the explanation work? One of my university physics lecturers asked this question and answered it in this way. "Some say an electron is a tiny blue sphere." The point is that, even if that is the only answer you can give, you can still work with the concept of an electron and understand a lot about how it behaves and what it can do for you. When that answer was given in the physics lecture, there were smiles all around the hall as well as a recognition of the valid point being made. There are a lot of blue sphere answers floating around in theology but we sometimes get the impression that theologians are not so able to smile at their blue sphere theories.

An even harder question to address in physics is *why* things act the way they do. I do not mean such interesting questions as why does the earth orbit the sun? The existence of gravity as a central force of attraction and Newton's laws explain that adequately. But to ask why two masses attract each other with what we call a gravitational force is a real show stopper. In theology "why" questions often end up attempting to interpret the reason God had in mind when he made things that way and that can be dangerous. Perhaps that is why there are so many anthropomorphisms in religion. Forcing God to act as a human might act can be as unhelpful as suggesting that a particular photon decides to reflect off the front surface of a lens instead of passing through to the image. Spiritual writers seem willing to tread such thin ice while scientists usually make every effort to avoid such tricky confrontations. The issue in question is not one of bravery but honesty.

A quantum explanation of the atom is a far cry from the traditional four elements - earth, air, fire and water - and all floating around in an invisible soup called ether. Historically, the first chemical element to be identified was oxygen in 1774 by Joseph Priestly. Ether was not discredited until the imaginative experiment devised by Albert Michelson and Edward Morley in 1887. Elements were thought of as solid spheres until J. J. Thomson proposed in 1897 that atoms contained particles which were later called electrons. Today the nucleus of the atom is known to be composed of hundreds of subatomic particles. It has been because of imaginative questioning by scientists that we have arrived at such a profound understanding of the world of the atom.

One wonders what might result if Christianity pooled its resources and created the equivalent of a hypothetical particle accelerator and invited good minds from around the world to become creative and imaginative about theology while maintaining good humor. In the Catholic Church specifically, it would also require that there be no insistence that all ideas must first be submitted to the Vatican for judgement. This requirement is frequently mentioned in papal encyclicals in phrases such as, "provided that all are prepared to submit to the judgment of the Church." (*Humani Generis*, §36) After all, peer pressure would be enough to police the process and that has served science quite well.

There is one final observation concerning ether that can contribute to the relationship between science and religion. The idea of the existence of ether came from the proposal in the nineteenth century that light existed as a wave. If this were so, then something had to be waving. A wave is a self-propagating disturbance in some medium so what was that medium? When instruments were devised to produce a vacuum, it was discovered that light and magnetic effects did pass through it. As a result it was assumed that there was something there and since its properties seemed rather ethereal, it was called ether. It did give answers to certain questions which made it somewhat convenient but, in the end, it was found to be something needed to answer questions which were not well understood. Further understanding eliminated the need for it.

A similar situation presents itself in the theological matter of determining why there is evil in the world. If God created humankind, it must be good so if evil exists, it must be the fault of the human and not God. At creation the state of humanity must have been ordered and free from pain or suffering. A loving God would not have it otherwise. If we find those evils now infecting human nature, it was certainly not God who caused them. According to Genesis, there had to be a fall from that original state of justice, original sin. This is the logic needed to accommodate the account we find in Genesis 2-3 composed some 2000 years before the birth of Christ. But does this also run the risk of being a colossal anthropomorphism?

Today, our understanding of human nature is enough to convince us that such a fall is not necessary to explain what we call evil. We can explain why there is pain and suffering not just in humans but all living things. We can go a good way in explaining the conflicts in human relationships. We can also explain why we could not expect to find those explanations in Genesis. Could it be that original sin is theology's ether? We will pursue this further in chapter 12.

By far the strangest aspect of quantum is that remark of Feynman about the probability amplitude of an event. The conclusion can be drawn about an electron that it is simply a probability wave in an abstract space. It takes up a precise position as a particle only when one attempts to measure its position. The mathematical probability wave expression is a valid description of the electron but the problem is how to interpret the description. In other words, can it be that the mathematical description is information out of which a thing is made and when we interpret it, measure it, we give it meaning in the real world? This implies that our consciousness influences or gives rise to certain physical realities. With the presence of conscious human involvement, physical reality becomes more than fixed, measurable and mathematically describable entities. It becomes a range of possibilities involving things like value and purpose.

The 1920s were an exciting time in science. There was a great dispute raging among certain leaders in the understanding of what quantum meant. At the heart of the debate was the interpretation of the way electrons jumped from one orbit to another without seemingly passing through every state in between, they were called quantum leaps. Erwin Schrödinger espoused a wave solution which came close to working but did leave some things in question, especially the particle evidence revealed in some experiments. The confusion was that if the electron behaved like a wave, it would have a measurable energy. But waves propagate out in some fuzzy pattern rather than proceed in the way a bullet does. In certain experiments, light certainly had bullet-like characteristics. Neither an acceptable mathematical explanation nor visualization could be reached.

In the 1927 Solvay Conference Werner Heisenberg presented his solution to the wave/particle duality of an electron. He proposed that the more certain you were about the energy or wave property of an entity, the less certain you could be about its location and vice versa. It became known as the Heisenberg uncertainty principle. Quantum theory says that every particle is described and determined by a probability wave function. If we try to measure the position or movement, this causes the probability to collapse into the value which defines the measurement. This raises the question about how objective and fixed the natural laws can be. This seems to imply that there is more to nature than what physical instrumentation, our eyes included, can detect.

The parallels in theology are striking. For example, conscience is an individual's measure of the rightness or wrongness of an act. The measurement is made from the perceived description of real possibilities. Just as the fields and forces described by the quantum mathematical expressions do not have a fixed correspondence with a physical reality, so too there is no fixed correspondence between the moral ideal and the complex experiences, judgements, understandings and influences acting on the individual which are the observational tools used to make the moral judgement. Conscience is the result of an experimental observation as surely as is the physical measurement of the energy level of an electron. The moral decision collapses into the particular judgement of conscience and not necessarily the objective ideal. Both examples are influenced by the observer and result in a reality, in one case physical and the other moral.

Let me dare to apply the Heisenberg uncertainty principle to another theological question. It might help us understand our difficulty when thinking about a human soul. Perhaps we should begin by picking away at some details about a soul which baffle us. Let's start with the question of location, where is the soul? Is my immortal soul contained within my skin, in all that is contiguous me? Of course if I lose a finger or cut my hair, I do not lose any of my soul. Or perhaps my soul is confined to my brain. After all the soul's operations in this life seem dependent upon it, at least as far as consciousness is concerned.

What then will happen to my soul when I die and the body disintegrates, loses its integrity, is no longer contained in anything? Theology teaches that after death the soul continues to exist and be me, the individual. Furthermore, if my soul continues after death, did it necessarily start when my body started to form or are there other possibilities since it does not depend on the body for existence? We have amassed a long list of uncertainties and perhaps the quantum experience can be of assistance. It may be for us a logical way for spiritual reality to interface with physical reality. It may offer a way to understand the spiritual universe in terms similar to those we use to understand the physical universe. That would be rather nice but first we need to look at the preconceived notions we bring to the idea of a soul.

The question of souls

What is a soul and the process by which the human person can be identified as ensouled? This also means that we are asking, when does a biological entity become a human being, a person with all the rights thereof? While the answers to these questions will never be completely satisfying, they impact directly such moral issues as stem cell research, artificial insemination and abortion, none of which can be approached casually. We will consider these issues in chapter 10 as moral questions. The fact and nature of the soul also impacts the concept of human spirituality as well.

Nothing about our nature stretches our ability to conceptualize an entity so much as the concept of the human soul. It has undergone many variations since Aristotle proposed the soul as the principle of all life. While there have been those who saw dual components in being human, physical body and spiritual soul, the theological conclusion of many today is that there is only one principle of life animating the entire human person, the human soul. In spite of this, it is difficult not to lapse into some degree of dualism when trying to come to terms with the idea. It is also a complex entity which involves the mind, consciousness, personhood, free will and life after physical death or immortality.

It is little wonder that while we use the term constantly, most of us devote little time trying to figure out want the soul is. This seems strange since we are the ones who are conscious of it, possess it and have the mind to investigate it using introspection. Yet we understand so little about it, especially how it interfaces with our physical nature. But it is precisely our physical component that science is discovering so much about. It is time for some fresh thinking on the part of theologians with the aid of these new understandings of the human body, especially the functions of the brain. Make no mistake, we are dealing here with the greatest mystery of our existence. We can at least clear our concepts of primitive simplicities and learn to respect rather than feel threatened by scientific discoveries. Doing this will also win theology respect and credibility from scientists.

Without going into the interesting history of the concept, the commonly accepted understanding was a dualistic nature in humans, a close union of body and soul, matter and mind, physical and spiritual entities. But recent neuroscience finds it difficult to separate the brain from consciousness of self, association of ideas, personality, making decisions or even assigning values. Traditionally, the body is the result of natural, physical causes and the individual soul must be the result of the creative and unique act of God. Extreme dualism would demand that mind and matter are completely different things. This dualistic view was championed by René Descartes in the seventeenth century.

Today, with a fuller understanding of the evolutionary origin of human nature, Cartesian dualism has fallen out of favour. The contemporary view is that there is a stronger oneness to an individual human identity. Perhaps our long-held view, that suddenly there was Adam and Eve, has prejudiced us toward an instantaneous creation of a soul which is somehow fused with a body. On the other hand, could what we call ensoulment be a process which is a part of a biological continuum rather than an event or instantaneous divine act, yet with a no less "spiritual" result? We have no hope of clarifying the question unless we keep abreast of the most recent scientific discoveries and conclusions. If our thinking is to have any credibility in the scientific community, we must be seen as participating in the intellectual enterprise of both science and theology, drawing on natural as well as Scriptural revelation.

Even in the dualistic view of humankind, there is no problem with physical evolution. According to this view, physical reproduction cannot produce a non-physical soul. As a result the person of faith must say that biology is not directly involved in the immortal nature of a human being, except as a body which in this life is the sensory input/output device used by the soul. Why, then, should not the physical, biologically functioning nature of Homo sapiens have evolved in the same way as the rest of living organisms? How does this idea tread upon the sanctity and uniqueness of humanity? God, it seems, must act to create each individual human soul and no amount of archeology is going to dig up evidence of that.

Considering evolution to be a problem may be a case of wanting to hang on to the Genesis inspired ideas of the origin of humanity. In the Galileo affair we saw how hanging on to preconceived notions can get us into trouble. To address these questions we must begin by taking a broad or holistic view of the notion of evolution. The greatest complication comes from the traditional idea that the first humans, Adam and Eve, were not subject to biological death until they sinned. But we will consider this in chapter 12.

To be consistent about the evolutionary nature of creation, it can be distracting to talk about ensoulment. It can sound like adding a computer to an automobile rather than a continuation of the single sweep of evolution. With a computer, suddenly our car can monitor itself - or become self-aware - and tell us what needs attention. It can guide us step by step to our intended destination using GPS and, in its most recent embodiment, park itself. It becomes truly anthropomorphic. We human beings are far more complex and sophisticated than an automobile computer so we can decide to go out and take a walk while, hopefully, the car cannot. The seemingly non-physical characteristics of humankind can be the assertion of potentials which have been for all time inherent in the material universe and awaiting the development of organisms complex enough to allow them to function.

The traditional soul

There is a less philosophical and more theological way to view the human soul. In principle, we believe that the human soul is made in the image and likeness of God. So perhaps our image of God is the best place to start if ultimately we are supposed to see a reflection of God in ourselves. The child's image of God, as often explained by adults, is the old man with a grey beard and a big black book assigning or deducting points based on how we behave. The adult creationist's image of God is the magical chemist whipping up worlds and species. The image of God for many evolutionists is a person who initiated the creation of material stuff which had such magnificent capacities that it can on its own produce everything we see around us, inert as well a living. The question becomes, to what extent and how often is this Creator, who is outside everything that was created, willing to intervene not only in the history of the human society but also in the individual life of each person?

In all of these images, God is still an external being. On the other hand, Christian theology traditionally explains the divine character of the human soul with the concept of grace, the way we become identified with the nature of God in some limited way. These traditional images of God can make the concept of grace like something that can be poured into or drained out of the human soul. Traditional theology also claims that the individual human soul, from its beginning, needs to be cleansed of the stain of original sin and receive first grace. Can we not admit that we should be able to do better than that? The only way to improve our concept is to become more imaginative, more adventuresome and willing to go down different paths of logic and reason always recognizing that we may reach a point at which we have to admit that we are wrong and need to readjust our thinking and submit to peer review, not to the primitive concepts of the past.

Concerning the location of a soul, Aristotle thought it was in the pituitary gland, or is it the heart - as in "have a heart" - or the brain because of consciousness and rationality? But this question is like asking "Where `am I?" All the organs of the human body support the individual that is human. We think of it in terms of location because we can detect that locality as within the skin of the individual, the person. Persons are the manipulators of their organs. The smile of a human being and all that it can communicate is identifiable with a particular person. Personhood is the agglomeration of all that is identified with a particular body. It is very much like the culture of a city or country composed of a large population of individual persons.

Asking when a soul exists can be like asking when a culture exists. If we had a vast land area completely uninhabited by human beings and could somehow draw a quota of individuals from every country in the world and suddenly in one week populate that area, that pristine emptiness of persons, could we say at the end of the week that it had a culture? Certainly it had none before the beginning of the week and how long would it be before we could say that it is developing its own culture? Surely we would all agree that there would result an identifiable culture over a period of time but would any of us speculate how long that would be?

From another point of view, when we look at the periodic table of

121

elements and shelves of pure chemical substances, we do not then start thinking of whales, horses, chimpanzees or the household pet dog with whom we find it so satisfying to relate. The distinction between pure chemical elements and living substances is molecular and organic complexity, not some kind of physical dualism. But the complexity of living organisms also produced Homo sapiens and here our primitive concept of God tends to lock our imagination into traditional terminology.

Traditionally, God seems external, outside the world he created, a magical chemist who not only produced all the jars of elements on his laboratory shelves but then, in the eyes of the creationist, he whipped up billions of species of plants, animals and finally humankind. He scattered them about this marvelous planet Earth which spins in a habitat we call the universe. These are, of course the only terms possible for the primitive imagination. They easily appeal to the imagination of the child today. The frequent complaint of those trying to explain religious beliefs to adults is that it becomes difficult to overcome the imagery accumulated in childhood. We deserve a better image of our universe and understanding the implications of complexity may be helpful.

A new possibility

For Teilhard, complexity is the key to producing a new entity greater than the sum of its constituent parts. Aggregates of particles lock together in a stable organization we call an atom. Atomic elements react with each other to form molecules. These systems of atoms have many properties which are not found in the individual atoms from which they are formed. The metal sodium which reacts violently with water and the poisonous gas chlorine combine to form table salt. Who would have foreseen that? Molecules can align into extremely complex systems and form a living cell whose characteristics are controlled by its DNA molecules. Cells differentiate into organs to perform single required functions in living systems of organs which take on the character of individuality.

Finally in a system of systems, the brain reaches a complexity that can sustain multi-tasking leading to imagination, creativity and self-consciousness, empathy and even love. This self-awareness makes possible decisions, choices and thus personality, a "me." These latter capabilities and implications of complexity lose all identification with the material lower levels of complexity. As Teilhard explained it, at the bottom level of complexity, it is chance which is instrumental while at the top it is freedom.

Perhaps there is a need for a Heisenberg uncertainty principle in describing souls as well as subatomic particles. It is not an absurd thought. Remember, when we define a unit of physical matter as a cloud of probability, that does not imply that it is any less real than if it were a well located, Newtonian particle. Nor does being uncertain about a soul imply that it were better to say that there is no such thing. It is not the reality that is uncertain but only our perception of it. We have as much trouble trying to visualize a soul as we do an atomic particle. What is more, our argument from complexity does not mean that everything is purely physical. Rather, complexity brings into play other realities which do not rule out what we usually think of as spiritual. This applies to organisms, societies and persons.

Would it be disrespectful to think of a soul as being present as a cloud of probability rather than in some point or region in space defined by our skin? The space the soul occupies will dissolve at death, dissipated into random and chaotic scattering. Could we not say that just as God arranged physical matter as a cloud of probability so too, in the interest of consistency, God he has done the same with the "spiritual" soul? All physical matter began, or should we say evolved, from one first creative act or Big Bang. Souls need not have begun that way but rather resulted from an evolving complexity. Scriptural revelation has no opinion in the matter.

Modern physics has led to what many see as a de-materialisation of matter. Quantum theory sharpens this focus away from mechanistic materialism. In our history, there have been many metaphors for understanding the universe. Genesis saw it as the result of a God organizing and separating the elements of light, earth and water and making living organisms. The Greeks described the universe in terms of musical harmonies and geometry. At the beginning of experimental science in the seventeenth century, the universe appeared to be a clockwork, deterministic system governed by the Newtonian laws of nature. Today, quantum physics describes a universe of probabilities which can depend on the observer. While the quantum approach is just getting started, it may well prove the most adequate way to describe human conscious awareness and our ability to communicate our understandings—or at lease until new theory is developed which gives us greater insight.

I do not suggest that theologians and spiritual writers must start using quantum speak. What I am suggesting is that, with a feel for how quantum concepts describe the physical world, theologians can be more secure in their convictions concerning our non-physical nature and more guarded in the way they describe spiritual realities. Philosophically, this new thinking is directing some academics to reassess the way we see God as present to the physical universe. These new views can be far richer than the concept of God as a designer standing outside the universe and working his magic. Quantum considerations allow us to identify the universe as, in the words of Henry Stapp, "a world of potentialities for future experiences".[6] This is in opposition to the Newtonian, deterministic world of material substances alone. One way to look at the human soul is as the personal identity making decisions about its relationship with God, the personhood with which all human souls as well as all physical reality are identified, and doing this as a self-determining, psychophysical entity.[7]

Immortality, a natural thing

One final characteristic of the human soul needs mentioning, immortality. In spite of the fact that Scholastic philosophers champion the idea that, since all creation is made from nothing and therefore it requires that the Creator continue to keep it in existence or else it goes back to nothing, the material constituents of atoms are immortal. The stability of DNA and its ability to replicate so accurately gives organic life on Earth a form of immortality so long as the Earth provides the proper environment. In other words, nature is immortal and so is the full identity of an individual human soul since it has evolved from nature, but once real, has no existential dependence on physical nature.

My overriding impression is that I am in my body, both controlling it and being controlled by it, yet as a conscious and thinking person I also transcend that body. My dependence on my body at present is the way I express my personhood to the world around me. But my existence as "me" no longer depends on my body enduring any more than I as a person would be diminished by the loss of an arm or leg, thus becoming a diminished person. With the total decomposition of my body, there remains the person who made use of my physicality to relate to others and to God in a very personal, creative and imaginative way.

At this point, our focus must turn to the nature of God as a Trinity of persons and how human persons are identified with God, in other words, through what Aquinas called grace. The concept of grace can take on new depth as a basis and foundation for the nature of the human soul. Such a consideration is beyond the scope of this book but it does identify it as one of the fields which opens up to the theologian who pursues this natural revelation of quantum. It would be an exciting adventure to walk that path.

Biology

We must not underestimate the importance of our biology. It is the home of my individuality. It is the physical instrument you and I use to work out the complicated task of human relationships. If we underestimate its potential, we handicap ourselves. If we overestimate its potential, we are destined to failure and disappointment. We will have expended energy and time with nothing to show for it but frustration.

The science of biology had its origin in the mid-seventeenth century. While for the next half century the progress may seem to have been slow, there was a great distance to travel and hardly more than the dissector's knife and Leeuwenhoek's primitive microscope to take us there. The existence of human egg and sperm were unknown and the theories of the ancient Greeks were still in vogue. The lower animals such as insects were "known" to be generated spontaneously.

The clever Leeuwenhoek had devised a method for observing liquids, a technique which he did not divulge to the Royal Society, and discovered in a single drop of water huge numbers of animals too small to be seen with the naked eye. The royal Society was in disbelief until the equally clever Hooke hit upon Leeuwenhoek's method of using a very thin glass tube to contain the water and he too observed this proliferation of microscopic living organisms which they called animalcules.

Using this method for observing liquids, in 1677 Leeuwenhoek observed human sperm and discovered living animals with tails in great numbers. In spite of this, a human egg would not be observed until 1827 and it was not until the 1840s that it was recognized that all parts of living organisms, egg, sperm, skin or leaves, were made up of cells. Louis Pasteur would demonstrate conclusively in the 1860s that even micro-organisms are not generated spontaneously. The first observation of the fusion of egg and sperm was not observed until the 1870s. The rest, as they say, is history. Mendel's genetic inheritance discovery in pea plants was rediscovered in 1900. The double-helix structure of DNA was discovered in the 1950s. Louise Brown, the first test-tube baby was born in 1978 and Dolly the sheep was cloned in 1996. Today we are challenged by genetically modified food and stem cell research.

With this last discovery, biology has bumped up against the difficult question of souls and it has not been a happy encounter. So what is the theologian to do? We can converse with someone only if we speak the same language. This means understanding the current state of biology. But language also has context and that means being aware of how biology arrived at its current position. This makes it possible to be sympathetic with the way someone thinks and the position they hold on a particular subject.

It would be hoped that the theologian might also recognize some parallels of this growth of biological science in the evolution of theological thinking. We might wonder why some scientists held the theory of spontaneous generation until such recent times. Are there theologians who might be accused of the same tenacious grip on ancient ideas? Yet should we not look forward to the satisfaction of a better understanding? This can be even more satisfying than not needing to change our mind about something. This approach leaves open the possibility of discoveries in theology and greater credibility in the eyes of the scientist as well as the general public.

Sex, genes and destiny

Sexual reproduction is key to the origin and survival of the human species. We have seen that natural selection, random mutation and time are the mechanisms of evolution. Sexual reproduction means that half of the genes in the new individual come from each parent. This means a constant exchange and shuffling of the genetic makeup of individuals and ensures that they are unique in themselves while perpetuating the general characteristics of the species, race and family group. This is an advantageous arrangement. Over time, detrimental genes can be eliminated through attrition and genetic quality does not deteriorate with the constant duplication of detrimental genes. It also means that diseases cannot affect a whole population at one time since there is bound to be genetic resistance in some individuals because of their genetic uniqueness. The only exception to this is the case of identical twins. It is by the study of such twins that we can get indications of what in an individual comes from genetics or nature and what from nurture.

The full genetic code of an individual is called the genome. While 99.9% of the human genome is shared with every other member of the species, that 0.1% leaves much room for individual variation. It contains some 3 million DNA elements which are the molecules containing the genetic instructions for the formation and operation of the living being. The influence of some are trivial such as eye color. Others can influence the susceptibility to disease or the inclination toward certain behavior. This is why we humans are such a mixed and interesting lot.

Sex gives each person a biological individuality. What is left is the social response of the individual and the moral evolution of society. This adds up to human responsibility and that is where religion comes into its own. We must decide in what direction we should go and determine what things we can control or change to travel that way. Without a well founded understanding of genetics and its implications as well as other components of our biology, making those determinations can be a risky business. We could have expectations which are not likely to be fulfilled and overlook possibilities we could pursue with every hope of success. We will treat this further in chapter 10.

People in different historical environments can benefit in different ways from the same human faculty. Take for example sexual attraction or the physical pleasure derived from engaging in sexual activity. In primitive times, when there was little understanding of diseases or how to avoid or cure them, early biological mortality was the big threat to the human population. The strength of physical attraction ensured that the species would reproduce enough to sustain it and even allow it to flourish.

In modern times, physical survival is not the major concern. For most societies, medicines and plentiful food supplies have moved physical disease well down the threat scale. Education and the economic stability necessary to maintain the desired living standard has moved up the threat scale. At first sight, there seems little connection between this new threat and sexuality but it is the physical and emotional satisfaction of human sexuality which can make family stability and emotional survival in modern living a reality. Sexuality is not just a matter of population numbers but one of emotional and social survival as well as personal identity. It requires addressing the human person in its fullness and we will consider these things in chapters 10 and 11. In the current state of humanity, we need to consider which of these aspects of human sexuality can best serve the purpose and plan of the Creator in the twenty-first century.

An intriguing question can be raised concerning the possibility that there might evolve within the human species, new ethnic genetic types. There is nothing to say that this could not happen but its probability is very small and getting smaller with the passage of time. This is because global travel and changing social attitudes are making it very unlikely that any ethnic group could remain isolated and not be subject to genetic and social mixing. This mixing of races, while thought of as an evil in the past, now appears to be beneficial. Different ethnic groups can have genes which have beneficial genetic characteristics that are lacking in other groups. By sharing these in offspring, the overall genetic makeup can be improved. It gives natural selection a broader base to work from as it preserves useful changes.

One final question concerns the difference between the sexes. There is a good understanding today of the role of the X and Y genes and the influence of what is called the sex-determining region Y (SRY), a gene on the Y chromosome. Curiously, for the first seven weeks of development, the human embryo is destined to be female. Only if this SRY gene then switches on, will normal male development begin. The result of the process is not only physiological but, along with culture and learning, is also responsible for behavioral differences and the characteristics which tend to be associated with the gender of the individual.

Aggression and risk-taking are usually stronger in the male. The ability to empathize, that is, identifying the emotions and feelings of another, on average is stronger in females. Thus it can be said that men and women are biologically different not just in their reproductive system but in their thought and behavioral processes as well. One must observe that the species is richer for that difference and all because of one gene on the Y chromosome. It also makes us wonder why any institution would want to limit its leadership to only men or refuse to include women in every aspect of its operations? This is clearly an unnatural decision?

It was scientists who, with encouragement from politicians, looked for and found arguments to support ideas like eugenics based on the total control which our genetic makeup was supposed to have over our behavior. This, of course, was at the expense of human rights and basic liberty. Genes exert a subtle influence but do not completely determine human health and behavior. Many diseases and mental disorders are inherited but they are usually the obvious ones and while they may be inconvenient for society to deal with, they are not the basis which would justify denial of human rights. This is a case where clearer science can correct social injustice even without making a value judgement. DNA studies have shown that we all have a close relationship to each other. Furthermore, it has demonstrated that we have a common origin in Africa.

Theologians often use the poetic formula which says the natural law, meaning the moral law, is that which is written in the heart of us all. We might also say prosaically that the natural law is to a certain extent written in our genes. This observation could explain why that law does not seem to be written as boldly in every individual. This raises the possibility that what is written in the heart of one individual is not quite the same as that written in the heart of another. This is very unlike the physical natural laws. We do not find gravity or electric forces differing from one electron to another, in spite of quantum strangeness.

Discoveries in biology should not be seen as a threat to theology but

128

as opening new opportunities to understand the human person better. Just as science in the past thought that everything physical was composed from the elements earth, air, fire and water, so the theological anthropology looked at humanity as a composite of body and soul and the soul explained all those things about us that did not seem to be physical in nature. MRI scanners have now allowed us to see the areas of the brain which are activated when we perform many of those things formerly thought to be the preserve of the soul. The genes which influence or control many human characteristics have been identified. To ignore such discoveries and neglect to rethink past assumptions lacks intellectual integrity and this does theology a disservice, especially in the eyes of the scientific community. Both scientists and theologian find themselves searching for truths which they can feel but cannot express.

Conclusions

Science in the last century has made astounding progress. Most of it has had theological implications to one degree or another. In other words, there is available new natural revelation about human nature and the created world around us, almost too much to keep up with it. If scientists are expected to respect and listen to the theologian, the complement must be returned.

Our theology is like a Newtonian model of physical reality, God and humanity in a fixed, determined, defined and predictable relationship. But human life is more creative and complex than that. Might we have a role to play in some of the definitions dealing with human nature? How much consideration does our theology give to human probabilities?

One wonders why some scientists scoff at the notion of anything non-physical and non-measurable when they are faced with the weirdness of the quantum world. It is rather rich when a scientist derides the notion of God as giving ignorance another name or being a delusion when physics has developed a mathematical expression for the uncertainty of physical measurement. In Heisenberg's terms, perhaps the more we try to measure the concept of God in physical units, the less we can know about God as a spiritual or supernatural being. This too can be a delusion. How can consciousness simply be a manifestation of the physical operation of the brain when it appears to have a role in determining the quantum state of a physical reality?

One also wonders why some theologians scoff at the idea of natural science making any contribution to theological considerations. In essence, theology is anthropology which includes God. What kind of anthropology would you end up with if your data included only those things about humankind or God which were discovered up to the mid 1500's? You would be including all the traditional time-honored concepts but your data would be impoverished and embarrassingly so. It would be lacking all the knowledge derived in the most prolific period of human discovery. By including this latest body of knowledge, theology would show respect for the work of those who brought us to where we are and be able to participate in the interpretation of discoveries yet to be made. There does seem to be room in the peer review process for theologians to comment on scientific conclusions and for scientists to comment on theological conclusions.

Notes

1. William of Ockham was a fourteenth century English theologian and logician who developed this principle.

2. Richard Feynman won the Nobel Prize in Physics in 1965 for his work in quantum electrodynamics. He warned an audience during a lecture that they would not understand it. He then added, "You see, my physics students don't understand it either. That is because *I* don't understand it. Nobody does." My purpose here is not to explain either of these physics topics to you, assuming that I understood them. They do make fascinating reading, especially in the many books by Feynman on the subject of physics and other issues.

3. He did not know that Michelson and Morley had already relegated ether to the dustbin of physics nine years earlier.

4. Oscar Williams (1952) *A little Treasury of Modern Poetry*, Charles Scribner's Sons.

5. One such dispute became known as the Copenhagen Interpretation. It occurred between Niels Bohr and Werner Heisenberg in 1941 at the Institute for Theoretical Physics in Copenhagen. It became the subject of a Tony Award winning play, *Copenhagen,* by Michael Frayn and was successfully staged in London and New York.

6. Davies & Henrik (2010) *Information and the Nature of Reality*, Cambridge University Press.

7. There is much scientific literature on quantum which is quite understandable to the general public and deserves to be read and enjoyed. Some authors to investigate would be Richard Feynman, John Polkinghorne and George Gamow. It can be so intriguing a

subject that we pursue it at our own risk. It is the ultimate in counter-intuition as well as the extreme intellectual boundary of our present understanding of physical, philosophical and thus theological reality.

9

A New Environment For Understanding

We began this journey by looking at Genesis 1 and its story of creation. Perhaps we should now consider how that chapter might have been rendered if God had waited until the twenty-first century to inspire its composition. After all, what is the wait of another 4,000 years added to the 150,000 or so years for the arrival of Genesis 1? I will not attempt to frame the story in the poetic form that Genesis uses so well but simply set out the facts it must contain. It is the complete story of evolution.

A full view of evolution

The idea of evolution becomes problematic when a blinkered, narrow view limits the concept to biological evolution. The material universe started to evolve some 13.7 billion years ago while biological evolution started a much more recent 3.5 billion years ago and both are continuing today. The understanding of this physical evolution began to develop in 1927 when the Belgian priest/physicist Georges Lemaître proposed an expanding universe. The British astronomer Edwin Hubble confirmed this by demonstrating that all the galaxies observed were indeed going away from each other and that the farther they were, the faster they receded. Lemaître proposed in 1930 that everything in the universe exploded from an initial point and Fred Hoyle coined the expression for it as the Big Bang and the name stuck.

In the first small fraction of a second after the bang, the primitive material of the universe went through a series of initial phases which are not completely understood. The Large Hadron Collider in Cern, Switzerland, is attempting to increase our understanding of just that. Within seconds of the Big Bang, electrons, protons and neutrons, the constituents of atoms, began to form. A few hundred seconds later as expansion increased and the temperature dropped, proton-neutron combinations formed the nucleus of hydrogen and helium atoms. It wasn't until some 300,000 years later that the temperature was low enough to allow these particles to form stable hydrogen and helium atoms by capturing electrons. Because of gravity, by which all matter attracts other matter to itself, the expansion of this hydrogen gas was not even or smooth but began to lump together. The larger the mass of hydrogen, the greater the gravitational attraction and by some 300 million years, stars and galaxies began to form.[1]

The pressures inside such large masses of hydrogen causes nuclear reactions to occur and the fusion of two hydrogen atoms into a helium atom resulted in the release of large amounts of energy which is why stars like our Sun produce so much heat.[2]

We can also observe that these stars formed into systems we call galaxies hundreds of thousands of light years wide and containing as many as a hundred billion stars. The universe is composed of billions of galaxies. Our Sun is probably a third generation star[3] in the Milky Way galaxy and as it formed it also acquired in orbit around it, large masses of heavy elements, one of which we call Earth. This formed about 4.5 billion years ago as a molten mass about eight thousand miles in diameter. In about a billion years, it had cooled enough to form a crust which was covered with water and land formed by the eruption of volcanos. Its mass was large enough that its gravity prevented its atmosphere of carbon dioxide from escaping.

Eventually the oceans became filled with minerals and organic compounds formed by lightening strikes in the atmosphere and the circulation of the sea water between hot and cold regions. They were in effect a nutritious soup. About 3.5 billion years ago, somewhere in that soup the first living organism formed as a single celled bacteria and biological evolution began.

In one of those bacteria there developed a metabolic process which released free oxygen. The forces of evolution soon developed organisms which could grow in size and support and protect themselves by hard exoskeletons such as clams and crabs and supported by the oxygen. When concentrations of oxygen became high enough, living organisms were able to exist out of the sea and plants and animals migrated out of the water and gills evolved into lungs. It may seem difficult to think of bacteria producing so much oxygen but remember that it had a billion or more years to accomplish that. Time is always a necessary ingredient in evolution.

When we take this more inclusive and realistic view of evolution, it is more difficult to dismiss it as just a scientific mistake. Rather, it becomes the method of choice of the Creator in the generation of both the physical universe and the biological universe. We agree that it is possible that God did it the way Genesis 1 tells us. But we should remember that, in the real world, most of the things that could possibly happen, don't. We should look not for possibility but probability. The above scenario presents the whole of the physical universe as a consistent and uninterrupted flow of events. It also gives us a whole new and awesome image of a powerful and reasonable Creator.

This story may not be as poetic as Genesis 1, it may lack the memory aid of three days of organizing and three days of populating but it is far more intriguing to the twenty-first century mind. Instead of symbolic events which require interpretation, it gives us the natural events which have stretched the best scientific and theological minds to their limit. These events have inspired awe in those who have the skill to speak the mathematical language which led them to these conclusions. It is no less awesome for those of us who cannot quite understand this language but can understand how these events fit the highest notions of a Creator God.

The reader of Genesis 1 is hearing about individual events which serve to set the stage for all that follows in the *Old Testament*. The reader of the twenty-first century version becomes more curious about the details of how each step in the story came about and what kind of God could accomplish such things. The story is an inexhaustible source of new questions and inspires more searching for answers. With each answer we are thinking God's thoughts after him. This is the beauty of natural revelation.

That the Genesis story might have been the result of divine inspiration is not so farfetched. It is full of details which humankind could see with their eyes and agree that this is a reasonable, possible account of how it happened. The problem of course is that it only seemed reasonable that it happened that way, in six days, but we now know that it didn't. The details of this twenty-first century version are also what we have observed but it is not only a reasonable and possible account but also one that is provable by physical data.

So what implications might this twenty-first century version have with regard to faith, religious practice and organization as well as spirituality, that is, the way we relate to the Creator? It is appropriate to rethink our ideas about God in this scientific age. After all, until the seventeenth century we thought it quite appropriate to think about God as described in Genesis 1 while we were completely ignorant of the physical reality into which we were formed. We have come a long way since then but that journey has not been one which drives us to conclude that there is no Creator to talk about.

The success of science

Science, as distinguished from natural philosophy, has only been functioning for about 400 years and at first the progress was slow. Most of its greatest advances have been in the last 150 years and in the last 75 years technology has produced a staggering amount of change in the way we think and do things. We might well ask what has driven this success and does it have implications for religious endeavors?

One driving force in science today is that nothing succeeds like success. The success of science and technology gave us better and more plentiful food, fabrics to clothe us, materials to house us, medicines to cure us, devices to transport us and means to inform us. It even gave us more dramatic ways to entertain us and more leisure time in which to be entertained. With such success came a greater willingness to fund science. It is also clear that the process used by science is satisfying to us. Scientific investigation and experimentation indulges our curiosity. It seeks the solution to mysteries. Epidemiologists, for example, deal with mysteries far more complex and of greater urgency than any Agatha Christie mystery plot. They apply their science to find the killer in an epidemic but that killer will most likely continue to kill at an increasing rate if not found.

Best of all, there is a natural appeal in the pursuit of science because we can usually see useful results in the technology it generates. Even the most tentative scientific theories create an atmosphere not just of mystery but wonder as well. Thus science is motivated both by our appetite for understanding and our desire to enrich life on Earth through that understanding and technology. We can also revel in the notion that we are the ones who can experience that wonder, the only ones in our solar system.

The success of the investigative and experimental approach of science has also encouraged us to try different ways of governing our society. These experiments involved our social nature motivated by the spirit of the Enlightenment. It was here that the principles of religion were most at home rather than with the scientific laws of physical nature.

But something underpinned this success and theologians should take note. In all human endeavors, the potential for success depends very much on a non-threatening environment which encourages creative thinking and curiosity. The questioning atmosphere of the Enlightenment was as important for science as were the developments in mathematics. Mathematics gave science an adequate language to deal with nature and the atmosphere of the Enlightenment opened up a world of things to discuss in that language. If the success of science seems to be promoting secularism and attracting people away from religion, it may be that religion has not maintained an intellectual atmosphere in which creative minds can demonstrate the true place of religion in the living of a human life in a scientific age. This does not mean ruling out the affective nature of humanity in religious expression but that the intellectual nature must equally be ruled in.

The result of scientific advances has not always been to everyone's liking. The same power used to generate electrical energy has also been used to destroy a city with a single bomb. The same technology that makes possible the global presence of the internet has also been used to promote radicalism and terrorism. The same almost ancient technology used to quarry stone and straighten the path for building roads has also been used to fabricate bombs for the suicidal killing of hundreds of innocent people in markets, buses and trains. The tragic use of technology developed by science has not been the fault of science but a moral failure of those who controlled its use. This is in part a failure of religion to sustain its credibility, priorities and values as a moral force in society. It is also a failure to recognize the evolutionary imperative religion has to promote the interests of all humanity and not just a particular sect, denomination or culture.

If, as we maintain, science can offer us new insights into God's created universe, we must ask what contribution has natural revelation made to our understanding of God? These insights should also be added to the successes of science. The first benefit was that science showed us where we were getting it wrong about written revelation. It made it clear that it was not a natural history we were reading in Genesis and that we needed to investigate how we were reading it and where to find the divine revelation in it. This was no small service. This happened, of course, only after science itself learned how to find things out about the natural world. We all learned that common sense was not a good guide. Repeatable experimentation with data collection and interpretation was the solution along with a precise mathematical language adequate to describe what was happening in natural events.

The new data which biblical scholars sought was to be found in biblical textual criticism within its historical context and this was a twentieth century accomplishment. The fact is that, if science had not uncovered the real nature of the physical universe, religion would have had no reason to question its interpretation of Genesis 1. Another benefit of natural revelation was in its contribution to our basic image of God. Until the ascent of science, we had no familiar vocabulary to substantially describe God. We strained at terms like infinite, immense, all powerful and the like. But when we began to understand the true size and complexity of this universe, we could use terms like millions of light years distance and billions of years passage of time to describe creation.

We could visualize the complexity of nature at the molecular and subatomic levels although we could not observe them directly. Still, these terms were like candle light trying to illuminate the mind that brought the universe into existence. The terms were not, however, the product of literary creativity but rather the measurements of physical reality inspired by theories expressed in the language of mathematics. We would expect that the physical nature and composition of the universe is a reflection of its Creator. By comparison, creation in six days only 6000 years ago is absurdly simplistic.

Clearly, science has strong, natural appeal. We can see the result of it in technology which serves our every need. We are dazzled because the facts of science are so much more interesting and no less imaginative than science fiction. This reminds us again that underlying the success of science is, at its best, an intellectual environment which encourages and rewards imagination, creativity, curiosity and the right to be wrong. Science learns things even from the process of proving a theory wrong. As a result, there is no stigma in having proposed a theory that is in error. Humanly speaking, no one sets out to enjoy that sensation but true scientists do not look upon it as humiliation. Discovering what a thing is not can be a major step in discovering what it is. Scientists are also human and, after supporting an idea perhaps too loudly, were sometimes loath to change their allegiance. We must now ask if an open atmosphere does or can exist in religion. But first we should ask to what can we attribute the success of religion?

The success of religion

The success of religion can best be seen from the viewpoint of the evolution of human society and the influence religion has had on it. In evolutionary terms, religion helps satisfy the natural urge to survive, not just as an individual, but as a species as well. That survival is not focused just on the present, but also on the future. It is observed that humankind is the only species who will plant a tree knowing that they will never live long enough to enjoy its shade. Only by tapping into natural revelation do we find an evolutionary reason for doing that.

The influence of religion has been exerted most intensely by the two largest world religions, Christianity and Islam. Both of these religions derive their theology from what they regard as revealed texts, the *Bible* and the *Koran*. While it cannot be denied that both of these faiths must have human appeal, the curious thing is that these two faiths owed their great expansion to imperialism. When the Roman Emperor Constantine converted to Christianity in 312, the Christian Church enjoyed material support and immediate exposure throughout the empire, both East (Byzantine) and West (European). Later, colonization spread Catholicism to Latin America and, through the British empire, reformed Christianity to North America and Australia. Missionary zeal carried Christianity to the Far East. It also meant at times an unholy alliance between Christianity and imperial government which certainly had its down side.

Islam saw rapid expansion through the Eastern and Southern Mediterranean. It was the Great Prophet Muhammad himself, to whom Allah gave the sacred text of the *Koran* early in the seventh century, who blurred the distinction between religious leader and political leader and formed Arab tribes into a strong military force and spread Islam through the Near East, North Africa and what is now Spain. But over time, Islam was greatly diminished by extreme fundamentalism and the failure to respond to economic and technological advancements. Both Christianity and Islam were also to suffer as a consequence of the political failure of imperial ambitions.

While in the West social concerns increased after the Enlightenment, the scientific movement grew in a religious culture. Society had been saturated by the religious traditions which were the foundation of its culture. The Enlightenment indicated new paths to follow without abandoning its basic principles. Islam unfortunately has not yet experienced a period of Enlightenment to force it to rethink its fundamentalist reading of its sacred text.

Both Christianity and Islam have at times fallen into the mindset that their purpose is to save those willing to accept the truth as embodied in their creed. Even today we hear Muslim extremists voicing condemnations of infidels. This exclusivity was also a part of the atmosphere found early in the *Old Testament* until the revelation in the book of Jonah whose moral conclusion was that God had concern for everyone, not just Israel, and the Israelite should do no less. Both Jesus and Paul pointed Christianity in the direction of a universal concern for all humankind. Christianity today, at its best, demonstrates efforts to promote human rights, justice, charity and reconciliation to every culture, society and gender no matter what their religious belief or disbelief. It exists for the whole of humanity, not just for its membership and least of all, for their own sake. To whatever extent religion can promote these things, it is helping human society evolve into one which more closely matches the perceived intention of the Creator.

After political imperialism collapsed, the danger was that scientific secularism would impose itself with a fervor equal to any political imperialism. Some think that this is what we are suffering from today. The number of Christian fundamentalists who are creationists is small, with the exception of the United States where it is approaching half the population and they are very vocal. Because they believe in creationism even in the face of the reasonableness of the scientific explanation of creation and the universe, they are causing many more thinking individuals globally to view religion as out of context and unreasonable. There is no limit to the number of people who will reject an unreasonable religion, one that is out of touch with reality.

Religious leaders are quick to indicate that secularism, indifference and the attractions of the consumer society are luring people away from religion. But could it also be that the intellectual atmosphere within religion is not attracting people to it? Nor have the intellectual arguments of science had much effect. Some contend that increasingly it is those religious believers who derive great emotional satisfaction from their faith as well as certainty about all questions that remain in it and that are its future. Yet surely there are other things about faith which should be attractive without the emotional intensity. Perhaps the answer to this will become clear when we determine how much of the intellectual atmosphere from which science has derived so much success is part of or absent from religion today.

The environment of religious thought

Let us start with Islam. There has never been any effective central defining body in Islam. Soon after Muhammad's death, Islam became splintered into different factions with what seem to Western eyes minor differences but with major enthusiasm supporting each. They can be identified as Sunni, Shia, Sufi, Wahhabi and within each of these there exist different schools. Christianity is also very divided but in modern times, with some exceptions, is not usually so militant and intolerant as some Islamic groups are. Most of society in the beginning of the twenty-first century watched in utter disbelief as daily in Iraq, Syria, Libya, Bahrain and elsewhere Muslims kill fellow Muslims.

As is so often the case, religion is not the only issue, just the identifier. Jobs, oil income and social status are what petty warlords and entrenched politicians are fighting for. Unfortunately some of those warlords are religious leaders and their followers shout "God is great" as they fire their mortars indiscriminately into city streets or blow themselves up in murderous suicides which kill innocent people. Christianity was also cursed with this situation in recent times. Fortunately there was a difference of degree although not kind. In the Northern Ireland conflict, euphemistically called the troubles, religion was an identifier of which side you were on but the root of the conflict was economics, jobs and housing complicated by historical animosities.

This is not the kind of environment we are interested in here. Yet intolerance and militancy are a product of the atmosphere in which religions operate. The intellectual environment which contributes much to the success of science is characterized by how it encourages examination of current thinking with an openness to new ideas and its ability to deal with uncertainty. This is the focus we will take in looking at the intellectual environment of religion.

There is one final parallel in science and religion which is seldom noticed but which has a strong influence on both. I will try to show a similarity between the satisfaction felt by scientists in the pursuit of their discipline and the effects of spirituality in religion. I am, however, going to limit my comments to the Catholic Church. It is easier to deal with a stationary target and, within Christianity, it is Catholicism which comes closest to being one. It also has a highly centralized structure with codified laws and organizational elements other forms of Christianity lack.

The arrival of infallibility

The early Christian Church relied on councils, meetings of large numbers of Church leaders and scholars to make decisions about belief and practice. It worked well and, being a new faith, there was much to decide. From these earliest times, there grew a presumption of a hierarchical structure which included authority. When the Emperor Constantine took Christianity under his protection, bishops acquired civil as well as doctrinal authority. The Roman Church began to organize along the model of the Empire and its center became Rome. The historical background and implications of this are outside our consideration here.

For our purpose, the major contributor to the intellectual atmosphere of the Church today is the doctrine of infallibility. Our interest is not in the substance of this charism nor the history of the doctrine but rather in the effect of its use. Infallibility means immunity from error. This should not be confused with meaning that a doctrinal formulation is adequate or appropriate, only that, as it stands, it is free from error. Furthermore, as defined by the Catholic Church, it is a quality of the Church, not the Pope in and by himself. He participates in this gift because of his central position in the Church but has no such power separate from the Church as a whole, as a community of believers. Beyond saying this, it does not help our interests to go any further into its technicalities.

The history of the definition of infallibility can help us understand the difficulties infallibility can create. When the Roman empire collapsed after the barbarian invasion, it was the Roman papacy that filled the vacuum with what is called the Holy Roman Empire. Eventually, Charlemagne was crowned emperor by Pope Leo III in 800. The price of Charlemagne's protection was that he could appoint bishops and exercise much power in Church affairs. When this empire collapsed, the Church found itself in what was later to be called the Dark Ages. There followed a movement to reintroduce councils into the decision making function of the Church but this was strongly resisted by the popes.[4] By this time the Church had acquired an imperial structure similar to the empire it replaced. With the Protestant Reformation in the 16th century, new challenges were made to the authority of the Catholic Church. The Reformation also provided a convenient way for civil rulers to escape the secular control of the Roman Church and this contributed to its success.

It was into this atmosphere of rising European Nationalism that Pope Pius IX entered the scene in 1846. While he saw his civil authority drain away with the annexation of the Papal States by the new unified state of Italy, he was determined not only to keep his doctrinal authority, but to preserve that doctrine from error. To this end he published his *Syllabus of Errors* in 1864 and called the First Vatican Council in 1869. With much pressure from him, the council defined both the primacy of the pope over the whole Church and his infallibility.

The Second Vatican Council (1962–1965) clarified that infallibility was in the hands of the Church and not just the papacy and perhaps this reflects the fact that there still remains to be further development of the doctrine. The purpose of infallibility is to ensure that the teachings of the Church are faithful to Sacred Scripture. I will not consider the recent introduction of the category of "definitive" teachings which was added in 1998 by the *Moto Proprio Ad tuendam fidem* which applies to non-scriptural teachings. Infallibility can thus be used to resolve questions so important that they could seriously impact the spiritual wellbeing or salvation of its members. Anything beyond that is to seek a feeling of security, or worse, to use such defined orthodoxy as a club with which to attack those who think differently or at least as a test of orthodoxy.

The difficulty with infallibility is not the doctrine itself but the decision when and how to use it. The purpose is surely not the elimination of all uncertainty from religious life any more than the purpose of the sacrament of anointing is the elimination of all disease. Infallibility is not meant to be a security blanket yet this is what it becomes if the Church is asked to give the definitive answer on any and all questions. Nor is it a way to maintain authority.

After almost 150 years of defined infallibility and centuries before that of deference to the pope and enforcement of doctrinal formulas, even under pain of death at times, there has grown up an atmosphere which dictated unquestioned acceptance of all decisions and formulations of doctrine issued by the pope and the Vatican offices. In practice, everything was best considered as being under the umbrella of infallibility, often referred to as the ordinary magisterium or teaching function of the Church. While some theologians might be able to distinguish the authority behind a particular decree, for the most part, the operative principal was that Rome speaks and the cause is ended. When this happens, great harm can be done. Theologians can find themselves walking backward into the future for fear that they will say something which does not conform to a formula devised many centuries ago. This stifles creative and imaginative thinking. It also encourages an unquestioning and passively obeying faithful while discouraging much thinking at a time when the institutions from which the faithful are graduating are rightly promoting independent thinking.[5]

There is also in our time a great disparity between the number of things which have been formally defined and those which are generally considered as infallibly defined by many in the Church hierarchy but in fact are not. It is surprising to most people when they learn that the Church has never made a formal infallible declaration on a moral issue, only dogmatic issues. There is also much uncertainty about what things are defined infallibly. In 1994 Pope John Paul II published the Apostolic Letter *Ordinatio Sacerdotalis* concerning the ordination of women which declared that it is impossible to ordain women to the priesthood. Theologians around the world expressed the opinion that this is not an infallible decision and that there is no Scriptural evidence to support it.

The papal document itself relied only on Tradition, or more accurately, custom and not Scripture to support the argument. It can be said with certainty that many scholars were not convinced by the arguments. Finally the head of the Holy Office, then Cardinal Joseph Ratzinger, issued a statement declaring that the Holy Father intended this as an infallible decision. The theologians then pointed out that if that was the case, the pope must make that statement himself. The director of the holy office is

142

not infallible. In the end, infallibility seemed to be used here not to clarify an understanding as much as to close any further discussion which might lead to further clarification.

Does religion need infallibility?

What would be the effect if the Vatican became a center for the encouragement of theological scholars and spiritual writers to remain at the forefront of religious thinking? Because of its status and credibility, it could influence policy in Christian countries throughout the world, debate theological issues in public and much more. It would be the place to find the best thinking of the day while being independent of any particular political interests. Its authority would be derived from the vast number of its members world wide and the integrity and openness of its methods. This would confer competence even in the face of uncertainty.

If this sounds reasonable, let me point out that what I have done is paraphrase the statement of purpose of the Royal Society which is the national academy of science of the United Kingdom. It was founded in 1660 and has had among its leaders and members such names as Christopher Wren, Samuel Pepys, Francis Bacon, Isaac Newton, Charles Darwin, Benjamin Franklin and Albert Einstein. It still flourishes today. It is a clearing house of new ideas and its authority comes from peer review and its reputation for credibility and openness. It is in an enviable position.

So where does or can religion get its credibility in a secular and scientific society? No institution can simply make an authoritative statement that it is credible and expect to be seen as such. Such a statement would have less credibility than the comic cliché, "Trust me, I'm a doctor." Nor does it help the Church when it gives the impression that it does not trust its own scholars and is unwilling to promote the ideas of its best contemporary thinkers. Evidence of this comes from the fact that in any encyclicals, decrees and apostolic letters issued by the Church, you will never find a reference to the ideas of a living scholar. The only references are from past encyclicals, council decrees, the *Bible* or saints who have been dead at least 500 years. One explanation for this can be that there is a mistrust of new ideas. This does not contribute to credibility. Rather, it gives the impression of insecurity.

The credibility spoken of here is not that which is seen through the eyes of the firm believer. The mandate of religion is not to save the saved. If Christianity is to fulfill the commission of Christ to teach all nations, it must be credible in the eyes of the general public, the non-believing world. What will make it credible from their point of view is the openness of the process of arriving at the best thinking of the day. Note that I did not say arriving at truth. As we will see in a moment, not even science uses that word since even its oldest and most trusted laws may prove to be incomplete and thus not the whole truth. I did, however use the word day and not century. It is often said that Rome makes decisions not in terms of weeks but centuries. That is just not good enough in the twenty-first century. By that time the issue has been decided by secular society without any contribution from the theologian. One would think that an infallible institution could do better than that.

One final point can be made here. We have been critical of Scriptural fundamentalism. But an exaggerated reliance on infallibility and authority has given rise to what can be called ecclesiastical or doctrinal fundamentalism. The stereotypical Christian fundamentalist is the Bible Belt preacher standing in his pulpit holding up the *Bible* and saying, "God said it, I believe it and that ends it." There is also a saying among conservative Catholics which goes, "Roma locuta, causa finita." or Rome has spoken and the cause is ended. In one case, the precise wording of a biblical translation is taken as the literal and last word in the matter. In the other, the precise wording of the Church's formulation is taken in the same way. In both cases, the authority behind the statements is thought to be God himself. Both can lead us to some very sticky conclusions.

Once you have said that the holy text is the word of God, there is nothing more to say unless it can be demonstrated that the interpretation of the words is faulty. But even then there is a reluctance to question the literal interpretation at all. The logic can also progress beyond the sacred text. It can apply to the traditional teaching of the Church by concluding that God would not let us be wrong about this for so long. But the "this" is always a human interpretation of ancient texts or philosophical conclusions which were drawn with, perhaps, an incomplete understanding of nature. In this way the fundamentalist conclusion is that any teaching which persists over a long period of time becomes sacred tradition and takes on the authority of Scripture e.g., the logic behind *Ordinatio Sacerdotalis*. Thus, every word issued by the Church must be given assent of conscience until such time as the Church changes it. This creates a Catholic form of fundamentalism. Once decreed, those issuing the decree believe that any retraction serves to weaken ecclesiastical authority so there is little appetite for reversing opinion. We know how long it took for the rehabilitation of Galileo.

In the past, crusades and inquisitions were waged partly because of the philosophical principle that error has no right to exist. As applied here,

144

the principle is questionable since rights belong to persons and not ideas. Science learned how to live with error and to enjoy the adventure of discovery and the indulgence of intellectual curiosity. Fundamentalists in the Catholic Church are undeterred by the warning that the church may become irrelevant or that believers may simply walk away. It would appear that fewer unquestioning true believers are preferable to large numbers of critically thinking faithful.[6] For some, religion becomes a deposit of self-styled truth to be preserved and revered rather than a pilgrim servant leading us to God.

To answer our question, does religion need infallibility, we might share the following observation. G. K. Chesterton pointed out that there are two kinds of people in the world: progressives and conservatives. The progressives are those who are willing to go through life making mistakes. The conservatives are those who are determined to prevent anyone from correcting those mistakes. Christian history reveals some of those mistakes which were made in the past: usury, slavery, the Galileo affair, the Inquisition and religious wars. We wonder how many mistaken ideas have not been recognized in a timely way because of the conservative fear of rethinking and reformulation.

The influence of Tradition

One final component which complicates the intellectual environment of religion is tradition. Catholic theology starts from a reasonable and useful principal about how we know about God. Stated most simply, we know about God because God formally reveals himself to us. Otherwise, how could we know him except through what his creation tells us, what we are calling in this book natural revelation. But God's formal revelation comes in two forms, written revelation and what is usually called tradition. Since there is only one source, God, and two forms, I prefer to think of tradition as living revelation. This is not only more descriptive but reduces the impression that there are two sources of religious understanding.

The awareness of two forms of revelation is a useful one. In the case of the *New Testament*, we could say that living revelation came first. It was the teachings which the apostles handed down verbally in their instructions and then much of it took written form in the *New Testament*. But since each book and letter in the *New Testament* had its own purpose and approach, not all those first instructions would be expected to make it into the sacred texts. In fact, some of those first instructions would be so widely understood and presumed as already known that there would be no need to include them. This body of knowledge is often referred to as apostolic tradition.

This tradition is not what causes any difficulty in the intellectual environment of modern religion. What can create a problem are those teachings or opinions which have no connection to apostolic teachings but have been part of the general instruction of the faithful for so long that they are referred to as being part of sacred tradition. The opinion that the Earth is at the center of the universe is perhaps the oldest example, predating the *New Testament*. While this was traditionally taught without question until the sixteenth century, it was wrong. The reason the centrality of the Earth was seen as important in the sixteenth century was because to change the teaching would dilute the authority of the Church. Yet in the twentieth century that erroneous belief was formally abandoned.

These traditional elements in religion not only involve moral issues but customs of worship, discipline and spiritual practices. A more contemporary example might be the traditional prohibition against contraception. This obviously has no connection to apostolic times or teachings. It is derived from the principles of moral theology and not apostolic teaching as lived by the early apostolic community. It, therefore, must rise or fall on the strength of its logic and reasonableness.

We might ask why any non-apostolic tradition is often considered sacred? No matter how long it has endured, it is not necessarily the product of rational methods of inquiry. Tradition is only as good as the good it generates in a society or culture. The tradition of bartering was replaced by the convenience of money which represented the value of an exchange. But this raised the moral question of loans and the charging of interest. This moral concern disappeared when the existence of a mature monetary standard produced a system of finance and commerce. Even an exaggerated sense of tradition could not hold back this evolution in society. So, given the light of better understanding of the workings of nature and society, tradition should not inhibit rethinking everything from principles of natural law morality to disciplinary regulations.

When traditions are impacted by nature, one can get the impression that new scientific discoveries are immediately held as suspect and a possible threat. There is a natural hesitation in human nature to change the way we think. The only threat can be a loss of face if the statement of traditional thinking was represented as far more certain than it turned out to be. Intellectually this is not an atmosphere which instills confidence or credibility.

We are not here intent on discrediting or doing away with tradition but rather expanding it to take advantage of new understandings about our physical and social world. Humanly speaking, it is always difficult publicly to change your mind but the Roman Church has done it. Natural philosophers of the time of Galileo had this difficulty but we know how natural science flourished when attitudes changed and broke away from traditional thinking.

Some things which science has discovered directly impact religious thinking. This suggests that we must be cautious in taking an absolute stand when making moral decisions involving our physical nature. Ignorance is not an appropriate foundation for moral belief. The famous remark of Cardinal Suenens during the Second Vatican Council still rings true. "Let's not have another Galileo affair." He said it concerning the inclusion of the birth control issue into the agenda of the council. It was not included and spared the council the reaction that followed the publication of the encyclical *Humane Vitae* by Pope Paul VI.

Sooner or later original thinkers in theology may encounter the tradition barrier. When this happens it is unfortunate. Tradition forms part of our intellectual environment and helps us interpret our experience. In this sense it is the wisdom of our age. But the primary characteristic of wisdom is that it never stops growing. The problem is that we see what happens when a person grows as change rather than development. The child and the adult are the same person, only wiser after much development. The transition from child to adult requires development which comes from new ideas, better understanding and new associations within these ideas and understandings.

Tradition must never be a limit on creativity, what some would call the movement of the Spirit in religion. Surprising and unexpected conclusions do not come from slavishly refusing to allow thinking beyond traditional convictions. When there is difference of opinion and questioning of traditional thinking, it should not be seen as a threat but rather a richness. Only institutions which fear decline exhibit such a defensive view of their ideas. The traditionalist mentality abhors mentioning the possibility of alternative thinking. Thus any attempt at creativity comes to a narrow dead end.

The body of knowledge which constitutes our understanding of God is often referred to as the faith. It must develop along with a better understanding of our human nature and the universe around us. Without this development, the faith will petrify. Ideas can become dated. This is true of elements of religious traditions of the kind we are speaking of here. This could include not only styles of spirituality or worship but also the verbal formulation of beliefs and morality. In the Catholic Church there have been profound changes in the way the sacraments of Reconciliation, Eucharist and Anointing have been practiced throughout history. At one time there arose a felt need for a place called Limbo where those children who were not baptized went for natural happiness outside the vision of God. Today the idea is dated and recent statements of the Vatican Theological Commission declared that it is outside Scriptural revelation and not absolutely necessary. Religion must remain vital and be able to shed those things which are dated and preserve what survives new discoveries.

Today we all would defend the moral principal that slavery is intrinsically evil. Yet it was an acceptable tradition in both the *Old* and *New Testaments*. Well into Christian history popes, bishops and canonized saints owned slaves. In fact it was civil governments which brought the practice to a halt. The first bishop of Florida in the United States owned a slave. John Carroll, the first bishop in the United States tolerated slavery and had two. Nor did the Catholic Church in the States play any influential role in the elimination of segregation, the remnant of slavery. It was not that the principles of universal love and respect for every human individual were missing from theology. A long history, a major constituent of tradition, of being able to dissociate these principles from the practice of society made it possible to overlook its evil.[7]

How certain do we need to be?

Religion needs to be credible but not necessarily certain. In business as well a science we are used to dealing with uncertainties. We exercise a bit of risk/reward analysis and then act. We do not simply close up shop because the path ahead is not clearly marked nor do we close our eyes to new ideas and proceed with business as usual. Who would deny that there are those for whom religion is an insurance policy against perceived risks? In the real world risk/reward analysis is a more reasonable basis for decisions than demanding or, worse yet, pretending to have absolute certainty about every aspect of the business at hand. Those who deny the realities of the changing marketplace very soon go out of business.

The credibility of science comes not just from the validity of the mathematics through which it is expressed and the experimental data from which it was derived. It also comes from the rigor with which science pursues understanding and its readiness to debate issues when conclusions are not so convincing. It demands evidence. As we have seen, its conclusions are not necessarily the ones that make most sense to us. Common sense does not serve us well in science. Scientific credibility is then further enhanced by submitting conclusions to peer review.

Nor do many of the beliefs of religion necessarily make sense in that they are what we would expect. The element of surprise works well both in science and religion and that should be seen as one of their appealing qualities. Reason says that light must be either a particle or a wave but not both. Fortunately, two scientists of different persuasions on this issue could share a drink together and debate it without shouting. Concerning the incarnation, reason would say that Jesus is either human or he is God but not both. Unfortunately, believers on either side have not always been so hospitable in dealing with their difference on questions such as this.

This situation is detrimental to Christianity and, if this is partly the effect of infallibility, then infallibility may be more trouble than it is worth. Once an atmosphere of authority is established, that authority feels less and less pressure to convince and explain. All it needs to do is simply formulate statements and expect obedience. In fact, in the past the opinion has been expressed that the role of the theologian is to determine the justifications for the Church's statements instead of being fully involved in determining their formulations. It is blatantly obvious that this is a process which is proceeding backward. This situation can only survive in an authoritarian community which has no means of self-correction and no motive for self-examination. It is preoccupied with conformity and authority yet the purpose of infallibility is to foster understanding and not preserve authority. This makes a parody of the primary commission Christ gave to his Apostles, to go and teach all nations.

In practical terms, if someone questions a dogma concerning a serious idea, of what influence can infallibility be? That individual is most likely to question infallibility itself so even a formal decree on the matter will have little effect. Most of the issues which are questioned openly are not the basic dogmas of faith. In our day, we are talking about issues which new scientific information calls into question or clashes with established cultural attitudes. These are teachings that clash with the expectations of informed people concerning the connection between religious beliefs and the latest scientific and social insights.

We can teach even while uncertain

Science was never given the command to teach but, because of the enthusiasm of individual scientists and scientific organizations, it is very successful at instruction. Proclaiming dogma is not the same thing as teaching. Humanly speaking, being able to claim freedom from error would lay the ultimate claim to authority. In recent years there is evidence

149

of the Catholic Church becoming more authoritarian as well as centralized, in spite of the direction given it by Vatican II. This atmosphere increases the limitations on individual thinkers. It does this by discouraging the contribution of original ideas. Yet it is just such freedom for creative thinking and original ideas that has contributed much to the success of science.

By its own definition, the Church is infallible only under defined conditions. This means that it must be fallible in all the rest. But what is there to fear from this? It is possible to trust someone who admits to making mistakes. We do not think any less of the Royal Society today because for the first hundred years of its existence it defended the idea of spontaneous generation. Nor do we today think any less of the Church because it was wrong about slavery, religious freedom or usury. Most of us would mistrust anyone who maintained that he never makes a mistake. The Church would not harm but rather enhance its credibility by acting as a clearinghouse for the best thinking of the day on controversial issues while admitting uncertainty about them. This is better than declaring certitude in the absence of incontestable proof. Openness is also an invitation for the best minds to focus on the need for further development.

How did Catholicism lose its tolerance for uncertainty? Uncertainty can be seen as a challenge to authority. It's not a sign of inferiority or weakness to admit that we are not absolutely certain about something. In fact it could be a sign of insecurity to abhor uncertainty. If anything characterizes the Christian Church as well as Islam in the minds of many people today, it is its insatiable felt-need for absolute truth and certainty, and the conviction that the Church or the revealed texts have it. It is natural to want to know the truth about things that concern us. This is what motivates both scientists and theologians. The problem arises when the lack of certainty causes us to feel insecure and to demand more from scholars or institutions than should be expected. Yes, there is a satisfaction, a pleasure in knowing things for certain. But there may be something else involved as well, what Russell Baker described when he wrote, "People seem to enjoy things more when they know a lot of other people have been left out on the pleasure." This adds an exclusive club mentality to membership in a religion.

How does science deal with uncertainty? At first glance it might seem that they do experiments which confirm the mathematical statement of laws and that gives them absolute certainty. Not so! The success of science comes not from eliminating uncertainties but from learning how to live with them. We arrive at truth through a progression of stages. When asked about something, we start out by saying that we don't know. In other words, we are ignorant. Then we come up with a new idea which we can investigate. This is little more than a guess. We say that it might be such and such. This means we are uncertain. We may investigate to a point at which we can say that we are pretty sure of it. This means that we still have doubt. To resolve the doubt, we need new ideas.

One thing scientists have learned is that old laws may be inadequate. As we saw in chapter 8, Newton's laws of motion and mass had exceptions when the movement was extremely fast or when we were dealing with things at the atomic level. The right observations had not been made to cover all possibilities. The statement of those laws served us well for a couple of centuries and, in fact, still do today but in the end nothing can be stated with absolute finality. This was discovered only because science had learned the excitement which comes from not being certain and seeking new ideas to eliminate doubt. The Nobel Prize winning physicist Richard Feynman devotes the first chapter of his book *The Meaning of it All* to the uncertainty of science.

In science there is always the assumption that there may well come along a better, fuller understanding of things. Our understanding of the atom and its nucleus is a perfect example. Each step along its history was so intellectually satisfying and seemed so final, one almost wanted to sit back and say that we have arrived and now let's enjoy it. The true scientist never does that. What is understood now can and should be used now but always be open to the liberating and expanding effect of the next step in understanding that is to come.

So how certain are we about science? Well, rather certain. We know how successful science has been with that level of certitude. We know how much credibility the general public is willing to give its ideas. It should be the same in theology. It seems that religion has neglected developing a philosophy of ignorance. And let us not forget the involvement of faith. Faith should engender self-confidence. It should not be a blinkered focus which turns off any informed criticism. Striving for orthodoxy can become censorship of thought, speech and critical enquiry.

There can be one final point of view, that of responsibility and liability. In the world of commerce, an accepted definition of corruption is this; the abuse of trusted power for private gain. In the world of global corporations, the power in question might be the ability to convince clients, on the strength of the corporation's good name and reputation, that their product is the best available for the price. The private gain might mean the gain to the corporate entity and not any single individual. Of course it was the decision of individuals which directed the misuse of power in the first place and, depending on the laws of a particular country, these individuals might be liable to prosecution. Engineering the wrong understanding of their product, perhaps an investment scheme, is certainly a dishonest or fraudulent conduct by those in power. Also involved in the trust we grant to corporate entities is the integrity of their method of securing data in order to make decisions which add value to the corporation and its clients. Any CEO who did not ensure the best procedures and up to date information gathering would not be long in his or her position. The market would soon see to that, and soon after, the shareholders.

Now consider a global organization whose product is information, a think tank which conducts research for other businesses and serves as management consultants to whom others turn to determine the best practice of the day. Can you imagine such a company ignoring certain bodies of knowledge because they do not seem to be directly connected to their primary concerns? Is it conceivable that they might forbid discussion of topics they had considered many years ago and nothing that has happened in the many years since should, in their judgement, change their decision? If, in an Annual General Meeting of the corporation, it had been decided that the company should change its practice to be more consultative and open in their internal processes, still management subsequently undid that directive and gradually reverted to the former management style and processes, would the shareholders continue to support and invest in them and treat their top management like royalty? How doubly sad it would be if that corporation had been given the divine commission to go and teach all nations? The charge against such management might not be full corruption but certainly it is malpractice, in spite of any good intentions.

Religion has been commissioned to instruct and advise on the best practice of living a healthy and rewarding human life. To be human on this Earth is to be physical and biological as well as social and spiritual. Our understanding of all these aspects of humanness is constantly developing as is the social and physical environment in which we live. To fulfill its divine mandate, theology cannot neglect any aspect of human nature or refuse to discuss any topic openly, especially on the premise that they have closed discussion on some subject in the past and that ends it. To put this consideration in the most practical terms, perhaps this is why some shareholders in the Church are voting with their feet.

If the scientific approach is used by religion, how do we get around the ideas believed in the past which might be superseded? There are some good examples that this has already happened. Since Vatican II, Catholics

152

discovered that they can pray with Protestants and not commit the sin of communicatio in sacris, that is, worshiping with non-Catholic Christians. Before Vatican II, this was expressly forbidden. *Mirari Vos*, the 1832 Encyclical of Pope Gregory XVI on liberalism and religious indifferentism taught:

> This shameful font of indifferentism gives rise to that absurd and erroneous proposition which claims that liberty of conscience must be maintained for everyone.... This also was of great concern to the fathers of Trent, who applied a remedy against this great evil by publishing that wholesome decree concerning the Index of books which contain false doctrine. (14)

Yet Pope Gregory's encyclical didn't stop Pope Paul VI from abolishing the *Index of Forbidden Books* in 1966. And it didn't stop Pope John Paul II in his 1980 letter on the eve of the Madrid Conference on European Security and Cooperation from saying; "Freedom of conscience and of religion ... is a primary and inalienable right of the human person; what is more, ...one can even say that it upholds the justification, deeply rooted in each individual, of all other liberties."

We need to be as certain as we can be about matters that contribute profoundly to our successful relationship with God. To desire more may be just a need for security. Would that some religious believers could relax a bit and, like the scientists, enjoy the real world in which we live, even its uncertainties. In the real world there are life-threatening diseases all around us and with ordinary precautions we manage to survive quite handily. If we get hung up on guarding against each and every threat to our health, we will die of a self-inflected nervous breakdown.

All around us there are erroneous theological ideas. Fortunately, very few of them are a threat to our eternal salvation or physical and mental health, especially the dogmatic ones. The enjoyment that comes from being relaxed about these things is not the goal. Rather, the enjoyment is the feeling that comes from knowing that the world is the way God made it and we will never fully understand it. But what we do understand, however inaccurate our expression of it, it is still so very wonderful that it could only have come from the hand of God.

Notes

1. Our Sun, for example, is 864,948 miles in diameter or 109 times

the diameter of the Earth.

2. The Sun is a nuclear reactor. Like all reactors, eventually the fuel begins to run out. The result depends on the size of the star but in the explosive last reaction, the heavier elements form and are expelled as clouds of space dust. This could happen anywhere between one and ten billion years depending on the size of the star. All the constituents of our body are thus the leftover result of dying stars.

3. The death explosion of a star leaves behind an increase of heavy elements formed by the nuclear reaction, the stuff of planets, as well as hydrogen gas. These can eventually form into another star and begin a new stellar generation.

4. The Council of Constance (1414-1418) called to end a schism of multiple popes, issued the decree *Haec sancta* in its fourth session which asserted "that this synod. . . has power immediately from Christ and that everyone of whatever state or dignity, *even papal*, is bound to obey it in those matters which pertain to the faith and the eradication of the said schism." Decrees of the Ecumenical Councils, vol. 1, ed. Norman Tanner (Washington, DC: Georgetown University, 1990, p. 408).

5. Unfortunately, this atmosphere exists today. Pope John Paul II issued his encyclical *Veritatis Splendor* in 1993 to address the fundamental principles of moral theology. Shortly after its publication, an academic theologian was in Rome and attended a social gathering. He recognized a member of the Roman Curia who was known to have been involved in the development of the encyclical so he engaged him in conversation with the hope of learning something about the background of the document. As soon as the individual realized what the theologian's motive was, he brought the conversation to an end by saying, "Don't analyse it, just believe it." To say this to a theologian who is devoting his professional career to the study of moral theology should have embarrassed the speaker. Unfortunately, it didn't.

6. The similarity of this thinking to the Donatist heresy which was condemned in the 4th century is notable.

7. Fortunately even moral insights can develop. I was a student at a seminary in a Southern state in the late 1950s. One day I was driving one of my theology professors. He was a Southerner. We came to a four-way-stop. I probably arrived at the intersection slightly before the car to my right. Nevertheless I waved the car on

in front of me. The driver was a black man. The priest looked at me and said in disbelief, "You let a black man go before you?" This is certainly an example of a serious disconnect of principal from cultural practice.

10

Twenty-first Century Moral Implications

It is one thing to consider the intellectual atmosphere in which science has thrived. It is another to investigate some of the implications of specific scientific data which bump up against religious principles. As always, the devil is in the details. The physical sciences have progressed at an accelerating rate in the last hundred and fifty years. The point can be raised that we have not adequately reconsidered some of the theological implications in light of this progress. Most of us show a reluctance to rethink things we have always believed. We do not enjoy being shown how we have been wrong about something much less how our concepts about God might be improved using science.

We also discover that our theology has attempted to draw on our understanding of nature in many ways, not only how we understand God's involvement in the created world, but especially in some conclusions of moral theology. This is the theology concerning how we use our nature in light of God's purpose in creating that nature, what the moral theologian Louis Janssens described as, "our active commerce with reality." Traditionally theologians use what is known as the natural law model of morality. This is the point at which the physical sciences impact religion most directly. This should be the starting point of our investigation into the implications of natural revelation today.

The natural law model of morality

While there is no single model which serves as a foundation for organizing moral principles, the natural law model is the one most often and most effectively used. Yet the term natural law has more than one meaning. Worse yet, it is often difficult to determine which meaning writers have in mind when using the term. Let me start by describing the meaning which I am NOT using anywhere in this study.

In 1993 the Pope John Paul II issued the encyclical *Veritatis Splendor, The Splendor of Truth*. It was written to address the fundamental principles of Catholic moral theology. The document maintains that, in order to freely choose good and avoid evil, we must be able to distinguish good from evil. We can do this through natural reason "which is the function of the natural law (and) is nothing else but an imprint on us of the divine light." The document is here quoting Thomas Aquinas. It goes on to

156

explain, "This participation of the eternal law in the rational creature is called natural law." (n 43)

The Vatican II document entitled *Pastoral Constitution on the Church in the Modern World* (*Gaudium et Spes*, 1965) equates this internal law with conscience. "Deep within his conscience man discovers a law which he has not laid upon himself but which he must obey…. a law inscribed by God. His dignity lies in observing this law, and by it he will be judged." (n 16)

This meaning of natural law cited in the above two examples has nothing in common with the laws of nature which the scientists discover. There is no physical way to measure or test it. Even the theologian has a problem determining exactly when it is in operation. After all, it has nothing to do with biblical revelation although much of what is in that revelation is human nature. Furthermore, it is found in the hearts of all men, not just believers. In other words, it is natural to all men. As you can see, this is fine in the saying but when faced with a specific decision of the goodness or evil of a particular act, there is bound to be debate and perhaps whole cultures which profess opposite views. *Gaudium et Spes* recognized that even an erroneous conscience must be obeyed. We must leave this view of natural law to the theologians and philosophers.

For the purpose of our discussion, natural law refers to any fact about physical nature which has implications for our view of the nature of the human person as a moral being. Goodness can here be defined as the ability of a thing to achieve the purpose for which it was made. A pen is good if it writes. A car is good if it runs. A pen which did not write lacks a physical good and this is a physical evil with respect to its purpose. Evil in this sense is a negative quality, a lack of a good which should be there. The laws of our physical nature impact the moral order because it is impossible to break a law of nature. The law breaks us when we try to disregard it. Sooner or later we will suffer the physical consequences.

The principle is simple enough. An act which attempts to violate our nature as a human being is morally evil. We are not talking about guilt here but the act itself. Guilt derives from the person knowing at the time the act was done that it was against the moral order and still the person did it. Gravity is a simple example. Since we humans are made of physical stuff, we are subject to the law of gravity. If I step over a cliff, it is not the law of gravity I break when I reach the bottom. The law breaks me because I tried to disregard it. Furthermore, life is sacred and if I knowingly push someone off the cliff, I am responsible for the effect that gravity has on their biological nature.

But this example is a mechanical one. There is no way to avoid gravity and the effect comes quickly. It is when we start to comprehend the natural world as a whole, as an environment in which we live and are a part, that aspects of its laws impact our notions of morality and contains an element of judgment. The physical operations which are at play in the Sun or the orbital motion of galaxies and solar systems are far simpler than the functions occurring in a bacteria much less a human body. The fact is that today we understand these astronomical processes far better than we do living organisms. More and more people are aware of this. If religion is to maintain any credibility it must be seen as recognizing these understandings and taking the fact of our physical nature as evidence to be considered in our moral decisions. There is, however, evidence that this connection is not always being made.

The natural law and the metaphysical

On 12 February, 2007, Pope Benedict XVI gave a short address to the International Congress on Natural Law which was organized by the Pontifical Lateran University in Rome. With reference to the "extraordinary development in the human capacity to decipher the rules and structures of matter" he pointed out that, "we see more and more clearly the threat of destruction of nature by what we do." Clearly he is here speaking about our increased understanding of how physical nature works. The nature we can destroy is our physical environment. Then he goes on to say:

> There is another less visible danger, but no less disturbing: the method that permits us to know ever more deeply the rational structures of matter makes us ever less capable of perceiving the source of this rationality, creative reason. The capacity to see the laws of material being makes us incapable of seeing the ethical message contained in being, a message that tradition calls lex naturalis, natural moral law.

The implication of what he is saying here is unfortunate. The title of his talk uses the term Natural Law. He begins with an observation on the danger of our understanding of physical natural laws as a possible destroyer of our natural world. Then he states that the more we understand this physical law, the less we are able to discern the natural moral law. His conclusion seems to be that since the sciences are empirical, based on experimentation and observation, those who practice it cannot also deal with what he refers to as "the metaphysical." Here metaphysical refers to those things or human capacities which are not based on our physical composition but are still natural to us such as the ability to make moral judgements, recognize right from wrong and establish value.

This proposed disparity between religion and science is difficult to justify. Isaac Newton concluded *The Principia* by commenting on how it was obvious from the unity of nature that one Being governs it all and we call him Lord God. Albert Einstein said that science without religion is lame; religion without science is blind.

We recognize that it is religion which is concerned with the questions we are all asking: how do we relate with others and God, what is the purpose of it all, what is good and what is evil? Natural science on the other hand is not asking any of these questions. Just because it is empirical, physical and not metaphysical, however, does not mean that it is of no use in discerning these important questions. It is simply more difficult to deal with metaphysical questions.

Nor does it mean that the metaphysical is not part of the reality of our universe and totally excluded from the interests of the scientist. When scientists today consider, as they do, the possibility of the existence of many universes, they are dealing with metaphysical concepts. Since by definition we will never be able to physically detect the presence of any universe except our own, the scientist is using abstract reasoning and arriving at a subtle theory about physical reality. Because the process is reasonable and about physical things, they are not scoffed at by fellow scientists or philosophers. There is always the possibility that simply being aware of the possibility and logic of the existence of other universes may give an additional insight into the one we know and live in.

These encroachments into the metaphysical not only demonstrate the possibility of science to find metaphysics of interest, it also implies a recognition on the part of science that metaphysics has a legitimate place in our search for truth about ourselves as a conscious and reflective species. But it is up to the theologian to make the connections between the two worlds of understanding, physical and metaphysical. After all, moral theology is not an empirical science. It is part of the humanities. At its best it is connective and embraces the whole spectrum of human understandings and attempts to relate and evaluate them. Yet it cannot do this without reference to the physical world.

Pope Benedict XVI maintains that the better we are at empirical science, the more difficult it is for us to comprehend "the source of rationality, creative reason." It is as if there is no use for creativity in scientific reasoning. Arthur Koestler deals directly with the place of creativity in three aspects of human thought. "All creative activity ... have a basic pattern in common: the co-agitation or shaking together of already existing but previously separate areas of knowledge, frames of perception or universes of discourse."[1]

Isaac Newton suddenly realized that what held the planets in orbit around the Sun and the moon around the Earth was the same gravity that held him on the surface of the Earth, not to mention makes apples fall to the ground. This was creative reasoning of the highest order. He was the first person in human history to make a connection between things everyone could see with their eyes but had not seen with their creative reason.

Can religion be creative or empirical?

It might be suggested that, if creativity is the shaking together of previously separate ideas, it is theology which needs to be encouraged to make the connections between religion and scientific understanding. Unless that encouragement is given, theologians will constantly bump up against the tradition barrier and creativity will be stifled. The two things which can depress creativity most are tradition and authoritarianism. Science is by definition too restricted in its scope to deal with things which its language, mathematics, cannot describe. When dealing with the origin of the physical universe, however, the physicist can become very philosophical. Science can deal directly only with things that can be physically measured or defined. But for the creative thinker, some of those measurements can be used to describe the dimensions of God and how we should form his image in our consciousness. The rest of God's dimensions can only be hinted at by metaphysical concepts and that is the role of theology.

In the scientific community, those who are good at shaking together ideas often face opposition. In some of the most pressing scientific issues today, for example the role of CO_2 in global warming, there are scientists who disagree. But when the experts disagree, that is a good sign. It means that wider consideration by more people is being brought to the question. This is the most effective way to a correct understanding. Theologians should also enjoy this intellectual atmosphere. When open discussion is not possible, the scholar is left only the possibility of writing books that no one in leadership is likely to read and we are all the poorer for that. If theologians could state moral principals in evolutionary terms they would get the attention of scientists and earn broader credibility than enjoyed within the narrower community of their theologian peers.

To express moral principles in evolutionary terms would not require a theologian who also had a degree in Biology. What the theologian often does not appreciate is the scientific method of drawing a conclusion. The reasoning goes from theory and evidence supporting the theory through experimentation to a judgement of the likelihood of its validity. Most important to the non-scientist are the implications the conclusions have to their areas of interest. One does not have to understand the details of the proof for a scientific conclusion to be able to use it productively any more than you must remember the way π is derived to use it in a computation. What is required is to have enough respect for the integrity and rigor with which scientists draw their conclusions to risk seeing what the implications are in a particular theological issue. After all, if it is a physical reality, then it cannot be in conflict with a valid theological conclusion.

All too often what happens is that the theologian tends to jump to the defense of the traditional theological position and dismiss or ignore the science. The most important requirement for anyone publicly entering into the debate on either side is that they possess the credibility which comes from broad understanding and a record of willingness to consider all aspects of the question before drawing conclusions. They must have a reputation for creative reasoning. These characteristics can also serve to moderate the language used in the zeal to promote religious or scientific principles.

In theology, the natural law principle works well when dealing with generalities arrived at by philosophical logic, e.g. murder violates personal and social good. We can reason to the principles of human rights although it has taken Western society a long time to codify them. Some of these involve our physical nature, even life and death. But what about the many prohibitions in the *Old Testament?* Many of its dietary laws were simply good hygiene and are no longer seen as moral precepts in themselves. The danger with the meat of pigs was the disease trichinosis. Circumcision can be beneficial in circumstances where good hygiene is difficult. Today, it is being recommended for sound biological reasons as a way of reducing infection with HIV in countries with high infection rates.[2]

The danger is that moral prohibitions which arose from strictly non-moral reasons soon become part of tradition and, in a moral system based on the natural law, are then assumed to be a violation of nature. In a time when the male was understood to have in his "seed" a microscopic but fully formed human being, masturbation could be portrayed as murder, and at times it was. Very often philosophical conclusions about right and wrong human actions are drawn from knowledge of the physical effects of acts and their implications. The accuracy of the conclusion depends on the completeness of the physical knowledge about the thing involved and our ability to make the proper logical connections independent of traditional thinking.

While at times it may be an uncomfortable liaison, ethicists have been forced to use empirical methods. Before ethical norms can be applied in a nuanced way, the extent and impact of ethical issues must be understood. In business ethics, this requires the use of standard empirical methods used by business itself. Nor are honesty or fairness the only issues. Ethnic or gender discrimination as well as the exercise of power and control require attention. Some data of ethical interest are difficult to quantify, for example degree of remorse, data privacy and security or the obligation of corporate entities to be open to shareholder scrutiny. It seems that at present empirical ethics is in a marriage of convenience with research methods. While the research results may not be the thing which drives the conclusion of right or wrong, it can inform and direct the proper application of ethical norms.

Some moral questions

We need to look more deeply into some specific examples of where natural law can contribute to theological considerations. Our purpose here is not to analyze selected topics with the hope of leading to a conclusion about them. Rather, I select these questions because they are current, important and demonstrate how better scientific understanding can contribute to theological considerations, if only by exposing their true complexity and the reason we find so many supporters on either side of the moral debate. To recognize that people can reasonably take sides in these issues is important because we must know that there are questions which, by their nature, will never be answered with certainty. Yet, because these questions cannot be avoided, decisions must be made by individuals, governments and society in general.

As we have pointed out earlier, science generates new technologies. These technologies make new things possible. Once this happens, we are faced with decisions about the value of these possibilities. Just because we can do something does not mean that it should be done. On the other hand, these possibilities might impose their own obligation to do them because of their beneficial effect. The issues raised here are not simply questions of biological procedures. They are also issues which affect persons and relationships.

162

Every human person is a fellow human person. This means that our moral judgments must be based on the dignity of the human person as well as the promotion of their physical, personal and social wellbeing. When science raises new possibilities, the moralist must consult science in order to gain insights into precisely what is happening in the physical process. Technology tells us what can be done with our physical nature but we must do it in a human way.

Consider the fertilized, single celled ovum which is the beginning of a human being. All the information needed to develop into an adult human person is there along with the physical capacity to protect, nourish and replicate itself with astonishing accuracy. It all seemed magical and in need of divine assistance or at least that of a spiritual soul. Although biology now has a better understanding of the physical reasons for this amazing behavior, it does not eliminate the eventual, non-physical (spiritual?) aspects of it, even altruism and an awareness of the transcendent, and this is more than hinted at in the quantum view of nature. We pass now to how biological science can possibly inform moral decisions in the matter of human reproduction.

First the egg and sperm

It was only in the seventeenth century that the role of egg and sperm was discovered. The details of exactly what is happening in the process of fertilization came much later as the science of embryology progressed. Today we talk of "the moment of conception" but which moment is that? Fertilization is a process, not a moment, and can take up to 24 hours. In such a process, could it be that the importance of what happens at any moment depends on its efficacy with respect to the future? For example, the formation of a genetically complete single cell at fertilization may have only physical significance in that it simply enables later separation at the multi-cell stage into two identical twin human individuals. If that first cell is genetically flawed in some way which prevents it from implanting when it reaches the uterus, how certain can we be that it was ever a human individual? The element of time begins to demand our attention and clarification and intrudes itself into our calculations of the beginning of a human individual.

Upon encountering the egg, the sperm cell must bind to the outer membrane of the egg. It then digests this membrane at the point of adhesion so that the sperm can fuse with the interior of the egg. When this happens, the membrane of the egg changes to prevent any further fusion by another sperm. Once fusion takes place, there is still much to be

163

accomplished. The chromosomes must be aligned to form DNA so that the single cell which results is genetically complete and can undergo cell division. Since this cell and those which immediately follow can develop into any of the numerous cell types and organs of the body, it is difficult to say that this cell has individuality or can be considered a person. In fact, if the first two cells formed after the first cell division become separated, each can develop into a unique individual and, as we pointed out above, we have identical twins.

All this has occurred in the fallopian tube and the original cell undergoes further division in the few days it can take to travel into the uterus. At this point, the organism implants in the wall of the uterus where it can develop to maturity. This lengthly process makes the moment of conception an arbitrary decision.

It is at this point that recent research has revealed data which impacts the moral questions surrounding the beginning of a human person. Different researchers have arrived at a range of values so we will deal with ranges and not specific values. It has been determined that from 15% to 30% of fertilized eggs do not implant but pass out of the body. This is called a spontaneous abortion. Of those which do implant, another 15% to 30% are released and spontaneously abort. As a result, it can be said that from 30% to 60%, or more according to some researchers, are spontaneously aborted within the first 20 days after fertilization and often without the woman being aware of it. The reasons for these natural abortions are numerous: infection of the uterus, poor health of the mother, chemical influences causing an imperfectly formed product of fertilization etc.

The observation which this suggests is that, if we maintain that the human being begins at the moment of conception, nature appears to have a very cavalier approach to human life in its first twenty days of existence compared to the way we look upon the embryo. Nature seems to reject as many as 30% of them. I do not raise this question as a way to disprove or refute the principle that we must consider the product of fertilization as being human from that first moment. We recognize that the exact moment when a human person begins life will never be known with scientific or theological certainty. Still, fertilization begins the dynamic process through which human life is generated. In fact, the dynamics of that process will continue to develop until the physical death of the person.

In stating that a human being occurs at the moment of conception, the moral principle being used is that in situations in which it is impossible to be certain, we must choose the safest option. Because of the importance of human life, we cannot argue with that decision. It can be compared to the debate going on within science about the causes of global warming. With so much at stake, can we risk not taking the safest alternative? Yet we must also recognize that those who find the application of this principle flawed in certain circumstances are not necessarily doing so unreasonably. It is also the case that by using physical natural law as the basis of moral decisions, this particular question is made more complicated and indecisive, especially when we consider how ill-defined the moment of conception is and how nature herself deals with the result of fertilization.

From an extremely traditional point of view, God must create each individual soul at conception. Being God, this can be accomplished at whatever stage God wants. It would seem most reasonable and advantageous to do this, not in a mechanical way when the chromosomes of egg and sperm are aligning themselves to form complete DNA, but rather at the point when the living entity has a good chance of reaching sufficient complexity and achieving birth and becoming a human person. Twins raises the question about how many souls were there at fertilization. We do believe in a reasonable God and try to take example from God's way of doing things.

It is accurate to say that personhood at the moment of conception is a theory. Evolution is also a theory but has much scientific evidence to support it while this is lacking in the theological case. All this suggests that theology needs to take these uncertainties into consideration when trying to deal with exceptional cases of individuals.

Reproductive science

Greater uncertainty arises when we try to engage this principle of conception in particular cases where humans, not nature, intervene in the reproductive process by deliberately causing the abortion or bringing about fertilization outside of the normal sexual function. It may well be that the moral solution is to use another model for arriving at our moral decisions. Artificial insemination is a case in point. As already stated, our purpose here is not to develop the moral arguments involved with the intention of reaching a decisive conclusion. Rather, our intent is to show how advancing technology makes new demands on the process of making moral decisions by offering new possibilities for human acts. These decisions are best made by taking an interdisciplinary approach to the subject.

Artificial insemination has four permutations. Fertilization can occur in the uterus by introduction of sperm through mechanical means (insemination in vivo) or outside the uterus (insemination in vitro) in a glass container and then introduced into the uterus. Both of these procedures can be done in two ways, either with the sperm of the husband or an anonymous donor. While each case has its own specific moral complications, we need only comment on the moral question common to all four.

If we use a purely natural law methodology, we conclude that none of these possibilities is acceptable. This was the stance taken by Pope Pius XII (d 1958). The basic consideration was that there is a natural physical function of the sexual organs which constitutes the nature of humankind and this controls the moral use of the sexual function. In artificial insemination, this function is violated in any number of ways starting with the manner in which the semen is obtained. But this approach does not take into consideration that a moral person is a subject and not an object or purely biological entity. A person is a conscious subject with conscience. We are also social persons with necessary relationships to others. A one dimensional biological approach is simplistic and inadequate.

It may be that the advent of so many technological procedures such as artificial insemination have made us keenly aware of the necessity to take a more personalist approach to morality. After all, why would a husband and wife be considering artificial insemination? It is to circumvent whatever barrier nature has placed in them which means that, without the procedure, they will be childless. Moral good should promote the human person adequately considered. To adequately consider a husband and wife, we must take into account their dignity as individuals, their mutual love for each other, their corporeal nature as sexual beings, their natural desire for the fulfillment of parenthood, the safeguard all this can be to their relationship and the social good that these elements can produce.

In any discussion of human reproductive science there is an elephant in the room and it is the physical and emotional pleasure which is given and received in the function of our sexuality. Ever since the negative and blinkered approach of Augustine of Hippo (354-430), theologians have not considered nor thought to develop a theology of pleasure. When Pope Pius XII refers to the natural physical function of the sexual organs, pleasure and interpersonal emotional satisfaction are not part of the consideration. We are limited to the realm of a biological function in the determination of moral use.

In recent years we have developed acceptable euphemisms. When I was young, the moral theologians talked about the moral sexual act as one in which there was "depositing of seed in the vagina." Today we say that which is "open to the transmission of life."[3] Enjoyment of sexual pleasure is also a major but unspoken factor in dealing with the question of homosexuality.

These are the lines along which the technology of fertilization has been pointing the moralist. As the theologian Louis Janssens put it, we must be "realistically led by an ethics of responsibility, one in which the objective criterion is 'the person integrally and adequately considered'"[4] By raising such considerations, this improved understanding of human reproduction and sexuality is providing another form of natural revelation. These moral considerations are no less complicated by the fact that ensoulment is not an observable phenomenon nor a revealed theological truth but rather a theory, a logical, ethical conclusion drawn through philosophical principles. When dealing with humankind moral decisions cannot be made simply from biological considerations. As conscious and rational persons, we seek a human existence which is worthy of our totality as unique yet related social beings. The natural functions of our corporeal nature must be dealt with in a human and not just clinical way.

How free are we?

Another area of study to which recent science can contribute is the question of free will and associated with that, our ability to relate socially to others. Today we would have to admit that our approach to free will has, in the past, been rather simplistic. The traditional assumption was that the human person was by nature free to choose and that is what constitutes a moral decision. Things which might reduce freedom were fear, force or coercion as well as physical impairments such as drunkenness or addiction. Beyond that, there was not much more to be said.

For the scientist before quantum physics, the physical laws of Newton determined everything in a predictable way. As science developed and the more the laws of physics were understood, it began to appear that all physical events were determined by them. If you had enough information about the initial conditions, you could predict the future events which they produced. This raised the suspicion among some scientists that since all physical events were determined, so too are all human actions and reactions.

If we knew enough about their origin, so-called free choices might also prove to be determined in some way. It is a parallel to the idea of seemingly random events being subject to a sensitive dependence on initial conditions. The appearance of free choice may be caused by the presence of such a large number of influences, motives and rules or physical laws influencing behavior, that there are infinite possibilities of apparently unpredictable behavior. As a result, it only looks as though the person is free to choose from all these possibilities. Thus either free will is just a feeling of freedom of choice which we enjoy but not a reality, or it is simply beyond the boundary at which physical laws end and so can be ignored by science.

It was a natural thing that science should turn its attention to how decisions are made in what is now called neurobiology. Since the development of Magnetic Resonance Imaging (MRI) and other devices, it has become possible to see which parts of the brain are active during particular mental activity. The electrochemistry of the brain can be watched in the process of making decisions and responding to stimuli. This makes it possible to see what is going on in the brain during the process of being conscious. It has also been found that a degree of influence can be had over those decisions by stimulating the brain in ways not detectable by the subject being scanned.[5]

Influencing behavior has also become a part of the science of psychiatry with the successful use of drugs to modify behavior. This raises the question of how much the chemical balance occurring naturally within the human body controls behavior and thus influences what looks like free choice. We do not think of mental illness as a defect of the soul but something which is physically based. This demonstrates how complex the concept of free will can be. Prisons are populated by many people who cannot see beyond the next hour and are not able to seriously consider the consequences of their actions.

This also begs the question, how much are human decisions controlled by nurture and how much by nature? The concern is about what we consider good behavior as well as undesirable behavior. Is there, for example, an altruistic gene which moves a person to act for the benefit of others that involves either cost to the agents or at least no gain to them? This gave rise to interest in evolutionary psychology which investigates the contribution altruistic behavior might make on the survivability of the individual or species.

The altruism question is complicated in theological terms by the fact that, strictly speaking, there is no purely altruistic act which does not bring anticipated reward, either in this life or the next. This can be a strong influence on motive. For the scientist, altruism is purely a secular consideration in which they look to police or soldiers and not to saints or martyrs as subjects. The necessary approach of the scientist to these questions is mechanistic in the sense of being physically based. Rather than see their conclusions as a threat, the theologian should see them as opening up our understanding of the human species. That understanding is a rich field waiting for cultivation with the spiritual and social values which only theology can bring to it.

The nature vs nurture question can be revealing. Nature is the bundle of instincts and proclivities our genes bring us. No human being was ever a blank slate. To admit of nurture implies that the demands of nature are not absolute. Free will and judgement allow us some control. Our nature is malleable and both nature and nurture evolve. There is no advantage in attributing things to a supernatural soul when it can be demonstrated to be physical and, perhaps, even evolutionary. Science describes what nature tends to do. Religion nurtures the individual and society toward beneficial, civilised behavior. Both influence the evolutionary survival of the species and individual.

Persons, souls and societies

The idea of a soul can accumulate a lot of baggage. It is where we reside as a person. As a person, we are aware of everything we consider as our self. It is the self within us which is the decision-maker and theology insists that we are capable of deciding and acting freely. Not all scientists insist that what we experience as self and free decision-making is simply a place in the brain where these functions reside and can be detected with the proper instrumentation. Yet everything we have said so far does not make the notion of a soul any easier to grasp.

Nor does it insinuate that the notion of a soul is a gratuitous one. What it should indicate to us is that it is going to take the best theological, philosophical and scientific minds to deal with the nature of the human soul. To be sure, the theologian has the more difficult task. He is the one who must take the best scientific and spiritual thinking and translate it into useful concepts and images which can help us all live meaningful lives. These can be understood as the practical implications of the personhood of the soul. We have the example of scientists and engineers who take the best scientific thinking and from it develop technology for the benefit of humanity.

Little progress in understanding the soul can be made if we cannot discuss possibilities other than those from longstanding tradition. Do we need to demand that God exercise in time a separate creative act in the origin of every human soul? What does this say about the wholesale loss of souls through natural, spontaneous abortions? Could there be another possibility which was not imaginable in the cultural setting which gave rise to our traditional view?

169

To understand the soul, it is not sufficient to consider only its origin. It is time now to reconsider life after death. Our understanding of the soul after death must be compatible with its nature before death. Perhaps it could be helpful to reconsider the traditional formulas about the resurrection of the body and the personhood of the soul before and after death. This would not be a technical exercise but a pastoral effort to bring spirituality into the twenty-first century.

The fact that we strongly experience the functioning of freedom in our decision making suggests that there is an evolutionary survival value in it for the human species and us as individuals. It cannot be just some kind of sensory illusion. It may be at this point that the evolutionary ideas of Teilhard de Chardin with respect to humanity become useful. In the postscript to *The Phenomenon of Man*, he summarizes the phenomenon or evolution of humankind as the product of a cosmic law of complexity-consciousness. Consciousness and later reflectivity are present in some rudimentary form in material substance but perceptible only in conjunction with great complexity. The very nature of physical substance guarantees that, with unlimited patience, greater complexity will take place as conditions allow and lead to a new form of biological existence. And just as we say that instincts, which are simply valid solutions to given problems, evolved in a species, so too future solutions to personal and human social problems will evolve into instinctive and thus natural responses.

Teilhard is sometimes dismissed as a creative dreamer or poet and neither a scientist nor theologian in his conclusions. This view fails to recognize the broad and unifying scope of Chardin's proposals. In quantum physics we learn that we cannot determine the position and the momentum of an electron at the same time. We resort to visualizing it as a cloud of probability or potentiality around the atomic nucleus. This does not make electrons less real or limit our ability to make use of them. Nor does it turn the scientist into a mere poet. What makes the electron real in quantum terms is that it is intelligible, not that we can nail all its characteristics down at any given moment. In the same way, the perception of reflection and consciousness in the human psyche, or could we say soul or person, depends on a certain minimum complexity but that makes it no less real.

The theologian Wolfhardt Pannenberg has been able to "shake together" ideas of the human person and the evolutionary future of the human species. For Pannenberg, revelation is not just in the word of God but in the actions of God as well. This is best seen in the approach we now take to the revelation contained in the *Old Testament* and how the events depicted collectively reveal the providence of God toward humanity. He states;

> The difference between human beings and other animals is not that the human being has a "living soul," but that it is destined to exist in a particular relationship to God, so that it is called to represent the Creator himself with regard to the animal world and even to the earth (Gen. 1:26).[6]

The insight that by being made in the image of God we are God's representative is not poetic trivia. It is the reason why human history is seen as a history of God's involvement with humanity and also why the human being is creative and can influence human evolution by influencing our cultural and social environment.

Moral issues involve the manner in which we relate to other persons as well as God. Moral judgments involve love, awareness of the feelings of others and how they relate to ourselves. Autism, for example, is a complex disorder of the central nervous system which impairs the ability to relate to others in these ways. While the causes of the condition are not well known, it seems clear that there is a genetic basis which influences the early development of the brain areas in which these functions reside. Research has shown that if one identical twin has autism, the chances are as much as 85% to 90% that the other will have it. In non-identical twins, the chances of both having the condition are as low as 4%. Findings such as these demonstrate that the freedom of choice in human behavior is not a simple matter which yields easily to general moral principles.

Again, evolution is a survival mechanism. Thus religion must be part of the survival mechanism of mankind by contributing to human wellbeing. This sometimes happens by resisting or transforming our physically and hard-wired impulses. Except for some perverted examples, religions throughout history have been aware of this although usually not with any nod to the analogy with biological evolution. Any religion which is not keenly aware of its influence on human survivability risks being simply an indifferent social phenomenon concerned only with preserving itself. In the Christian sense, religion must concern itself not just with salvation but survival for the individual, society and species.

The whole human rights movement, the global health concerns for developing countries and the economic benefits of fair and free trade are also mechanisms of survival for individuals and societies in a world in which the social and economic climate is constantly evolving. This includes support of realistic means of achieving good reproductive health and family stability. This is an expression of respect for individuals, family and society as a whole. These are also examples of the human person adequately considered. It is of great value to humankind that religious concerns can promote these efforts.

Notes

1. Arthur Koestler (1967) *The Ghost in the Machine*, Picador.
2. *The Lancet*, 24 February 2007. There may have been a social motive for the prohibition. The pagans also ate pork so the prohibition became a rejection of and separation from paganism.
3. We shudder to think of the implications this approach might have if applied to our social practice of dinning and food preparation. We have a hint of this in the revulsion some people express to the preparation of foie gras, all for a minimal increase of taste sensation, or the price paid for some fine wines.
4. *Louvain Studies*, 1980-1981
5. This topic is considered so important that, in June of 2010, a $4.4 million four year grant was awarded by the John Templeton Foundation for the study of free will.
6. Wolfhart Pannenberg (2008) *The Historicity of Nature*, Templeton Foundation Press.

11

Twenty-first Century Spiritual Life

The way we relate to another person depends on who they are, the type of person, their character, how they are involved in our life. People of faith are also in a relationship with God. Religion, however, is not like our relationship with a bank where we put money into our account and expect to collect so much interest or expect to be able to withdraw it from a cash machine at a convenient time and place. Religion is a relationship with a divine person and we refer to that relationship as our spiritual life.

The way we relate to a person on a daily and informal basis changes as time passes. We change because of new experiences and, therefore, have different interests than we had before. Our understanding of the person to whom we relate changes as well. Thus the character of our relationship changes. Since the first chapter of this book we have been investigating the things that God has done, things brought to light by our better understanding of the natural world of which we are a part. We have labeled this natural revelation. In a number of places we have pointed out how our image of God could change because of our better understanding of the natural world.

It is valid to say that the broader our understanding of the created universe, the greater are our possibilities to relate to the Creator. An infant or young child relates on the level of emotions and need fulfillment. It is true to say that while we look at an infant and think how loving it is, in fact that infant is at the most selfish stage it will ever be in its life. And so it should be. Nature contrives to give them every opportunity and support to grow not only physically but in experience, to understand the world around them. The things they need and seek from their parents and the way they seek them are very different from the way they do these same things as they age and mature.

When we look at Homo sapiens as a species, as an evolving society, the same is true. In the oldest physical evidences of human society we find indications of primitive methods to express relationship with the superior being who controls the nature and events which society depended on but could not understand. Stonehenge and cave paintings appear to contain such evidence. In more recent times of which we have detailed record, or have participated in ourselves, it is still a record of how we relate both as a community and as an individual to a perceived divinity and what we expect from that relationship.

For some individuals their relationship with God is very much like the relationship they want to maintain with their bank. They are willing to pay reasonable charges so long as the service is there when needed and being known by the bank may help one day when a large loan is required. But other relationships we carry on with individuals are done not so much from what we can get or the chance of future need. Instead, they are relationships that we enjoy. We value relationships because these people are good to be around. At its best, they are people with a bit of wisdom upon which we can rely and against whom we can project our own thoughts and decisions and seek their opinions. In the comparison with a maturing child, the relationship of Homo sapiens, of human society, with God must progress from the stage of fulfilling needs and receiving affection to enjoying company, appreciating what the other person has accomplished and respecting their opinions. The relationship must become more adult.

The fact that natural revelation changes our image of God should offer possibilities to change the way we relate to God. Furthermore, human society is not static. Increased population density and technology have altered the survival focus of Homo sapiens. Globalization has increased our opportunities to relate to our neighbor who may just live on the other side of the world. Our ability to be aware of such neighbors and affect their lives is magnified and that magnifies us. This is a major change in the perspective of religion. The practical result is that the language and method of worship, in other words our formal and informal conversations with God, is bound to evolve.

There are more than nine hundred stone rings in the British Isles. The best known, Stonehenge, appears to be the celebration of the alignment of the Sun at the winter and summer turning points of the seasons. Even today self-styled druids find satisfaction in showing the god of the Sun recognition of his fidelity and regularity by assembling each year at Stonehenge. Perhaps those who built Stonehenge went away from their celebrations feeling more secure, feeling that their future for the next six months would be more favorable because they incurred the favor of the Sun. Such was the nature of their spirituality. That feeling of security was not unnecessary, unneeded and in that sense did no harm and was a positive influence in that primitive society.

What about us today? I am not trying to raise some odious comparison by asking this. Through the ingenuity of human society and the science that it developed we now have a more sophisticated understanding of that Sun, how it influences our lives. I suppose we could say that natural revelation has taught us that we are correct in relying on it. It follows all the Newtonian laws which are immutable and make the Sun 's position predictable. Astrophysics tells us that it is very likely to remain that way for another billion years or so. I suspect that with that knowledge we come away with an even greater feeling of satisfaction and security than did the original worshipers at Stonehenge.

We need now to investigate further our understanding of God as a person. The question then remains how we choose to relate to that person. Has that relationship been influenced at all by natural revelation? Perhaps the first judgement to be made is in the characterization of our relationship. At what stage of maturing have we arrived? Are we the infant or young child seeking need fulfillment and affection? Are we just emerging from our teens and very much filled with our own abilities and trying to express our independence and keen to express our own opinions which were formed in an atmosphere of very little experience? Or have we reached the age in which we can relax with our friend in a coffee shop or over a bottle of beer or wine and engage in enjoyable as well as informative conversation? We may not have thought of our spirituality in these terms but isn't this the stuff of human relationships? And the only way God can expect us to relate to him is through our humanity. It is only possible here to take a cursory view of how natural revelation can affect our spiritual lives but it should be worth doing.

Defining spirituality

What we usually refer to as our spiritual life includes all the ways we respond to our understanding of God and the way we think he wants us to relate to him. This includes such things as prayer and worship as a person and a community. Spirituality tries to make sense out of a world in which we as physical, biological as well as social creatures try to come to terms with so many aspects of our life. These are aspects for which we can find little physical basis. Unless we take all these things into consideration, we are not dealing with the human person as a whole.

Healthy spirituality should lead to growth into the full person we are capable of being. Does self-abasement and constant focus on ourselves promote growth as a person? Spirituality is the constant striving to be as fully mature as I can be at the particular stage of my life. This must be measured by my relationships with God as well as the people and physical environment around me. The development of my spiritual life never reaches a conclusion. We never arrive, but only search.

Spirituality must take into account that we are by nature physical, intellectual, artistic, social and moral beings. Keeping physically fit is part of our responsibility to ourselves. Our intellect formulates the rational basis for the way we think and act and must constantly be informed. Artistic creativity is the celebration of one of the most human characteristics we possess on both the intellectual and emotional level. Our social skills are what contribute to our survivability as a species on Earth and make human life worth living. Our moral principles reflect not only our self-image but the value we place on our relationship to others, the world and God. To be properly realized, all this must be executed out of a full recognition that these capabilities reside in a biological organism with all the aptitudes/talents/abilities and demands with which evolution has endowed it.

A relationship with God can only happen if God is a person. The way we relate to a person very much depends on how we understand that person and how we perceive the way that person has dealt with us in the past. This is true not only with our relationship with people we know but with God as well. In the time of the *Old Testament*, the world and God were understood through primitive and faulty common sense views of our world. In fact, these faulty notions lasted into the sixteenth century and beyond. The Old Testament image of God was dominated by all the images which society had of their earthly rulers. Most often, and even into recent times, these biblical rulers were thought to be chosen by God. Although not exclusively, they were honored as wise legislators and judges, great military leaders and very one-sided on behalf of their own subjects at the expense of any outsiders. They demanded obedience and could be very jealous. They usually dealt harshly with enemies.

With the advent of the *New Testament*, Jesus softened that image and emphasized love and social concern for everyone. In the mystery of God's incarnation as a man through the birth of Jesus, God revealed the ultimate nature of our relationship with him. By taking on our human nature, God revealed that we are capable of sharing his spiritual nature. This happens by being metaphysically incorporated into the life of Christ by what we call divine grace. This is the great and central mystery of Christianity. Although our identity as a person includes a material, corporeal entity, our relationship with God, however that is implemented, cannot be physical or material. It is non-physical or spiritual.

If religion means taking due notice of God and acting accordingly, in Christian terms, a difficult question presents itself. How much notice does God really require? There is also the possibility that we are using the wrong word here. Does God need our notice, or does he require or demand

176

our notice? These are not the same things. And why would God need anything from us? The answer to these questions must be reflected in our spirituality. A healthy spirituality promotes an awareness of the connections between our self, our neighbor and the physical world. Anything short of that makes it shallow and nearsighted.

Finally, we must not confuse spirituality with religiosity or piety. Having a sense of what is spiritual about us does not mean sprinkling our speech with pious vocabulary or phrases such as "God willing", "Praised be God" and the like. Nor does it require changing the way we dress or groom ourselves. Spirituality is an internal conviction and disposition. It may manifest itself in external signs but not necessarily. It is based on our perception of ourselves, God and the world around us. But all of this is the result of the design built into creation. Revealed texts as well as natural revelation have much to tell us about that design.

Is God a person?

When we talk about a personal God, we do not mean that there exists three separate persons in God, in other words, the Trinity. This is a separate theological question. But we can logically deal with God as a person. In practical terms, we could not pray to God if he were not a person. People who like driving enjoy spending time using their automobile. They may even personify how the car responds to their control. But while they may become skilled at controlling the car, they cannot form a true relationship with it. The car responds only as it must by virtue of the way it is designed and the driver can become sensitive to the way it handles. This can seem like establishing a relationship with the car. We can, however, establish a relationship with another person.

It is in this way that we can say God is a person and it is possible to relate to God. By custom, we use the personal pronoun him. And, as in all personal relationships, any relationship with this God can be characterized by love, mutual concern and sharing of understandings and experiences. History shows that we tend toward such relationships not only with other humans but with God as well. Relating is a natural human instinct. For pagans the gods were a solution to the problem of trying to understand and influence things around them which they could not otherwise explain.

Today believers consider the general history of Israel which is recorded in the *Old Testament* as demonstrating that there has been an intervention of God in the progress of the people of Israel even if not in the specific details related in the *Old Testament*. Storytelling was the primary method of teaching in that period of history. The *Old Testament* also offers directions from God on how to relate to him. More directly, Christians understand Jesus as the incarnation of that God as a human person so that he could instruct us more personally and demonstrate the extent of God's love and concern for all humanity.

The concept of a personal God is a difficult one and not within the scope of this book. I briefly touch upon it here to show the scale of the difficulty and to indicate how this might engage the scientist. As we saw in chapter 8, physics has become fully involved in the mysteries of cosmology, the origin of the universe, and as such, analogously shares many of the uncertainties with which theology is faced. As mentioned earlier, however, scientists seem better able to handle that uncertainty than some religious thinkers.

A Creator God could be thought of as some form of force or energy that existed before the beginning of the physical world we know. But this idea is as unsubstantial as when someone might say that you could feel the energy in the room. Perhaps, but it cannot be measured nor is it detectable by everyone present. If by person we have in mind a distinct individual locatable in the sense we ordinarily use that term, then we are severely restricting the notion of a personal God to the inherent limitations of human knowledge and language which is based on physical experience. This falls far short of the notion of a God who is a person.

Our language can only deal with God by drawing analogies. As soon as we say, "God is..." we must immediately add, "But of course he really isn't." When we talk about a particular person we know, the things that make them different from any other person are not so much their physical attributes as what they have decided to make of these attributes and how they choose to relate with us and others. From the viewpoint of evolution, relationship is a survival mechanism. It is what produces a caring society and promotes the good of society as well as the individuals in it.

At its root, religion is meant to promote and enhance the evolution of individuals and society toward a higher state of perfection. This means enhancing survivability. While great progress has been made at the community as well as the international level, it is clear that this evolution has a long way to go. Furthermore, the historical evidence of the involvement of religions in things which worked against the good of society has produced some cynicism. The numerous examples of an apparent absence of the hand of a caring God have led such people to reject the notion of a personal God. Some of them are scientists and this is understandable. This does not make science the enemy of religion. For some, scientists and non-scientists as well, it is enough to tangle with the concept of a Creator God without introducing the question of a personal God.

On the other hand, some of the most convincing evidence that God is a person can come from the personal experience of individuals. Of course this evidence only works for the individual having the experience. Such experience is eloquently expressed by Francis Thompson in his poem, *The Hound of Heaven*. Francis, "Fled him, down the nights and down the days;" yet, after recounting his complaints, all of them reasons to flee this absent God, he discovers God still pursuing him out of love.

The great delineating characteristics of the human person are reason, creativity and personal relationships. Does it not seem reasonable that if the Creator is a person whose creative act evolved into persons capable of relationships, it should also be possible for them to relate to that Creator? Through reason we are capable of decision making, abstraction and planning. All this leads to the dominance of the strong presence of individuality. It also appears to lead to religion, that is, the willingness to take due notice of God and act accordingly. The notion of a God has evolved dramatically throughout history and not just as a result of divine revelation.

The hesitation of some religious people to pursue the scientific description of the universe may be a subconscious but real fear that it will undermine the notion of a personal God. We as persons could get lost or recede into insignificance in a universe of such unimaginable size. But is a simplistic imagery of God a better alternative? The *Old Testament* imagery of God which we frequently find in religious expressions today portray God in terms of royalty. There is even a Christian celebration of the feast of Christ the King. But royalty are usually at a distance and inaccessible. In reality royalty is an artificial status. There is no such thing as blue blood and history is full of examples of royalty who were not worthy of the deference extended to them. The populace was simply stuck with them and their many self-serving decisions.

On the other hand, the true scale of the reality to which God's creativity led is obvious to anyone willing to observe it. The fundamental evidence of a personal God is found in revelation and that is accessible only through faith. The evidence of the universe comes from instruments which technology has put at our disposal. As a result, the size of the universe should not constitute any threat to belief in a personal God. The conclusion of the person of faith is that, in spite of the vast universe, revelation singles us out as having a special place and purpose in it and a choice in how we decide to promote that purpose, or not.

Does God care about us?

For those who accept that God has communicated with us, Sacred Scripture and, most of all, the person of Jesus Christ is direct evidence of a personal God. All religions exist as a way to approach, respond to and influence this divine person in some way and are confirmed for individuals by their personal religious experiences. Just as personal experience can give evidence of a personal God, so too contrary experiences can suggest his absence. Tsunamis, genocides, injustice, plagues and earthquakes can leave us wondering where God was at the time. This question has inspired books on why bad things happen to good people and different religions find different way of working this out.

Admittedly it is easier to feel comfortable with the notion of a personal God if we think God has been acting through and controlling nature as required in an Earth only 6000 years old through a creation which took place as related in Genesis. But the factual understanding as established by science does not eliminate the possibility of a personal God. It does, however, expand the notion of God. It is Jesus and the *New Testament* which give us the clearest understanding of God as a person but in Christian theology this requires the gift of faith to recognize it.

Many accept without hesitation that there exists a supreme being we call God. But it is another matter altogether, and a difficult one, to accept that this God is a person still acting in our universe and, possibly, in response to our requests. This is a question which, strictly speaking, has nothing to do with science. But whatever we maintain about that personal God, it must comply with what we observe in the real world. If, for example, we extol God's care and universal concern for us, we must be ready to address the examples of his apparent lack of concern. The mass deaths caused by plagues, famines, tsunamis and earthquakes do not discriminate between those who pray and those who do not.

Repeated assurances of God's care do little to explain these events on the ground. The *Old Testament* image of a God who is quick to take offense and is jealous does not help. These events could be used by such a God to extract atonement for offenses but what does a Creator God consider as offensive? If we could come to terms with the physical world in which we live and how we relate to it, how it affects us and how that impacts our relationship with God, it might also mean that our explanations for these terrifying events are more reasonable and credible. In simple terms, it may mean that we become more comfortable with our position in the world and with God. Then we might become more realistic about our expectations of God rather than attempting to explain away those examples where our expectations have been for naught. Explaining these things is the job of the theologian and the spiritual writers. In this twenty-first century writers should be addressing these questions of substance, not simply stroking our spiritual sensibilities as is sometimes the case.

Natural revelation can influence spirituality

You and I can only deal with God on a human level. That does not imply that God must always be dealt with in the same way as we deal with other humans. The dominant characteristic of Old Testament imagery of God is anthropocentric. God is pictured acting toward us in the same way that human leaders dealt with their subjects. Sacrificing the first fruits of your crop is in effect a tax on your harvest. But now that our understanding of what God has done in creating the universe has changed so drastically, it is surely reasonable for us to expect to change our image of God and the way we relate to him.

Where is there any evidence or logic that God the Creator is like any of the Old Testament images as an earthly ruler? If, at a particular time in history, that is the only basis upon which a culture could build an understanding and relationship with God, then so be it. But when that culture moves on to a fuller understanding, then one would expect that our response to God would change as well.

An essential part of Old Testament spirituality was the idea of offering sacrifice to God. When someone offered his fatted calf to God as a burnt offering, the idea is clear enough. It is equivalent to saying; God, if you needed this I would give it to you. To prove my point, I will destroy some of it so that I cannot use it. Christian theology teaches that the death of Jesus was an ultimate sacrifice done once for all and there is no longer need for burnt offerings. In fact, not even Orthodox Jews offer such sacrifices any longer. In the case of the Orthodox Jews, the requirement of sacrifice stopped with the destruction of the Temple. God had designated the Temple as the only place such sacrifices could be offered. (Deut. 14:12-13) Reform Jews see it as unnecessary now. Without it they can adapt Jewish tradition and identity to the modern world. They try to be faithful to the sacred text while at the same time employ critical scholarship.

Jesus added another dimension to this view of sacrifice. In his emphasis on love and the importance of our dealings with each other, he said; "Go and learn what this means, 'I desire mercy, not sacrifice.'" (Mat 9:13) He was making reference to the Old Testament prophet Hosea, "For I desire steadfast love and not sacrifice, the knowledge of God rather than

181

burnt offerings."(Hosea 6:6) In evolutionary terms, it is a socially moral life which serves humanity, not sacrifice. If it seems that we have not evolved very far morally, remember that evolution is an extremely long term phenomenon.

The survival of humanity is not just a matter of physical characteristics. Our social needs and potential have also evolved. For primitive humanity, survival concerned the individual and family, often in isolation. With the rise of population and the stability which came with farming and herding, the community became a force for survival. Further population increase produced cities and survival began to depend on issues of public health and law which resulted in an awareness of basic human rights. In the twenty-first century, these concerns have evolved into issues of global dimensions involving the social as well as the physical environment. Could this be why, in the long history of humanity on Earth, the divine revelation found in textual revelation could only have been effective in the last 4000 years? Yet much of that revelation is aimed at human survival as a society, but not one with the global dimensions it now has.

Spirituality can suffer from language

Spiritual writers need to be careful with language. It can at times sound like someone commenting on a work of art. There is a profusion of words to which you cannot take exception but you do wonder where the ideas came from. Perhaps we need an enlightenment movement in spirituality. The Age of Enlightenment made Christianity rethink many aspects of religious belief. Theology was asked to substantiate these ideas. This led to rethinking how we read the Scriptures and that proved to be a good thing. A similar enlightenment could foster a greater sense of spirituality in the twenty-first century based on how natural revelation has altered our image of God.

On closer inspection it can be seen that some common spiritual principles may have been overplayed. Are we unnecessarily attributing some things to God without cause? Take for example the often heard statement, "All good things come from God." What is the real spiritual value of that statement? How does it help understand the bad things that happen, either man-made or natural? What does it say about something which turns out to be very good for me but very bad for someone else? What image of religion does this give someone struggling with the concept of religion and who is also well versed in science as the explanation of most of the cause and effect evidence in the real world? This statement is not the meaning St. Paul intended when he wrote, "We know that all things work together for good for those who love God." (Rom 8:28)

We can find examples of terminology used in religious practice which is fine for someone borne into the faith but creates difficulties for others. It is traditional to refer to Mary as the mother of God. This expression is completely rejected by Islam and gives heartburn to many who have a strong belief in a God but find some of the details as expressed in popular Christianity difficult to accept. Mary did not literally give birth to God. Strictly speaking, what Christian theology teaches is that she gave birth to the human form of Jesus who is God Incarnate, the fleshly reality through which God appeared to us under the attributes of God the Son. Like so many real things, this is completely against common sense and unexpected. But considered in the light of God's plan, it is fitting and advantageous for us. Dropping the term "incarnate" when referring to Mary's motherhood of God does not help promote understanding of this dogma. While we do not look for the mathematical exactness of science in the terminology used in discussing God or religious matters, poetic license should not be allowed to obscure concepts which can be clearly defined.

We saw that scientists need to be creative. This does not mean that they indulge in science fiction. Creativity is not used to state the principles of science but how to both discover and use them. Creative thinking by Newton led to the explanation of gravity. Creative thinking about the electrical properties of solid state semiconductors produced the transistor. A fuller understanding of the physical universe should be able to inspire spiritual thinkers to fitting and appealing ways to explain and relate to God. The ultimate question for the spiritual writer should be, has this conclusion been too creative and gone beyond what we can legitimately conclude from divine revelation or well-reasoned theology? It may be because much spirituality is motivated by pastoral concerns that there is a tendency to overstate some ideas. This may explain the excess but does not justify it.[1]

The difficulty for those who compose liturgies, the format for public worship, is that they become trapped by the language and imagery of the *Old Testament*. For many in the twenty-first century, indulging in Old Testament terminology is not attractive. Christian theology has much to say about the nature and purpose of humankind which is exciting and cosmic in scope. It can show why humanity can be considered central to creation without placing his planet at the center of the universe. But this capability is not well served by much of the Old Testament imagery which is found in abundance in Christian liturgy. It is hard to argue against the inclusion of any individual phrase or term but when considered in respect of frequency of use, it has an effect opposite what is intended. These Old Testament images in the liturgy can be like so much background music rather than something that attracts and interests us.

The solution is not to strip the format of worship of all these poetic and dated images. Rather, the end should be to introduce new imagery which appeals to a better informed audience. The challenge to spiritual writers is to replace insubstantial or gratuitous statement with an approach which eliminates the need to explain away all the exceptions in an attempt to justify the words used. I mean no insult in comparing this process to replacing the idea of Santa Clause with an adult celebration of the feast of Christ's birth.

This is not an easy task but it can yield great rewards. No psalm in the *Old Testament* expresses the nature of God's creation using imagery which reflects the real universe and yet that real universe is far greater than even poetic language can express. This implies that we may need to introduce more contemporary poetry into the liturgy. Perhaps the liturgists could add a new feast to the calendar celebrating God the Creator. Architects and artists would find much inspiration in designing a building dedicated to God the Creator as understood by modern science. To my knowledge, none yet exists.

The use of language can have great influence on credibility. Science enjoys the highest level of credibility in the things it claims to understand and an admirable sense of mystery concerning the things it cannot yet explain. How can our claims to spiritual truths also achieve a similar level of credibility or at least the presumption of reasonableness and probability? Perhaps one of the reasons for the lack of credibility is that theology never proposes anything as a theory, which science always does, until evidence is overwhelming. Often science keeps the term theory for things which have been overwhelmingly demonstrated, such as relativity and evolution. For some reason, many demand that religion be certain about everything and this brings us back to our comments in chapter 9 about how certain we need to be. Yet it is theories in science which increase its wonderful sense of mystery. The same would be true for religion if we would only allow ourselves to admit to and live with uncertainties. The sense of mystery comes from being aware of the depth of the things we do not understand, not the incomprehension we experience when we pray in a dead language we do not understand, as advocated by the pope and others in the Catholic Church today.

Christian worship has a long history of accommodating and taking advantage of developments in music, art and architecture. The willingness to do this has inspired the highest levels of creativity. Should it not be the same with the language and intellectual imagery we use? After all, the music and discipline of worship is for us, not for God. We are the ones who need them, not God. We take advantage of new building materials and architectural design, install the latest sound technology to ensure that everyone present can hear the words used. Should not the imagery which those words express match our twenty-first century image of the Creator God we worship?

There is a strong parallel between the satisfaction which the scientist derives from the pursuit of his or her discipline and the personal rewards of a religious spiritual life. In both cases the satisfaction can be on both the emotional and intellectual level. In the end, a sense of satisfaction may be the primary motivating force behind both science and religion. On the personal level, spirituality satisfies a strong felt need in our personal life. It is rewarding on a number of levels and that gives it value in itself. But in the twenty-first century, it is important that religion be rational. Spirituality is based on that which identifies us as a unique person and much of that is determined by how we understand the world around us. Spirituality must not leave reason behind. It is not an activity at the surface of being human but an activity of our whole identity as a person.

Twenty-first century spirituality

Spiritual writers today need creative thinking, not thinking locked in the framework of past cultures from a different era. Not everyone is equally attracted to the same form of spirituality. In part, this is the influence of culture which evolves within a social group. Not everyone likes public demonstration of emotional forms of praying as found in some evangelical groups or the extreme rigors of the Neo-Catechumenate or Opus Dei. Those who are attracted to this type of response to God have it open to them but it must not be seen as somehow superior to less rigorous ways of expressing twenty-first century spirituality. The public exercise of spirituality must fit the local community and national culture. Changes to make them fit need not be rapid but they can be expected to be as constant over time to track with cultural and intellectual changes.

It is not easy to change long-held ideas. The erroneous notions about the physical reality of the universe found in the *Bible* were relatively easy to circumvent. It was pointed out that the *Bible* is not a science book and simply relied on the faulty common sense notions of that period. This is not what was being revealed by God. But with spiritual matters it is not so simple. A conclusion once drawn, especially if by someone of notable sanctity, tends to remain sacred and permanent.

The importance given to the ideas of mortification and self-denial is an example. What made life difficult in Old Testament times are not the same things which make life hard for western twenty-fist century populations. The spirituality of the *Old Testament* and early *New Testament* was fit for purpose - to get those of that day through their hardships. So denial and hardship were made part of spirituality, the way we relate to God and a path to virtue. Food supplies were not always adequate so it helped to sanctify fasting. In the extreme, a premium was put on suffering. Although there are still places and populations in which physical hardship and suffering is endemic today, for a great part of the global community, this is not the case. We must now devise a spirituality which better fits this new condition.

Recently there are encouraging examples of change. As these words are being written, Lent has begun. The letters of some bishops, Anglican and Catholic, have suggested some remarkably twenty-first century ways of observing Lent. One archdiocese containing a large city has organized a six-week arts festival comprising concerts and exhibitions through which people are encouraged to greater appreciation of things God has brought into being, including human creativity. Another is encouraging people to ask who their neighbor is rather than concentrate on abstinence. "Take time this Lent to get to know someone better" is the advice. Another bishop has recommended that we cut our carbon output rather than our chocolate intake. Not too long ago these suggestions would have been shocking and foreign.

Nor are we today so much in the no pain, no gain school of spirituality of the past. What is more, suffering today can be seen not just on the cross of Christ but around the word. Rather than manufacture artificial discomfort for ourselves, is it not more within God's plan that we concern ourselves with the genuine suffering of people around the world due to corruption, injustice, ignorance, natural disaster or a combination of all these things? It is the globalism of society which makes us aware of these possibilities. Our TV screens and internet browsers bring them into clear focus.

As we have pointed out, nature has revealed the evolutionary character of human life, even in the survival aspects of its social characteristics. It is encouraging to see greater emphasis on the social aspects of morality rather than limiting it to our personal relationship with God alone. Can any sin be considered on its own as an offense against God without any reference to our relationship to someone else or ourselves? This is a point which Jesus made and some spiritual writers in the past tended to neglect it.

Christian spirituality as well as morality is based on love. But desire is an integral part of love. Even in loving our enemy, what we desire is their good and the greatest good for them and us is that they are no longer our enemy. For someone who is not our enemy but our loved one, our desire is to be more aware of their presence, their personality and to know everything they do and celebrate their accomplishments. We learn these things about God not just through his revelation but through the revelation we can discern from even the physical things he has created, in other words, natural revelation. Thus, the greater our understanding of the physical and social universe, the more constantly aware we will be that we are in the presence of an awesome and all-pervading creative power which we call God. The challenge to twenty-first century spiritual writers and directors is to find ways to share and express that awareness.

Traditional Christian spirituality has made use of what we call sacramentals. All the sacramentals involve an action and something physical: candles, incense, a blessing. But recognition, understanding or making associations are also actions. Sacramentals are human activities which start from something physical. In them we can make connections between spiritual and physical realities. They do not confer grace but rather a sense of reasonableness and fittingness. To recognize humankind's evolutionary step up from biology to grace is to use our physical nature as a sacramental. Sacramentals make us at home on this planet and in this body of ours. They can support a healthy spirituality and give us hope for the future.

The sacramentals I am speaking of were not established by religious practice but by God through physical nature. They involve: the size and complexity of the universe, the awesome possibility of all life forms to exploit, accommodate and populate every part of our earth, the ability of humans to understand this creation and put that understanding at the service of others. These things are sacramentals of the highest form and greatest value. They require a correct understanding of realities, physical as well as spiritual. Some spiritual writers seem not to be aware of the possibilities of sacramentals in modern spirituality. The secular scientists may not be able to travel with us to our spiritual conclusions. They will know, however, that we are not creating something spiritual out of things which they understand have physical causes. As a result, they can respect our conclusions while disagreeing with them.

187

Twenty-first century saints

A twenty-first century spirituality requires a new mode of sanctity, one that is down to earth. This will rescue it form the accusations of being rather airy fairy or lacking substance. Take for example the notion of sanctity. The lives of particular individuals are offered as examples of success in the spiritual life and they are declared saints, people certainly enjoying the presence of God because of the way they lived their life. Of course, if they are saints after their death, they must have been living, breathing saints the moment before they died. Death did not change their sanctity or spirituality.

Often, the declared saints are people who lived extremely difficult lives of self denial or even martyrdom. Their sanctity was deemed to be heroic. In practical terms, it would be difficult for the ordinary person to emulate them to any great degree. There are three criteria for sainthood: what they did, why they did it (their motive) and how we think God valued their lives. Let us apply these criteria to two people of our time, Mother Teresa and Bill Gates.

We all know so much about these two people that we need not list their achievements. At first glance, the comparison seems disjointed and inappropriate. But is it? Mother Theresa valued the effectiveness of suffering. After all, this was the means which Jesus used for our redemption. She used this theological concept to give dignity to the death of the poor in their last days. The medicine she offered was minimal and she could do nothing for the causes of the poverty which was grinding down those who came into her care. She did all this with much personal deprivation but it was all she could do and we honor her for that.

And what of Bill Gates, one of the richest men on Earth? He established a foundation for the purpose of eliminating ignorance and diseases which afflict the poorest people on earth. Endowed with over $38 billion, generous portions have been allocated to research and development of vaccines and techniques to prevent and cure some of the world's biggest killers, malaria and tuberculosis. Most of the victims of these diseases are children in developing countries. They are funding research to develop health solutions that are effective, affordable and practical. This is what the foundation is doing. And why? "The foundation is guided by the belief that all lives, no matter where they are lived, have equal value."

As for the third criterion of sanctity, how do we think God views the work of the Bill & Melinda Gates Foundation for establishing such ambitious charitable programs? We know the answer to that. But do we know how God would compare Bill Gates to Mother Theresa? One gives value to life while the other gives value to death. A disease-free life certainly leads to a greater possibility of spiritual growth. Perhaps the answer is in the difference between a philanthropist and a saint. The philanthropist surely displays a deep respect for humanity in an effective and practical way. Andrew Carnegie built nearly 3000 libraries around the world, one of which is today my local library built in 1914. Who could discredit the intellectual and spiritual benefit of such an undertaking?

It is tempting to say the difference is that the philanthropist gives from his surplus while the saint experiences personal deprivation in some way. This implies that self-giving must be uncomfortable to be of any value in the sight of God, the no-pain-no-gain school of sanctity. We are dealing here with extreme cases in order to clarify the notion of sanctity. The spiritual writer must deal with the formation of saints who have a mortgage and credit card debt, children to raise and educate and employment to maintain.

But the majority of these saints are well educated. They keep up with global news as well as social and scientific documentaries. Their spirituality will not come from a haze of Old Testament images. The more it is founded on the real world they know and experience, the more credible and productive their spirituality will be. It is unfortunate that recent declarations of sainthood have not ventured into this group of saints. One also wonders if the day will ever come when the Catholic Church will canonize a non-catholic who ticks all the boxes except orthodox beliefs. Can these never enjoy a life with God? Such an act would go a long way to clarify what constitutes a meaningful human life.

Spirituality is the technology of religion

Just as technology is the practical spin-off of pure science, so too spirituality is, or at least should be, the spin-off of theology. In science, a better understanding of light improved the technology of optics and new microscopes improved the health sciences. A better understanding of the electrical properties of materials led to more complex and efficient devices such as computers and body scanners. So too, the better we understand the universe God created and especially as it involves human participation and influence, the better we will be able to relate and respond to what the Creator has done and intended. By universe I mean the realms of atoms, stars and generations of living organisms. Moreover, by taking this view, religion will escape the suspicions from some reasonable quarters that it is governed only by myths and unsupportable when subjected to rational investigation.

The transition to this situation is most difficult. Pastoral clergy do not want to shake the simple faith of sincere people. Yet it is also easy to underestimate the intelligence of people in theological matters. Thus it falls on the shoulders of just such pastors to craft spirituality to augment and not necessarily replace all traditional elements of popular spiritual practice and belief. To do this requires an understanding of how God's creation functions at all levels.

Technology has made mistakes. Thalidomide, asbestos, freon and radium are clear examples. When I was a child, all clocks and watches had radium dials which glowed in the dark, that is until it was discovered that radium caused cancer. The problems were caused by incomplete understanding. Technologists admitted the mistakes and set about devising remedies and replacements. Is it impossible that spiritual direction in the past could have devised harmful usages, forms of spirituality or, perhaps, some which could not be given a substantial theological basis? These things are far too important for the flourishing of a human life and should not escape periodic review and assessment.

Theologians and spiritual writers should feel the excitement which the physical scientists are experiencing. There have been many discoveries and accomplishments in which scientists and inventors can take pride, things which have a great impact for good: vaccines, scanners, genetic discoveries. Spiritual writers too should be able to experience such satisfactions. To be sure, there have been some on the periphery. Take for example Taizé and monasticism. They reflect two distinct images of God while using the common elements of silence and music. The former supports the inner human spirit through daily life in the world with a joyful experience of God through human solidarity while the latter supports the spirit by withdrawing from the world and self-denial.

There is no questioning the legitimacy of either spiritual style but we might ask which model more closely matches the image of a God who created such an awesome, fertile and evolving universe which was able to generate the human species? In practical terms, which has greater influence in increasing our survivability as a social species today? In relation to the size and complexity of the universe and the extent to which we are capable of understanding it, which celebrates best what the Creator has done? These questions make obvious why monasticism started in the fourth century and Taizé in the twentieth century.

Some traditional spiritual models emphasize self denial and mortification. Physical pleasure and satisfaction are thought to be dangerous, suspect or evil. In evolutionary terms, is it healthy or accurate to insist that flesh always be equated with sin? Yet in the liturgy of the Christmas season, a communion antiphon refers to God's Son as coming "in the likeness of sinful flesh." This expression clearly reflects an attitude toward the perceived human condition rather than an image of what God's universe brought about in the human species. It certainly contradicts Genesis 1 in which we are told that God saw that it was very good. It can also spoil the image of the birth of God's son as well as the image of the birth of any human child. After all, it is not human flesh which indulges in hatred, injustice or prejudice. It is not flesh which crushes the human spirit of another person or misleads them with falsehoods or denies them justice. Perhaps if we better understood and appreciated the physical components of human nature, we could better prioritize the elements of our spiritual lives.

Adjusting priorities

At the biological level, the usually perfect copying of genetic material assures the stability of living organisms. Chance mutations insure adaptation to a changing environment through the mechanism of natural selection. DNA driven reproduction also creates opportunities for new species with more advanced capabilities. Our Earth today is the evidence of this through the presence of an almost infinite variety of living organisms and species in every cubic inch of material on its surface. This is how biological laws serve all living beings. Should there not be a form of natural selection within our spiritual practices which keeps pace with changes in our physical and intellectual environment? One could ask how religion serves the human species in particular and the rest of the sphere of living things in general. At the biological level, instinctive behavior remains genetically locked into a species because it has enhanced its survivability, at least in the past. As a parallel to biology, religion should contribute to the stability, survivability and adaptability of humanity as a whole as well as individual good. Could not the phenomenon of denominations be comparable to variety of species? The concept of a personal God focuses not just on the good of the individual but the human species as well.

We should ask how we can expect religion to serve humanity? This consideration must also be guided by what we can reasonably expect from a God who created the world which evolved into material and living things, a universe of size and complexity that baffles our common sense and exceeds our ability to understand it. We evolved with the ability to

191

understand and contemplate the world and use it for our survival and enjoyment. With this in mind, would such a God dictate the killing of those who have not come to a particular human understanding of him? Would he wish the liberation of a particular nation by the killing of masses of people of different religious convictions who occupied it because of the quirks of history? Would this kind of God desire the burning to death of people who were convinced of ideas foreign to what was otherwise perceived as the orthodox view?

These are extreme examples but what of lesser things? Of what possible concern can such things as dietary laws, strict dress codes or bodily appearance such as facial hair be to the Creator of our universe? Some of these things can be seen as wise hygienic codes which were given the force of divine law for the good of society. We could continue through a long catalog of curious things which have taken on such importance in identifying those who accept a particular religious belief that they have become, in the minds of many, essential parts of it. There is nothing wrong with these things so long as they are done freely as a personal expression of faith and not forced as a divine requirement of faith.

What priority does the Creator of the universe place on such things as praying in Latin, full face veil, fasting, circumcision or mortification? The way to approach these practices is to have a sense of priorities in light of what our best understanding of the physical universe tells us about its Creator. Placing humanity in a larger evolutionary context is the way to escape from a parochial and blinkered view of how to relate to God.

The problem of parochialism can even infect the concept of church. On 29 June, 2007, the Congregation for the Doctrine of the Faith in the Vatican published a document answering certain questions about Catholic doctrine concerning the meaning of church. The document explained that the term church could only rightly be used in reference to the Catholic Church while all other Christian denominations are only ecclesiastical communities. The reason for this opinion is that the Catholic Church has formulated the definition of church as requiring apostolic succession and valid celebration of the Eucharist.

All the feelings of alienation which this document caused among other Christian were the result of giving a high priority to a traditional formula for church and doing it at a time when there seemed to be no reason which required insisting on the formulation. An alternative might have been to creatively attempt to recognize, as science does so well, the uncertainties of our understandings and their formulations. We can say this while passing over the question of the diplomacy it involves. There is little chance of growth as a human society when we resist the need to reformulate our understandings of the world. Even if we are convinced that our formulations are correct, by pursuing a better understanding of the natural world including the society in which we live and human nature, we can begin to have more respect for those who do not share our priorities.

We frequently hear the lament that Christianity is on the wane, especially in Europe. Church leaders form the Pope to the Archbishop of Canterbury and many Imams have been telling us that a large part of the problem is secularism. Some believe this is the reason for a drop of interest in religion and why vocations to the priesthood have fallen to unsustainable levels. Such questions are extremely complex. But can it be that, if the problem lies with society in general, religion beares some of the responsibility for it. It did not contribute enough to that social thinking in a credible way. It did not hold its own in that wave of scientific discovery and provide an image of God which could fit the new understanding of the physical reality of the world in which we live.

The Catholic Church still clings tightly to Old Testament imagery in its liturgy. Shouldn't we expect that the Creator of the universe would act a bit better than an earthly, pre-Christian king? Yet this is the image of God throughout the *Old Testament*. In the liturgy of the feast of Jesus Christ Universal King we read from Psalm 92. "The Lord is King, with majesty enrobed; the Lord has robed himself with might; he has gird himself with power." These words no longer resonate with well-educated people who live comfortably in modern communities and face mortgages, inflation, the high cost of educating their few children and still try to accommodate their innate yearning for a relationship with their Creator through a spirituality which seems more and more out of touch with the world in which they live.

Trapped as the Catholic Church is in a concept of infallibility which has been extended beyond its definition, it is loath to rethink its formulas about issues involving our physical nature or even our improved understanding of human nature. This sort of fundamentalist thinking is seen by many Christians as being so out of touch with twenty-first century reality that it is simply ignored, even by a sizable segment of its active members. A twenty-first century Christianity which strives to promote the evolution of human society toward God's goal for us must become a learning body instead of one that repeats formulas from the past. It must draw on the new natural revelation which deepens every day and make that effort a priority.

Science has been good at discovering the what and the how of the natural world. It is time for the Christianity to take up the challenge to discover the why of the universe in modern terms. It can only do this by a fresh reading of modern natural revelation and working out a way to express religion in the evolutionary terms which have bought about the current state of humankind on Earth. It is not intellectually acceptable to simply let science and religion go their separate ways. Science and the technology it produced has changed our world. Fast global travel and communications have changed the meaning and scope of the command to love your neighbor as you love yourself.

Unfortunately, a parallel example can be found in Islam. The thinking Muslim world has recognized that science and technology have driven the progress of the western world. But too many have failed to appropriate these tools of progress into the Islamic ideals. Fundamentalist religiosity has made much of the Islamic world a place of social turmoil which falls farther and farther behind in economic, social and intellectual achievements. In the extreme, it is a place where doubt and dissent are never tolerated. This is in spite of the fact that within itself beliefs are so fractured that different Islamic factions are at physical war with each other and their primary tactic is suicide bombers. These are misplaced priorities in the extreme.

A richer image

While the picture of the universe as portrayed in Genesis has a lasting beauty and poetic appeal, natural science revealed to us that the Creator had a much better idea. His creation was so potent that it could generate the things we see in the natural universe from its own natural functions and potentialities. Yet this image of God should not be seen as making God remote or less a mystery. Nor does it make impossible the idea that God also has the attributes of a person who inspires a loving relationship with us as individuals. As part of that relationship, people of faith believe that God is able to hear and address the prayers of every person on Earth at the same time. Is this a greater capability than being able to conceive of and create the universe we find ourselves in, a universe whose magnitude and complexity we are just beginning to understand? We have physical proof of the physical universe while we have evidence of God's intentions through textual revelation and experiences in life that we cannot otherwise explain.

Although one of the humanities and not a science, theology is not an embellishment or decoration to real living. While logic and reason are defining characteristics of human capability, so too are intuition as well as instinct about goodness and empathy in relationships. Science is good at focusing on something and defining it. The humanities are good at comprehending things in the context of the whole in which they exist. In a sense, comprehension radiates outward instead of inward. While poetry cannot meet the rigors of proof that science does, it is often the only way to express some aspects of human life and, in its own powerful way, put things into perspective. This is what poetry does best. We cannot overlook the physical world when considering things human nor ignore what it reveals to us about God. Scientists can use their profound knowledge of the physical world as a foundation for their spiritual life.

Notes

1. It also may explain other excesses when talking about the Virgin Mary. Spiritual writers often tell us how Mary thinks and why she thinks that way. But how do we know? We are told precious little about how she thinks in the Gospels except that she pondered many thing that she did not understand in her heart. We know nothing about what she concluded from these pondering. In reference to the recent Year of Priests, it was remarked that Mary had a special affection for priests because they are more similar to Jesus and, like Mary, they are dedicated to the mission of proclaiming, witnessing and giving Christ to the world. One could legitimately ask what the effect of this affection has been? How much more clerical abuse would there have been if she had not had this affection? This question is not asked out of cynicism but out of hard nosed practicality. What good is there talking about the affections of Mary if we can see no effect on human lives? It might be a way of complimenting Mary by attributing this affection to her but I don't think Mary needs to be complimented.

12

A Theology of Evolution

The premise I have been trying to support in this study is that from the beginning of humankind until the development of natural science in the sixteenth century, humanity turned to nature to support philosophical answers to basic questions of our existence. Conclusions were drawn using reason and not by experimentation. Practically from the first moment that natural science began to replace natural philosophy, science became suspect and a perceived threat to the idea of God. This was because, until the last 500 years, powers of observation were severely restricted by a lack of instrumentation and conclusions were drawn which matched these inadequate observations. The conclusions may have been scientifically invalid but to whatever extent they satisfied the inquiring mind and inspired stories as explanations, they were adequate for the time. Because human reason demanded that every effect have a cause and because there were so many effects whose cause could not be determined, an explanation was often found in the existence of gods who, while they could not be seen in their person, could be recognized in their actions.

Finally, some two thousand years before the birth of Christ, verbal and then written accounts of the actions and involvement of one of these gods were collected by a group of people who ultimately became the ancient nation of Israel. The text concluded that there was only one God who cared for them as a nation. The text was the account of that concern and was ultimately accepted as sacred revelation inspired by God. While we may look at this text today and observe that it is severely restricted by a primitive understanding of physical nature, this does not mean that the primary inspiration of the text was not of divine origin. After all, the limitations of human understanding also limited the Revealer. The only terminology available was that which was explainable through human language and experience and only as far as that experience had matured. As a result, while the world revealed much about the Creator, the understanding was still primitive.

Today natural science has become so profoundly competent in explaining the physical world that it is now time to again turn to what nature can reveal to us about ourselves and the Creator. This does not imply that now we will find the full answer to all our questions but the answers we do find today will potentially be far more adequate than humanity's first attempt at them. It will also eliminate some longstanding errors. I have tried in the previous chapters to explain the need for this reconsideration and suggest ways this might be accomplished. I should now provide an example of what I have been suggesting. So why not dive Into the deep end and see how far we can swim by considering the possibility of a theology of evolution.

The main flashpoint is going to be the fall of the first human beings. We are not talking about an event in a garden and a piece of fruit. We are going to want to consider what the condition of the first human was when he received the state of original justice. Was he adult or infant? What would have happened if he never sinned? How could he have been given birth in the real world and yet never be subject to death? Finally, what does this story say about the type of God we are dealing with who would condemn all future generations to death and disoriented relationships because of an act of disobedience by the first human to exist?

A theology of evolution

A theology of evolution would be a Christian anthropology informed by contemporary scientific findings. It would have the effect of broadening the physical picture of the human species found in biological science by merging it with the theological understandings of the human spirit. Since the theological aspects of the human person are not in the remit of physical science, this merger is no threat to the scientist in the sense that it could refute scientific data. Since the sciences work on the hard evidence of experimentation and repeatability, theology should be eager for the additional input from the sciences to augment philosophical conclusions and Scriptural interpretations.

A theology of evolution would differ from all other theological topics in one major aspect. It would need to explain itself in very physical terms. The strongest criticism of the current anthropology in Christian theology is that it does not give adequate recognition to the biological side of our nature. This may have been understandable at a time when the main interest was the spiritual nature of humanity and there was little understanding of the physical reality of our biology or the natural functions of our body. That situation no longer exists and it is time for theology to catch up with our understanding of human biology. The benefit of calling it a theology of evolution rather than a theology of the body is that this would not only include the physical origin of human nature and thus the involvement our biology has in everything we do, but also investigate the origin and development of what we call the human spirit or soul.

197

The motive for developing a theology of evolution is the same as the motive for reconsidering Genesis 1 and the six days of creation, and more. The net effect today of taking the six days of creation as historical fact is to look silly and perhaps miss the revelation it contains and end up with a shallow image of how God works and relates to humanity. But in that case those who hold that view are the losers and no one else.

To be wrong about Genesis 2-3, however, is far more serious. It would mean that we are wrong about our own nature and the effect could be a blight on human well-being and prevent the flourishing of a human person. Nowhere is such deprivation more likely and potentially devastating than in the moral considerations of human sexuality. To get it wrong here could potentially distort a young person's self-image or hinder the ability of two people to navigate the tribulations of married life. These are not matters to be treated lightly.

Theology usually limits itself to theory, reason and Scripture. Unlike all other aspects of theology, a theology of evolution can be considered an empirical theology in that it will frequently look to data derived from the senses for direction. Sense data may take the form of the analysis of the effects of certain physical acts upon the physical and affective senses of the human individual. Thus the degree to which the presence or absence of a particular gene affects the aggressiveness of an individual would be physical data. The degree to which mutual sexual satisfaction, independent of any reference to reproductive intention, promotes the stability of a marriage and the sense of a flourishing human life together is affective data. In both cases there are physical actions and causes with moral as well as emotional and social consequences.

The physical capacity for these effects are elements of human nature which are the result of biological evolution. They reflect the historicity of the human species. In so far as the moral implications look toward the future, that is to say the flourishing and survivability of a healthy human individual and society, these moral consequences are themselves an evolutionary mechanism without being purely physical. They contribute to the survivability of the species by adjusting to the cultural and economic changes in society.

Empiricism and theological investigation may at first seem like odd bedfellows. This is a consequence of the dualistic view of the human species. It also means that this is not just a theology of the human past but a living theology flourishing in the intellectual atmosphere of the twenty-first century. What is not needed in this theology is a new set of definitions, with a capital D, with all the implications of finality that come with them.

What is required are expressions of best current thinking. The intellectual community must not see such statements as the products of a know-it-all authority. They would be welcomed as the concerns of thinking realists willing to promote understanding.

More than any other branch of theology, this would forever be a work-in-progress because science is always a work-in-progress. Vatican offices with responsibility for theological content must see themselves as a clearinghouse of best thinking and a source of direction, not as the authority which determines when discussion of a topic should cease. More than any other branch of theology, the theology of evolution must be able to deal with uncertainty. As we have seen, science has learned how to do this and it is time that theology learned this as well.

The starting point for a theology of evolution would be a clarification of how literally the interpretation of the first sin in Genesis must be taken. This requires that we confront in detail the demands which the traditional account make for a creationist origin of Homo sapiens. Can we reconcile biological evolution with the traditional idea of the state of original justice? Is such a state likely or even possible in the real natural world? Is this state necessary for maintaining Scriptural integrity? I would suggest that the answer to those questions is a resounding, No. The idea of original justice and the fall in the origin of human nature described in Genesis 2-3 is exactly equivalent to the six days of creation and the conclusions we came to in Genesis 1, that the earth was at the center of the universe. This situation begs to be addressed by theologians in light of evolution and what contemporary genetics, anthropology and neurology can tell us about human nature.

Genesis 2-3 is out of sync with what we know about the real world and, without reconsideration, theology becomes unreasonable and appears to be founded only upon myth and mysticism. The first age of enlightenment forced the reconsideration of Genesis 1. It focused on the world we live in, our position in it and how we learn about it. Theology not only survived that upheaval but was the better for it. That Enlightenment was made problematical for Christianity because the Church was more concerned about a loss of authority than it was about being open to new understandings.

It is time to begin a second age of enlightenment concerning Genesis 2-3. It should be driven by a fuller understanding of the nature and origin of our human species found in and enlightened by contemporary understandings in physical science. To avoid the turmoil of the first Enlightenment, it should be characterized by openness to new insights. Its focus should be on the nature of the human species, how it got that way, how it works and the theological implications of these things and all driven by the revelation contained in the incarnation. Our current understanding of Original Sin or the fall of humanity has not progressed beyond that which was developed in the fifth century. Does it matter? If we place importance on the credibility of theology, it matters greatly.

Such a reconsideration would not devalue the crucifixion and the theology of redemption. The very act of reconsideration would rehabilitate the contemporary view which many hold of theology. It would go far to reinvest theology with credibility in the eyes of twenty-first century society. It might reasonably suggest that evolution produced not only a physical humanity, but a religious humanity as well. It could explain more fully how the physical/spiritual dualism found in humanity is not two irreconcilable worlds but part of a seamless progression from the first act of creation. Seldom in history has theology been offered such potential rewards for its efforts. Unfortunately, some religious institutions are still ambivalent about science and not open to reevaluation of long held dogmas. As we said earlier, gee-whiz science which causes us to respond with, "Isn't God great!" is one thing. But when science suggests that what has been taught for the last 1500 years might need some rethinking, few will admit to being interested.

The history of dogmatic development has often been one of reaction to challenges made by individuals suspect of heretical ideas. The theological community was uneasy with an idea, made further clarifications and, perhaps, reformulated their explanation. The heresy was tagged with the name of the person who espoused the idea. In the case of the erroneous interpretation of Genesis 1, it was Christianity which held the faulty notion. That was understandable since all the natural philosophers held the same notion. When natural philosophy was replaced by natural science, Christianity was, some would say, dragged into accepting the new interpretation. We have the same situation today with respect to the evolution of the human species. If we have any intellectual integrity and sensitivity to history, we should not need to be dragged into reconsidering Genesis 2-3.

Evolution, the science of humankind

For many today, the area of human study in which science and theology seems to lock horns most stubbornly is the question of evolution. Although in his exposition of the theory of evolution, Darwin seldom touched on humans and limited himself to other animal species, the

200

conclusions were obvious and no religious person wanted to admit to the popular misconception that he or she was descended from an ape. The sacred texts had already dealt with the origin of humanity, his fall from grace, the existence of evil in the world and the redemption by Jesus Christ. So why does science think it has a contribution to make to our understanding?

I would suggest that a scientific understanding of the origin and nature of the human being can bring us to a simpler and more reasonable understanding of humanity than the *Old Testament* story. It can contribute to a theology of humanity which has far more credibility and intellectual satisfaction for the twenty-first century mind than was ever before possible. This is a satisfaction we should not overlook. Philosophy has been described as thinking beyond what we know. Theology seeks understanding beyond what our senses can detect or revelation has made known. With such understanding we can develop a theology of evolution which should lead to greater spiritual as well as intellectual satisfaction.

Perhaps the best place to start is to review briefly what was discussed in chapters 6 and 7 about scientific evolution. Life forms started on earth about 3.5 billion years ago. As long ago as 65 million years animal species had developed into the primates. Starting some 2 million years ago, one strain of these, called hominids, developed in parallel with the rest and became Homo sapiens. All other branches of the hominids have become extinct. The primary reason for its survival success was the increased brain size and complexity over other lines of primates developing at the same time.

Biologically, what makes any successful species stable is the reproductive role of DNA. DNA imparts a form of immortality to a species. In fact, the bacterial life which first evolved 3.5 billion years ago still survives today. In conjunction with stability is adaptability. What makes a species able to adapt to a changing environment which threatens its survival is the slight fragility of DNA when replicating itself under certain physical influences. This mutation and the appropriate contribution it might make to subsequent survival insures adaptability as well as a degree of variety.

Thus the first humans to walk the earth were the result of all the biological mechanisms which produced all other life forms. Humans shared in all the biological functions, requirements and capabilities of all the most complex forms of life - and then some. The "then some" is difficult to enumerate because we are discovering that some are the result of the genes rather than evidence of a spiritual causality. There are others which are considered characteristic of that which makes an individual human a unique person. We will develop this a little more in a moment. We will simply say that at the arrival of Homo sapiens we are dealing with a thinking, reasoning, feeling, empathizing, imagining, creative as well as physically biological mammal. Physically it is born, reproduces and dies in the same manner as all other species of animal life.

It also engages in a complex social structure of its own devising which it can modify to fit immediate needs. Most of this is made possible because of the development of sophisticated spoken language. But the important point is that this is what biological evolution bequeathed to the human species, assisted by the much more difficult to determine personality of each individual of the species. While personhood is outside the capability of biology, this problem does not make biology useless to the theologian.

As a result, every individual of the species experiences the need for food and to protect itself through physical provision as well as intelligent planning. Each is driven by the sexual desire to reproduce as well as provide for offspring and close kin within the social structure. In great part this is in response to the demands made by genes. While these genetic directions are not absolute and many are holdovers from primitive ancestral instincts, they are certainly not easy to overlook. While there is a genetic immortality of sorts, individually we all biologically die, as do all other individual living organisms.

Revelation, the theology of humankind

Given this biological picture, we must now consider what revelation adds to it. The first difficulty is that the biology we have been considering is very recent while the theology is not. Under other circumstances, we might be accused of an unfair analysis were it not for the fact that all too often people of faith insist that every detail of their theology is as valid and useful today as it was when first developed in an age when biology as a science did not exist. For this reason, we must let the facts speak for themselves.

We are talking about a physical, historical, real-world situation. If the first humans were in a state of original innocence, when did they get that way? Were they born that way or did God wait until they were adults and then elevate them or worse yet, create them as adults, first one and then the other, and thus we must all be creationists to be orthodox? If they were adults, then what kind of biological change was required so that they would not suffer death or pain and is this the effect of having a soul? And if it was not an effect of the soul, then it was a perk which God was soon to snatch away from them. Is such a state with no physical death or suffering possible in the real world? What kind of God is it who imposes an arbitrary requirement on the first parents and then condemns all future generations to death, suffering and disoriented relationships because the conditions were not met? How well could those first primitive human beings have understood their situation?

Finally, the physical state into which the first humans fell, or returned, is the state humanity would have had by being the result of the same biological evolution which governed all other species. How does original justice fit in? We cannot expect Genesis to answer any of these questions. They arise from philosophical and scientific considerations which were impossible to make at the time Genesis was being composed. This raises another question. The stated competence of the teaching authority of the Catholic Church is the mission of interpreting authentically the Sacred Scriptures. Under this consideration, how bound are Catholics to the traditional, literalist and uninformed interpretation of Genesis 2-3?

We might also notice that the Earth humankind was put on cannot last forever so freedom from death was a shallow promise. Astronomically speaking, our Sun will die the death of all stars and obliterate the earth in the process and that is just one scenario for the disappearance of life from earth. The promise of no death is not absolute. Physically, the whole earth construct is a temporary one. But the writers of Genesis were not to know that nor the readers of Genesis more than 1500 years after the birth of Christ. So it is little wonder that the idea of original justice has persisted. But should it persist into the twenty-first century?

There is no need for a fall to produce disorientated relationships as some commentators insist today. Natural evolution is the cause of that. It is the conflict in us between the survival value of social behavior and the instinct to self-preservation. We can observe this same conflict in other higher animals. So how can we insist on a fall when there is such strong contrary indications against it and no need for it to explain what we observe about humanity?

What then is the revelation contained in the story of Adam and Eve? Just as we find in the revelation of the six days of creation that all creation is good and not evil, so too we find in Genesis 2-3 a deeper consideration of the existence of evil. Today we appreciate that life in the animal kingdom is cruel but, at the primitive animal level, that is the way to survive. The human animal is left with the residue of these instincts in our DNA. Furthermore, Genesis tells us that humanity as a species has a purpose in the grand scheme of things. Humanity is meant to be steward of creation and use the earth's resources to promote our social existence. We can now influence the social evolution of the species and even provide for the elimination of genetic flaws. Humanity is meant to flourish with abundant life in its physical and social environment.

Another difficulty Genesis 2-3 creates is that theology has become encrusted with centuries of hyperbolic and inaccurate language which, in turn, has become regarded as part of authentic tradition and, for all practical purposes, thought to share in the inerrancy of Scriptural revelation. This may be the primary reason for the hesitation of some theologians to reconsider the teachings of the origin of humankind in light of scientific evolution. As a result, while today there is little hesitation to accept Genesis 1 as metaphorical and in no way revealing that God created the universe in six days, for all practical purposes, the fall of Adam and Eve in Genesis 2-3 requires a fundamentalist interpretation. It is little wonder that some scientists and others see the notion of God which this implies as suspect.

As a result, while the details such as garden, trees, fruit, snake etc. may be metaphors, for many the basic scenario is not. The scenario is this. There was a unique creation of the first humans which made them independent of much basic animal biology. Then, through an act which they freely decided upon, their nature was reduced to one containing concupiscence, suffering and death. To think otherwise is to walk blindly through a minefield of possible heresies. There must be a way around this intellectual blockade which is acceptable to both the scientific and theological communities.

The contribution of science

A theology of evolution is one which concerns itself with the origin of the ensouled human species and all the implications of its physical makeup as well as its divinely established purpose. Science can make a contribution to the development of such understanding beyond using a scientific methodology. Everything science can tell us about the human body is potentially useful. It cannot offer ways to test a theological theory. Science can, however, clarify those characteristics in human nature which have a physical, biological basis. Scientific methodology has been extremely helpful in other seemingly unrelated fields such as economics, psychology, sociology and political science.

Often it is the absence in theology of certain elements of the scientific method which bothers the scientist most. It does not demean theology to require that it take a scientific approach to its reasoning process. Since there is no possibility of an experiment to prove a theory in theology, the logical process should at least be unassailable. There are at least two aspects of the scientific approach the absence of which can weaken theological propositions.

Science recognizes that most things which are possible don't exist or happen in reality. To say that it is possible that God created Adam and Eve just as Genesis 2 states is meaningless. It is true that God can do anything except contradict himself. You could also say that it is possible to roll dice 100 times and come up with the same numbers every time. A claim of possibility is meaningless. Just because you can think of it does not mean that it exists or is likely to. This principal has application to theories. Since the beginning of experimental science there have been countless theories but the fact remains that only a small percentage have proven to be true.

In the statement of any theological proposition, the minimum starting point is to show not that it is possible but that it is probable, likely or at least reasonable. It also demands that there is nothing to indicate that it is not or cannot be true. We should demand this of any consideration of the first humans because what we are dealing with are real physical persons, real biological entities. It is different when dealing with things like the nature of God, the Trinity, which does not touch physical nature in any direct way. The scientific method is at a loss to help in such cases.

A second principle of scientific reasoning is a very old one. In his great work *Principia, Book III*, Isaac Newton set out his rules of reasoning in philosophy. The first rule states: "We are to admit no more causes of natural things than such as are both true and sufficient to explain their appearances." He added by way of explanation that "Nature is pleased with simplicity, and affects not the pomp of superfluous causes." Ockham's razor again. Had Ptolemy understood this, he would have quickly abandoned his complex system of circles within circles to explain the motion of the solar system.

Theologians might also observe this rule for investigating nature. If we can now explain human origin and what we observe in the human conduct through understandings of genetics and the evolution common to all living things, then we need not complicate it with additional explanations involving an original state of justice and the first human's tragic fall from that preternatural height. The fact that this account originated in a primitive culture a few thousand years before we knew anything about biology strongly recommends that it is too exceptional. This approach does not eliminate the idea of sin. With the elevation to personhood came the responsibility of contributing to the fulfillment of the divine plan for humankind. It involves everything we now categorize under the headings of love, respect for all life, our natural environment and the human rights of every individual.

So how would scientists view Adam and Eve as interpreted by the *Catechism of the Catholic Church*? Clearly there is no scientific problem with the situation after the fall. What resulted from the fall is a normal, natural human species brought into existence by biological evolution, exactly what one would expect. The problem is with the situation before the fall. Is it reasonable, probable, likely that after 3.5 billion years of evolution, during which death is the ultimate fate of all living organisms and a part of the mechanism of evolution, suddenly there evolved a creature which was immune to disease, fatal accident, pain and death? In spite of the fact that it eats food and thus would experience hunger, it appeared as an adult in a garden and was destined to reproduce and multiply, it had no appetite or instinct it could not completely control and found itself in perfect harmony with the only other member of its species, Eve. How reasonable or probable is that?

Most scientists are happy to grant that humanity displays a difference of kind from the rest of the animal kingdom, the ability to feel shame for example. But this account of human origin violates every fundamental characteristic of how nature works. It does not seem reasonable that nature would function normally for 3.5 billion years and suddenly everything changes, but only temporarily and for only one species.

The final scientific insult is to likelihood and comes from the way in which we end up being what one would expect of biological evolution, humanity as we are today. It happened through an act of disobedience to an arbitrary prohibition imposed by the creating God. This Original Sin returned everything back to normal. And what if there had not been a fall? In practical, physical terms it does not bear thinking about.

Finally, scientists expect that any scientific truth has the potential of being predictive and contribute to the understanding of other aspects of nature. Does Original Sin really solve or contribute anything to our understanding of the problem of evil in the world? Does it contribute anything to the science of evolutionary anthropology? Does it clarify the question of ensoulment? Given that the state of original justice was completely unnatural, one could predict a fall affecting every future generation just to get us back to a nature state. Finally, what are the implications behind the fact that God waited some 150,000 years after the fall to bring about redemption? Questions like these call into question the reasonableness of the whole idea of a fall. Any theologian who expects to dialogue with a scientist about evolution will have to address these issues.

All of the above highlight a frame of mind on the part of scientists and we suggest that evolutionary theology would benefit from it as well. It suggests, for example, that whatever theological conclusions are drawn, the theologian should ask what the implications are for those who lived 4,000 years ago, or 40,000 or 120,000 years ago and what are the benefits of knowing it? For example, how do our theologies of grace, redemption or sacraments work out in practice for these ancient generations? Their nature as human persons was the same as ours. Our theology should be the same for them as us.

The human in paradise

These traditional ideas concerning original justice and the fall are clearly defined in the tradition of Catholic theology. In order to represent the authentic teaching of the Catholic Church in these matters, I will draw from two sources: the *Catechism of the Catholic Church* and the *Enchiridion Symbolorum* by Denzinger and Bannwart. The *Catechism* is a compendium of Catholic doctrine which was in preparation from 1985 until finally approved in 1992. The *Enchiridion* is probably less familiar to most readers. Its complete title continues, "definitions and declarations concerning matters of faith and morals." It is a collection of official Church documents and decrees by councils of the Church and was started in 1854 by Heinrich Denzinger. Clemens Bannwart updated the tenth edition in 1908. It is now in its 30th edition.

In a section entitled "Man in Paradise" the *Catechism* tells us about the first human. We must, however, keep in mind that the only competence which the Church claims is the authentic interpretation of Scriptural revelation. This does not extend to scientific understandings or historical fact. I excerpt the following paragraphs by way of a summary of the Catechism's teaching about the first human beings on earth and containing my underlines.

374   The first man was not only created good, but was also established in friendship with his Creator and in harmony with himself and with the creation around him, in a state that would be surpassed only by the glory of the new creation in Christ.
375   The Church, interpreting the symbolism of biblical language in an authentic way, in the light of the New Testament and Tradition,

teaches that our first parents, Adam and Eve, were constituted in an original 'state of holiness and justice.' This grace of original holiness was 'to share in. . .divine life'.

376 As long as he remained in the divine intimacy, man would not have to suffer or die. The inner harmony of the human person, the harmony between man and woman, and finally the harmony between the first couple and all creation, comprised the state called 'original justice'.

377 The 'mastery' over the world that God offered man from the beginning was realized above all within man himself: mastery of self. The first man was unimpaired and ordered in his whole being because he was free from the triple concupiscence that subjugates him to the pleasures of the senses, covetousness for earthly goods, and self-assertion, contrary to the dictates of reason.

While this summary of the authentic interpretation of the Scriptural account of the first human being was written in the twentieth century, it contains nothing that could not have been written by Augustine of Hippo in the fifth century. In fact, the term Original Sin, and thus original justice, comes from Augustine. The picture is not one which bears any resemblance to the scientific description of human origin but then no one in the fifth century knew anything about that.

So what are we to think about this "harmony with himself and with the creation around him?" Genesis 2-3 does not discuss this issue. Its purpose was to explain the existence of evil in the world. Since there was no understanding of the genetic remnants in us which might cause an individual to place a higher priority on the instinct for self-preservation than altruism, it had to find some other metaphorical explanation for selfishness. Since there was no understanding of the genetically based biological drive and evolutionary need for sexual reproduction, the eventual loss of the first innocence into lust seemed an adequate way to express the perceived disordered sexual relationship between man and woman which made them see their nakedness.

This metaphor does not exclude a subsequent and more informed explanation based on observable science. The authors of Genesis 2-3 were not trying to explain how humanity came to be. They were trying to explain why we are the way we are and do it with almost total ignorance of what we are. We must not turn the metaphor into the thing revealed. Further more, what is this "harmony … with the creation around him"? It is one thing to say that I am in harmony with my world as I sit basking in the warmth of a sunny beach listening to the gentle waves lapping at the white sands. But what happens when there is a hurricane blowing.

The most difficult claim to understand is that man would not have to suffer and die (376). The Genesis account does tell us that if Adam ate of the tree of knowledge of good and evil he would die but it does not tell us that he would never suffer if he did not sin. Physically, this could be dangerous ignorance about the health of his body. Suffering, physical pain, is part of the body's mechanism for telling us that there is something physically wrong and, according to this traditional picture, Adam never experienced any discomfort until he sinned. If this were the case then, at the time, he was not a biological creature that we could recognize and we are dealing with the world of creationist hypothesizing.

According to the *Catechism*, this original harmony also extended to all creation. The meaning of this is not clear. Even work was not a burden but rather, "the collaboration of man and woman with God in perfecting visible creation." One might ask how a human has perfected or could ever perfect visible creation, with or without the original state of holiness or justice? Rather, this is one of many examples of hyperbolic language which today only serves to cloud the issue. We have already pointed this out as a tendency suffered by many writers on spiritual subjects and even official documents of the Church are not spared. It is not possible to describe this perfecting of visible creation as metaphorical. Why add a metaphor to a metaphor? Instead it is offered as a clarification of the meaning of the metaphor of the first humans living in the garden to till it and keep it. Yet he would never work up a sweat in the process nor grow tired. Only after he sinned would he work by the sweat of his brow.

The *Catechism* makes it clear that the language of Genesis is metaphoric. Nevertheless, that language is relating to a real biological entity, the first human being, and so to be meaningful it must be reasonable. Since all life forms are the result of an evolutionary process, we are forced to recognize that the state of original justice is an unnatural one. I refer here to the statement that the first man was not subject to, "the triple concupiscence that subjugates him to the pleasures of the senses, covetousness for earthly goods, and self-assertion, contrary to the dictates of reason." (377) The metaphor Genesis used for this is that Adam and Eve were not aware of their nakedness. Being unaware of nakedness is a perfect metaphor for human evolution within the animal kingdom. No animal is ever aware of nakedness. This, however, would not have concerned the original writers of the text. Of course, the alternative is that humanity originated, both body and spirit, in a different act of creation which was not subject to biology, in spite of being made from the dust of the earth, and we are back to creationism again. But is this necessary?

The *Catechism* accurately places the revelation of Genesis in proper perspective.

> Among all the Scriptural texts about creation, the first three chapters of Genesis occupy a unique place. From a literary standpoint these texts may have had diverse sources. The inspired authors have placed them at the beginning of Scripture to express in their solemn language the truths of creation - its origin and its end in God, its order and goodness, the vocation of man, and finally the drama of sin and the hope of salvation. (289)

The difficulty arises when concern for the truth of creation, expressed in symbolic language begins to dictate the physical events through which humanity originated. The scientist reasonably asks why it was necessary that humanity suddenly had to be unlike the biological nature which gave him form? The state of original innocence does precisely that. The scientist does not deny the possibility of ensoulment, that is God's associating the individual human person with His own divine existence, making the individual immortal in preparation for a life with God after physical death. Science has no interest in that and no way to deal with it. But since the human biological nature at present is constituted genetically and metabolically the same as all other animal life and when the only reasonable explanation for this is the process of biological evolution, then any interruption of this process seems unreasonable and unnecessary. This is the objection scientists have to creationism and our theology would be well advised to agree.

Paradise lost

So what happened to that original state of innocence? Before addressing this question, we must recognize that we have reached a point of extreme danger. Christian theology is so focused on the concept of sin that to reconsider the slightest detail automatically invokes a fear of the domino effect and one can stand accused of all manner of errors. Our theology of sin, grace and redemption must be more robust than that and not because of the authority behind it but its essential reasonableness. What is more, the theology of sin, grace and redemption are not so much solutions as descriptions of a problem and the problem is the human soul. But ensoulment is probably the most elusive question in theology. So how can our understanding of things based on possession of a human soul be so firm when our understanding of the soul is so vague? Anyone who thinks that they have such a perfect understanding and explanation of any topic that there cannot be further adjustment or fine tuning is dreaming.

While admitting that the language of Genesis is symbolic, metaphorical, when it comes to the loss of original innocence, the interpretation of the fall from original justice tends to favor the literal. We have seen that evolution would produce a being with all the tendencies we find in ourselves today. This is to say that all our instincts, proclivities, and even the frustrating tendencies to do the things we would rather not do but find attractive, are natural to us. As noted earlier, St. Paul put it, "For I do not do the good I want, but the evil I do not want is what I do." (Rom 7:9)

On the other hand, the culture which gave rise to the *Old Testament* believed that everything was under the direct control of God. So it must be that God brought about everything and that would include the present human condition. Those who composed the Genesis account of creation could only think of God as acting in a very human way. When they wanted to make something, they had only the stuff of the earth to use. It was the same with God. God reminded Adam and Eve, "By the sweat of your face you shall eat bread until you return to the ground, for out of it you were taken; you are dust, and to dust you shall return." (Gen 3:19) No distinction is made here between before and after the fall.

It is curious how selective we are in the details of the *Old Testament* we choose to hold on to and those we have no problem dismissing as not part of the deposit of revelation. For example, after condemning women to painful childbirth, God adds, "yet your desire shall be for your husband and he shall rule over you," (Gen 3:16) While there are cultures and religions today which share this principle to a fault, here is what amounts to a moral principle for human society which we now consider to be in violation of basic human rights and dismiss it. Yet in the case of a detail contained in a story written for a primitive people to explain the existence of evil and not the physical origin of the human species, we act as if the fall is essential in explaining the present human condition.

The disobedience of our first parents is stated in Genesis but with little else by way of details of what this implied beyond work, pain and death. Oddly, it is only attributed to Adam and not to Eve as well. Nor is it seen as some kind of Original Sin. In fact, the term sin is only used once in the first seventeen chapters of Genesis. In Genesis 4:7 it is used to warn Cain who showed displeasure that his offering was refused while his brother's was accepted. God says, "If you do not do well, sin is lurking at the door." Everything else which we associate with Original Sin is a result of the theological development which continued into the sixteenth century. The major contributions came in reading the *New Testament* by Augustine of Hippo who made the association between Original Sin and concupiscence, Thomas Aquinas who linked it to the question of grace and finally the Council of Trent which saw it as a loss of that original holiness and justice.

Today, as we will see in the next section, it requires a careful balancing act between attempting not to run afoul of past definitions and still offer reasonable alternatives. Perhaps the best suggestion is to remember that Genesis is trying to deal with the problem of evil and not a detailed analysis of what the first human was like. What we are suggesting is that evil is more clearly explained as a residue from physical evolution than a fall as a consequence of disobedience.

The final horror of God's punishment of our first parents was not that he threw them out of the garden so that they would have to work if they would eat. Rather, "at the east of the garden of Eden he placed a cherubim, and a sword flaming and turning to guard the way to the tree of life" (Gen 3:24) so that they could not get to that tree, "and eat, and live forever." This is one angry God, even to the point of vindictiveness! Today we know that their subsequent death has not been because of the fall. It is because of a fact of evolutionary biology and the nature of all living things.

To say that we have a fallen nature is a biological statement, not a theological one. It says that humanity has all the animal instincts that evolution has given it. That it "fell" is a euphemistic way of saying that our nature changed. We became a different kind of being. But the only one who can change the essence or nature of something is the Creator of that thing. Therefore when talking about our "flawed nature," and remembering that we have a fallen nature, we are in effect saying that this is the way God made us. Thus God is the one ultimately responsible for our having distorted relationships and inclinations. All of these details create an interesting and memorable story but they can also cast a rather uncomplimentary light on God.

We again find ourselves up against a problem of language. We say that God created humankind. We might say that a particular architect built a building. The fact is that the design he devised existed in his creative mind and was later transferred to drawings on paper. Civil engineers drew up technical specifications to make it a stable structure. Then an army of skilled workers translated those drawings using the materials at hand into the building you and I can look at and walk into. To say that the architect

212

built the building is symbolic language at best.

It is in this sense that we say that God created the world or humanity. God designed the nature of the material out of which the universe and humankind are made. The tradesmen and laborers, if you will, who actually did the work are the natural laws which these physical elements must infallibly obey without exception. As a result, when we say that God created everything we see, it is true but not in sense that an artist sculpts a particular statue. It is symbolic language just as are the words of St. Paul, "For every house is built by someone, but the builder of all things is God." (Heb 3:4)

Perhaps Genesis has put things back to front. This was not done to mislead but to help people understand at the level possible for the time. In the Genesis story, those unique gifts in the garden when humankind first came on earth were a way of telling us what we are striving for, not what we had and then lost. That was a clever way to do it. Instead of God telling us what we must strive for, he convinced us that it was possible by saying that we used to have them once but lost them through disobedience. It made the possibility of achieving them more real rather than just baiting us with promises.

Now that we have fuller knowledge of how we got to where we are in the universe of things, we should be able to understand that the natural flow of evolution can bring us ever closer to that divine end where we control our actions in order to achieve clearly perceived goals. We now have reason to hope for the future and not lament the failings of the past. It also puts the future squarely in our own hands even as individuals. Our starting point is not the failure of our first parents but the unfinished evolution of our species and the residue of primitive needs embedded in our genetic makeup. In the final analysis, Original Sin is not the name of an event but the name of a condition with which every human being that ever lived had as part of their nature and will have for the foreseeable future.

A metaphor becomes history

A severe challenge for any Catholic theologian attempting to reconsider the interpretation of Adam and Eve comes in the *Enchridion Symbolorum*. Paragraph 101 states;

Whoever says that Adam, the first man, was made mortal, so that, whether he sinned or whether he did not sin, he would die in body, that is he would go out of the body not because of the merit of sin but by reason of necessity, let him be anathema.

This understanding draws heavily from the thinking of Augustine of Hippo. The 1943 encyclical *Divino Afflante Spiritu* encouraged biblical scholars to use historical, textual and scientific methods in determining the meaning of the Scriptures. We must also use these methods when reading the documents of the Church. Paragraph 101 is quoting the Council of Carthage of 418 CE. It was attended by 200 bishops and was concerned with the doctrine of grace as challenged by the Pelagians. There would be no natural science for another thousand years and, for all practical purposes, Christians were Scriptural fundamentalists, taking the words of the *Bible* in a literal sense, and would continue to do so for well beyond the next thousand years. To insist that this statement closes the issue of the physical status of Adam and Eve is to become a doctrinal fundamentalist and demand stricter interpretation of ancient documents than we demand of the *Bible*.

By introducing the question of Original Sin, the *Catechism* appears to head off any attempt to rethink its assertions by overstating, through implication, the importance of the details of the fall. "The Church, which has the mind of Christ, knows very well that we cannot tamper with the revelation of Original Sin without undermining the mystery of Christ." (Par. 7, Pt 1, 389) This sounds like the house of cards argument. Touch this card and the whole thing will collapse. This is equivalent to saying that we can learn nothing more about the meaning of the Scriptural account of the creation of humanity nor about the nature of salvation and thus the mystery of Christ. It implies that theology is finished in this matter. Yet is it not the nature of a mystery that while we may never fully understand it, we constantly seek better understanding and often fruitfully discover new insights? Mysteries are inspiration for creative thinkers. It would be a sad thing to prevent such intellectual investigation.

At the time of its composition, Genesis was trying to explain the existence of evil in the world to a people with no physical science and a completely erroneous image of the physical universe in which they lived, nearly universal illiteracy and few developed philosophical principles to guide the process of reasoning. Learning and memory were accomplished through stories. Genesis eminently achieved its purpose. In fact, many today see this quality in Genesis as a strong indication of its divine inspiration, the presence of a guiding hand behind the human author's creativity. All the more reason to expect that, with fuller understanding of our physical nature, we will also find a fuller understanding of the human vocation in the divine scheme of creation by evolution. With each subsequent book of the *Old* and *New Testament,* our understanding of God and our relationship with him evolved further. It is not enough to say that Genesis may not have the details of the fall exactly as it happened but something happened to damage our nature. Can we honestly say that something we have by our very nature as a biologically evolved species can be called damaged? It is now time to let the development of physical science play its part in that evolution of understanding.

I emphasize that I am speaking here of the species and not the individual who could be damaged by a faulty genetic replication. In evolutionary terms, there may be room for improvement but damage means regression and deviation from the norm. Improvement means better adaptation to the environment and make no mistake, the human social and therefore moral environment changes. Globalization and communications has opened not only greater opportunities to give assistance to other societies and cultures but has also opened new opportunities for greed, dishonesty and violence against others. It would seem that biological evolution better explains why there is evil in the world than does the story of the fall. Evil is essentially our inability to rise above purely biological instincts when called for by our spiritual nature.

Pope Benedict XVI, in his 2009 encyclical *Caritas in Veritate*, explains this by saying that "man has a wounded nature." (34) He observes that modern man can be "selfishly closed in upon himself" and adds, "it is a consequence – to express it in faith terms - of Original Sin." By saying that it is in "faith terms" and not literal terms does not force the conclusion that it is necessary to maintain that there was definitely a fall or wounding of our nature. The writers of Genesis knew nothing about the genetic source of human inclinations and appetites nor the evolutionary mechanisms which made these valuable for survival. To insist that there was a fall or wounding puts the blame on God for he is the only one who could have inflicted that consequence.

On the other hand, if we maintain that what ancient and primitive cultures saw as a wounding was in fact the natural result of the biological evolution of our species, what was needed was some indication that this was not the end state of humanity. From the evolutionary point of view, we needed to know that the human person was capable of better things through evolutionary progress. This can be understood through our evolutionary concept of soul which we discussed in chapter 10. Theologically what was needed was for God to elevate human nature to the point of incorporation into his person.

215

The fact of this was revealed to us by the incarnation of Jesus, which exposed the possibility of a freedom from death as an individual person but not freedom from biological death. As we saw in our discussion of the human soul, this took place as a part of the continuum of evolution. This approach recognizes the scientific understanding of human nature while preserving the redemptive revelation of the *New Testament*. But remember, this elevation must apply to all human beings from the very first one. The revelation of this came only with the birth of Jesus. The impact of this elevation of the soul on the concept of redemption invites further and exciting study.

We have become acclimated to hearing chatter about Adam and Eve. It easily pass over us without any impact and without any feeling of intellectual satisfaction either. It simply fulfills an expectation that this was another occasion to mention it. Reminding us of our fallen nature is not a theological statement. It is a statement about our biological makeup bequeathed to us by evolution and couched in the language of a metaphor found in the oldest book of the *Old Testament*

But how can we say that we must remember our fallen nature without making the connection between the way our nature functions and how that nature evolved to possess that set of characteristics? The key is in what we think are the aspirations of being fully human. The hope to rise above purely physical impulses and the difficulty of doing so does not require a fall and redemption. Rather, it requires the elevation to an ensouled state and the realization that it has happened. Because the *Old Testament* explained the source of evil in terms of a fall, which was a useful metaphor for the time, Jesus continued the metaphor by introducing redemption which served us well until such time as we had a better understanding of human nature and its origin. We are now capable of a fuller understanding.

Speaking about Original Sin without reference to human biological nature can lead to distortions and immoderate language. Pope Benedict XVI, in his address to the general audience on 3 December, 2008 in which he insisted on the existence of Original Sin, referred to it as a "filthy river of evil … that has poisoned human history." He had earlier explained this river as "injustice, lies and lust." The only creature that can indulge in these three activities are human individuals. No brute animal can ever be accused of these evils. In the brute, they are mechanisms of survival.

One of the reasons we have become trapped by the story of Original Sin is because there is circular logic at work. New Testament theology teaches that Jesus came to redeem fallen humanity and restore what Adam and Eve lost for all humanity. But then we cannot rethink the story of Adam and Eve in the *Old Testament* because it is confirmed in the *New Testament* in the purpose Jesus came to accomplish, restoration after a fall. Arthur Koestler makes the following suggestion.

> The ancient doctrine of Original Sin, variants of which occur independently in the mythology of diverse cultures, could be a reflection of man's awareness of his own inadequacy, of the intuitive hunch that somewhere along the line of his ascent something has gone wrong.[1]

Perhaps what has gone wrong is that, all too often, we refuse to use our rationality and divine grace to change our behavior. Clearly, the story is an ancient attempt to explain the evil in the world and not much more. One would expect that we could explain it better today.

If we remove the fall from grace from the history of humanity and focus rather on the relentless evolution of the species, there comes a moment at which a quantum leap is needed to elevate an intelligent and feeling creature into Homo sapiens, a being with which the creative God can relate at the level of a personal relationship. An expanded view of evolution sees this as a natural possibility brought about through increased complexity as discussed in chapter 8. Traditional theology has maintained that this is more than a matter of brain size and complexity and requires a special divine act to create the individual soul and then, because the soul is fallen, another act of redemption. Could this be an occasion to invoke Ockham's razor? In the evolutionary scenario, the redemptive act demonstrates the level of relationship with God that is possible and the importance the Creator places on it. This approach eliminates obstacles one must face when dealing with the origin of the human species in the *Old Testament*.

It is difficult to think that the God who created the universe would set up a situation in which the whole human race would suffer such dire consequences and disorientation of relationships because of an act of disobedience of the first human beings he created. It is genes, inherited DNA which causes all humanity in history to display the so-called faults we see in us today. With the scientific understanding we have of human biology and its origin, it is also difficult to accept the idea that there was ever a time when humanity did not have these inclinations to act contrary to our better judgment and was not subject to physical death.

The sequence of events is also a problem. In the traditional

Scriptural view: the first humans were created in a supernatural state (able to communicate and relate directly with God) and a meta-natural state (would not experience physical death), fell because of an act of disobedience through which they lost both of these favorable conditions, and then had the supernatural but not the meta-natural nature restored by the redemption of Jesus. The most difficult part of this scenario is that humanity began in a creative act which was completely out of the natural sequence of events which generated all other life forms, that is, evolution. Yet everything we were left with concerning biological life is exactly the same as all other forms of life on Earth.

Paradise regained

This evolutionary elevation scenario is based on the theological observation that the redemptive grace of Christ is something which raises humanity up above the purely natural state. This is the traditional view. While the act of redemption happened in time, the elevation of human nature was present in the first human person. We find this explained in the Enchiridion which quotes from the letter of submission of Lucidus the priest to the Council of Arles in the fifth century.

> I declare further that by reason and through the regular succession of centuries some have been saved by the law of grace, others by the law of Moses, others by the law of nature, which God has written in the hearts of all, in the expectation of the coming of Christ: nevertheless from the beginning of the world, they were not set free from the original slavery except by the intercession of the sacred blood. (160b)

Because the statement is conditioned by the fifth century concentration on sin and death, Lucidus frames his explanation with being set free from sin rather than being elevated above pure physical nature.

Today we say that all individuals who lived before Christ's redemption through shedding his sacred blood were redeemed through his foreseen merits. We do not need to be slaves to the metaphor of a primal fall from an original innocence, the effects of which were then biologically passed on to each successive generation. The moment the first human existed, he was a biological entity endowed through an evolved complexity into what can be called a spiritual state with a divine purpose and a free will to cooperate with that divine plan written in his heart. He was at that moment redeemed. In this sense, that first human person was the same as a

218

person today.

The essence of Christ's incarnation was the revelation of how we can be incorporated into the personhood of God by the informing of a human body with the life of God, the Son. The essential theological point is that when God became a human in the person of Jesus Christ through the incarnation, it demonstrated that human nature was forever and always capable of sharing in some way the nature of God. That, of course, is the essence of the concept of soul and there is no need for any kind of retrofitting after the event. The event, the revelation simply needed to be historical and God chose the time and place to do this. The incarnation of the second person of the Trinity in Jesus Christ was the God-human relationship made visible. It revealed the intersection of the "eternal now" with physical time.

With this scenario, we escape any need for literalist interpretation of a scriptural metaphor. We avoid any necessity of an interruption of the natural flow of God's creative plan in the physical universe. We allow the redemptive grace of Christ to work on the nature of humanity by recognizing the evolutionary process of being elevated to its intended state of union with God. We avoid a need for that initial and unnatural state in which the first humans would never suffer or die. We avoid the need of an artificial cause of the loss of original justice through an act of the first human which then was passed on to all his progeny symbolized in Genesis by eating the fruit of the forbidden tree and being expelled from the garden. This means that we avoid an image of a God who created an artificial situation and then punished a whole species for the failure of the two first members of that species. In the end, Genesis 2-3 is not a very good character witness for God.

Every person alive today has life because all of their ancestors reached the age of physical maturity, copulated and successfully gave birth. The genes which were passed on to us through that human reproduction give us all the physical proclivities which theology calls concupiscence. They are, after all, natural to us and have been from the first moment of human existence and we have never been free of them. They are part of what made our species survivable before there was any philosophy, science, formalized religion or population centers.

What is more, genetics tells us that the structure of DNA is so stable that the basic set of genes we possess today are essentially the same as that of the first human being. That is quite some design and worthy of a great and creative God! The important thing to understand is that we can overcome the genetic residue of evolution in us. We referred to this in

219

previous chapters. Our relationship with God is our redemption and makes us eligible for forgiveness when we fail to overcome this residue and cause harm, fall short of our potential.

This scenario does no violence to the theology of grace or redemption. Theologically, we know little about the details of life after death and we know equally little about the specifics of a soul which marks the beginning of our life as an individual person. Science, on the other hand, can instruct us in great detail about our physical origin, both as a species as well as an individual. We do not need science or theology to tell us what happens to our body after biological death or why it happens. So why do we allow vague generalities derived from primitive metaphors to override demonstrable scientific evidence and by so doing diminish the credibility of theology for many thinking people? Genesis 2-3 ends in death, the revelation of the incarnation of Jesus ends in resurrection and life.

We should rejoice in what revelation tell us about the human vocation as well as rejoice in what science can clarify and confirm about our potential. Since Biblical revelation is finished, we can only await what further scientific discoveries will be able to tell us about our physical nature and thus our potential as social and spiritual human beings. It is up to creative theological thinkers to arrive at new insights from these discoveries and by doing so, make religion more appealing by making it more rational, more understandable, more recognizable as part of the real world we know. In the process, we may discover that some of the things we originally attributed to activities of the soul, spiritual faculties as we thought of them, are explained by neurological processes within us and genes being turned on and off. We should value the clarifications. There are today theologians doing precisely this but it is happening in an atmosphere which suppresses creative thinking and leaves original thinkers at risk of offending simple or conservative souls. The recent history of biological science has made astounding discoveries, revelations about our human nature. Can anyone point to recent advances made in theology concerning the human soul?

Quantum Philosophy

There is, perhaps, one final observation which can be made about modern science and the theological view of humankind. In his 2010 book, *The Grand Design*, Stephen Hawking states that because of gravity the universe could have created itself. At first this seems to contradict all conventional thinking about the necessity of a prime mover or first cause.

220

These concepts are so much a part of our natural and primitive logic and were so well championed by Thomas Aquinas and the Scholastics, that self-creation seems absurd. On closer inspection, however, it can seem quite reasonable and plausible. Stephen Hawking is proposing a conclusion about the origin of the physical universe based on the implications of quantum physics of which we spoke in chapter 8. If you have read anything of quantum physics, you know that it is an extremely strange account of time and the physical reality of things all served up with measurable uncertainty. It goes against all our inclinations about the universe as we experience it. Physics got along quite well with the principles derived in the 17th century by Isaac Newton. We did not take note that we were dealing with the macro universe, large scale chunks of matter and space on a grand scale. But when we began to deal with individual atoms and discovered that electrons orbit the nucleus in what we thought was the same manner as planets around the Sun, we discovered that Newtonian equations did not work. We had to resort to quantum speak.

Perhaps we have reached a similar point in our philosophical understanding of causality because of our ability to deal with things on a scale that neither Newton nor Aquinas could have imagined. So if gravity can bring about the physical universe and biological evolution can produce the entity Homo sapiens, then this makes the incarnation, God becoming a human person, the most profound and counter-intuitive element of all divine revelation as well as an important event in human history.

How very clever of the divine creator to devise a physical universe which can take care of itself without his constant intervention and direction. But don't be distracted by macro philosophy. We are now dealing with quantum philosophy where things can appear to be turned on their head. This is the level at which logic does not behave in the same way it does in macro philosophy. We are now philosophizing about philosophy instead of about the physical world.

At this level in the quantum physical world, we are dealing with entities which change their properties because they are being observed. At this level of quantum philosophy, we are dealing with the evidence of how God gets involved with Homo sapiens. It shouldn't surprise us that it is not an easily observable process, one very unlike all other processes. In the oversimplified macro philosophy, the closest Aquinas got to it was the term grace, the fact that humanity shares in some way with the divine nature. Now how does one even start to understand that? No wonder it needs a different philosophical approach.

But getting back to self-creation and the evolution of human species, the pressing question is, What is it for? Gravity or the universe for that matter has no value or purpose, it just happened. It would simply mean that the creator was enjoying himself. But when the human species began to question the world, had a desire to discover what it was about, then what was self-created had a stake in what needed no creation, God. When Homo sapiens realized that it had some control over its own evolution (a la Teilhard de Chardin) and the character of its social environment, when it became creative and altruistic, it was then on a new level of existence. Things become purpose-driven. Gravity has no purpose of itself, nor does the electron. If they are present or not, it makes no difference to the next generation of physical stuff. But you and I do make a difference to the next generation as well as to ourselves.

The reason we make a difference and stand out in self-created stuff is that we give things value, we understand, appreciate, we are creative. But how did that happen? Creativity is not just a spark that goes off in the electric circuitry of the brain. The pull of relationship between two human persons is not some primal bio-magnetic force within physical nature. These are phenomena within and between persons, not within the nuclei of atoms or aggregations of molecules.

What evidence do we have of the difference in our species from all others besides the intellectual conclusion we derive that it is so? I suggest that the strongest indication is the incarnation, the birth of Christ. The incarnation is the revelation that humanity is different, has been elevated to a new level of existence from its very beginning. Jesus was also God (more need for quantum philosophy). Now that we know that we physically got to where we are by evolution, all that was needed was an elevation to a new level, the inclusion of grace as part of human nature. I call this a revelation because, while the incarnation happened in time, it applied to every human person in the history of Homo sapiens.

The strongest recommendation for this scenario is that it is a natural and uninterrupted progression of evolution. It does not require the unnatural creation of humanity in a state of original justice free from concupiscence and not subject to death followed by the loss of all that privilege. And doesn't God come out in this second scenario as more loving and creative than shortsighted, vindictive and condemning? In the 16th century the telescope freed us from the metaphor of Genesis 1 and the six days off creation. In the 21st century we should now let evolution and genetics free us from the metaphor of original sin and the fall of humankind. It is time to take a quantum philosophical look at Homo sapiens. It will certainly make theology more credible to the secular society in which we live.

Conclusion

What I have presented here is simply an outline indicating one direction in which these ideas might proceed with benefit and I submit it for peer review. It is up to better and more imaginative minds to take us into further possibilities. Our theology of grace needs creative thinking in an intellectual atmosphere of adventure, not safe rethinking, or worse, damage limitation. A renewed attempt must be undertaken to arrive at a theology of the body which is not limited to mystical spirituality and is willing to dirty itself with the physical realities of human nature. What is at stake is credibility in the eyes of people who are scientifically aware and morally sensitive. Genesis successfully spoke in the symbolic language of its day. Today theology must speak with the scientific symbols of the twenty-first century.

As already indicated, it is not irrelevant to ask if Christianity must bear some of the burden for the success of secularism. If an institutional church is loath to rethink its teachings on issues involving our physical nature then it deserves to be ignored. It is out of touch with twenty-first century reality as understood even by a large segment of its active members. Many Old Testament images and metaphors for God no longer resonate with 21st century life. We need to become a learning religious community rather then one that declares formulas from the past. We must draw on the new natural revelation which widens and deepens every day. But make no mistake. This must be seen as a pastoral and not a purely intellectual or academic exercise. It remains for pastors and spiritual writers to translate the facts of our physical nature into religious experience. To assist in this effort, I would recommend two sources: *Christianity in Evolution* by Jack Mahoney and *Human Evolution and Christian Ethics* by Stephen J. Pope.

Science has been good at discovering the WHAT and a bit of the HOW. It is time for theology to take up the challenge to expand our understanding of the WHY of the universe in modern terms. It can only do this by a fresh reading of modern natural revelation and working out a way to express it in the evolutionary terms which have bought about the current state of humanity on Earth. It is neither intellectually nor morally acceptable to simply let science and religion go their separate ways.

Notes

1. Arthur Koestler (1967) *The Ghost in the Machine,* Picador.

TIME LINE
of people and events

384 – 322 BC Aristotle, Greek philosopher

~85 - ~165 Claudius Ptolemaeus, Ptolemy, Egyptian astronomer and Mathematician

354 – 430 Augustine of Hippo

1225 – 1274 Thomas Aquinas, monk, scholastic philosophy

1473 – 1543 Nicolaus Copernicus, astronomer, Earth centered universe

1483 – 1546 Martin Luther, priest, Protestant Reformation

1545 – 1563 Council of Trent

1546 – 1601 Tycho Brahe, astronomer

1561 – 1626 Francis Bacon, philosopher

1564 – 1642 Galileo Galilei, astronomer, Sun centered universe

1571 – 1630 Johannes Kepler, astronomer, laws of orbital motion

1581 – 1656 James Usher, cleric, Earth created 23 October 4004 BC

1596 – 1650 René Descartes, mathematician and philosopher

1632 – 1723 Antoni Leeuvenhoek, microscope observations

1638 – 1686 Nicholas Steno (Niels Stensen) geologist and paleontologist

1642 - 1727 Isaac Newton, mathematician and physicist

1809 – 1882 Charles Darwin, naturalist, theory of evolution

1822 – 1884 Gregor Mendel, monk, genetics

1840 – cell theory

1860's - Louis Pasteur, biologist, disproves theory of spontaneous generation

1869 – 1870 Vatican Council I, primacy and infallibility defined, Pius IX

1879 – 1955 Albert Einstein, physicist and mathematician

1881 – 1955 Teilhard de Chardin, anthropologist

1943 - Diveno Afflante Spiritu, encyclical concerning Scriptural interpretation

1953 - Watson and Crick, DNA

1974 – Henry Morris, Institute for Creation Research

1991 – Discovery Institute

1992 - Catholic Church exonerates Galileo

Index

Descates, René 45, 47, 49, 113
Diderot 51
Discovery Institute 93, 94
DNA 63, 74, 75, 79, 86, 89, 122, 124-126, 128, 164, 165, 191, 201, 203, 217, 219
Dollo, Louis 76
dualism 118, 119, 122, 200

E

Einstein, Albert 87, 111, 112, 113, 159
energy 90
Enlightenment, Age of 12, 44, 46, 48, 49, 52- 54, 92, 135, 138, 182, 199
ensoulment 68, 167, 204, 206, 210
entropy 62
Eratosthenes 24
ether 115
eugenics 128
evil 116, 206, 216
evolution 73, 83, 85, 87, 88, 89, 96, 97

F

faith 95, 96, 100, 101
fall see sin, original
Feynman, Richard 16, 114, 116, 130, 151
flat Earth 23
Franklin,Benjamin 51
fundamentalism 82, 91, 93, 95, 98, 99, 100, 101, 102-104, 138, 139, 144, 193, 194

G

Galilei Galileo 11, 12, 27, 34, 38-43, 48, 50, 52, 57, 58, 62, 72, 85, 89, 111, 120, 144, 145, 147
Gates, Bill 188
Gaudium et Spes 157
Gelson, Etienne 8,
genes 74, 75, 78, 80, 106, 128, 129, 217, 219
Genesis 1 14, 18, 20, 22, 28, 54, 93, 100, 110, 134, 136, 180, 191, 198, 199, 200, 204, 222
Genesis 2-3 55, 56, 92, 101, 116, 120, 198, 199, 200, 203-205, 208
genome 126

Leibnniz 51
Lemaître, Georges 132
Leo III, Pope 141
Leo XIII, Pope 51
limbo 148

M

Mendel, Gregor 73, 125
microcephaly 80
Morris, Henry 92, 93
Muhammad, Prophet 138
mutation 65, 74, 76, 126, 191, 201

N

natural law 156-158, 161, 162, 166
natural philosophy 27,
natural revelation 4, 5, 42, 88, 100, 119, 129, 134, 136, 137, 145, 156, 167, 173-175, 177, 182, 187, 193
natural selection 73, 86, 89, 98, 99, 126
Newton, Isaac 7, 25, 34, 38, 43, 44, 49-51, 52, 112-115, 123, 124, 129, 151, 159, 160, 167, 175, 183, 221

O

Ockham's razor 110, 130, 205, 217
original justice 71, 197, 199, 203, 205, 207, 209, 210
Osiander 34

P

Paley, William 78, 79
Pannenberg, Wolfhardt 170
Pascal, Blaise 51
Pasteur, Louis 125
Paul III, Pope 34
Paul VI, Pope 147, 153
Piue IX, Pope 141
Pius X, Pope 51
Pius XII, Pope 52, 166
Plank, Max 113
Plato 5, 28, 30, 58
praeternatral gifts, see original justice

T

Teresa, Mother 188
tradition 145, 146
Trent, Council of 34, 40, 212
Tertullian 41
theory 86, 87
Thomson, J. J.

U

Usher, James 93

V

Vatican Council I 141, 150
Vatical Council II 71, 141, 147, 150, 151, 156
Veritatis Splendor 156
Voltaire 51

W

Watson, James 75

Printed in Great Britain
by Amazon.co.uk, Ltd.,
Marston Gate.